CHALLENGES OF CONTEMPORARY POLICING

This edited collection reflects contemporary challenges faced by police forces across the globe and the role of technology in addressing them. The use of science and technology raises questions about ethics, training, the well-being of people, and freedom. New technologies promise to foster police practices based on intelligence, accuracy, and preparedness, and are considered necessary to overcome challenges such as declining budgets, lack of personnel, and legitimacy. However, technologies can also be used for authoritarian and nefarious purposes. For those reasons, this book aims to discuss related topics from various contexts to establish connections among common problems in the field of policing across the globe.

This book provides an internationally relevant assessment of the use of technology in the field of policing, as well as the impact on training and police well-being. It is ideal for an academic audience at both graduate and undergraduate levels in the fields of criminal justice studies, police studies, legal sociology, and public policy, and will be of interest to police practitioners, legal professionals, social service workers, and public-sector managers.

Vicente Riccio holds a doctorate in Sociology from *Instituto Universitário de Pesquisas do Rio de Janeiro* and was the coordinator of the graduate program of Law and Innovation at the Federal University of Juiz de Fora (2017–2023), Brazil. He also has worked as a consultant for many public institutions in Brazil, such as the Ministry of Justice, the Public Security Secretary of Rio de Janeiro, and the Civil Police of Amazonas. His research interests are police reform, legal systems in developing democracies, media, justice and video evidence. He has coedited *Police and Society in Brazil* (Routledge) with Wesley Skogan (Northwestern University). He has also published articles and book chapters in both international and Brazilian publications.

Di Jia is Associate Professor in the Department of Criminal Justice and Criminology at MSU Denver. After receiving her Ph.D. from the College of Criminal Justice at Sam Houston State University, Dr. Jia has committed to teaching in criminal justice. As a former law enforcement officer in emergency and crisis policing, she applies her research and working experience to the classroom. Her teaching/research interests include Police Systems and Practices, Crime Analysis, Homeland Security and Crisis Management, and International and Comparative Studies on Criminal Justice Issues

Dilip K. Das is the Founding President of the International Police Executive Symposium, IPES, and the Founding and former Editor-in-Chief of *Police Practice and Research: An International Journal.* He is the current editor of *Advances in Police Theory and Practice*, and *Interviews with Global Leaders in Policing, Courts and Prisons.* Dr. Das has also worked as Human Rights Consultant for the United Nations and is professor of Criminal Justice. He currently teaches at the Coppin State University in Baltimore. He has also authored and coauthored diverse books in the field of Criminal Justice

ADVANCES IN POLICE THEORY AND PRACTICE

Police Performance Appraisals: A Comparative Perspective
Serdar Kenan Gul and Paul O'Connell

Policing in France
Jacques de Maillard and Wesley G. Skogan

Women in Policing around the World: Doing Gender and Policing in a Gendered Organization
Venessa Garcia

Police Behavior, Hiring, and Crime Fighting: An International View
Edited by John A. Eterno, Ben Stickle, Diana Peterson, and Dilip K. Das

Translational Criminology in Policing
Edited by The George Mason Police Research Group with David Weisburd

Exploring Contemporary Policing Challenges: A Global Perspective
Edited by Sanja Kutnjak Ivković, Jon Maskály, Christopher M. Donner, Irena Cajner Mraović & Dilip Das

International Responses to Gendered-Based Domestic Violence: Gender-Specific and Social-Cultural Approach
Edited by Dongling Zhang & Diana Sharff Peterson

Gender Inclusive Policing: Challenges and Achievements
Edited by Tim Prenzler

Challenges of Contemporary Policing
Higher Education, Technology, and Officers' Well-Being
Edited by Vicente Riccio, Di Jia & Dilip K. Das

CHALLENGES OF CONTEMPORARY POLICING

Higher Education, Technology, and Officers' Well-Being

Edited by Vicente Riccio, Di Jia and Dilip K. Das

Routledge
Taylor & Francis Group
NEW YORK AND LONDON

Designed cover image: Ignatiev

First published 2025
by Routledge
605 Third Avenue, New York, NY 10158

and by Routledge
4 Park Square, Milton Park, Abingdon, Oxon OX14 4RN

Routledge is an imprint of the Taylor & Francis Group, an informa business

© 2025 selection and editorial matter, Vicente Riccio, Di Jia & Dilip K. Das; individual chapters, the contributors

The right of Vicente Riccio, Di Jia & Dilip K. Das to be identified as the authors of the editorial material, and of the authors for their individual chapters, has been asserted in accordance with sections 77 and 78 of the Copyright, Designs and Patents Act 1988.

All rights reserved. No part of this book may be reprinted or reproduced or utilised in any form or by any electronic, mechanical, or other means, now known or hereafter invented, including photocopying and recording, or in any information storage or retrieval system, without permission in writing from the publishers.

Trademark notice: Product or corporate names may be trademarks or registered trademarks, and are used only for identification and explanation without intent to infringe.

Library of Congress Cataloging-in-Publication Data
Names: Riccio, Vicente, editor. | Jia, Di, editor. | Das, Dilip K., 1941- editor.
Title: Challenges of contemporary policing : higher education, technology, and officers' well-being / edited by Vicente Riccio, Di Jia, Dilip Das.
Description: 1 edition. | New York, NY : Routledge, 2024. |
Series: Advances in police theory and practice | Includes bibliographical references and index.
Identifiers: LCCN 2024007440 (print) | LCCN 2024007441 (ebook) | ISBN 9781032589695 (hardback) | ISBN 9781032589671 (paperback) | ISBN 9781003452379 (ebook)
Subjects: LCSH: Police administration. | Justice, Administration of. | Management--Technological innovations.
Classification: LCC HV7935 C43 2024 (print) | LCC HV7935 (ebook) | DDC 353.3/6--dc23/eng/20240223
LC record available at https://lccn.loc.gov/2024007440
LC ebook record available at https://lccn.loc.gov/2024007441

ISBN: 978-1-032-58969-5 (hbk)
ISBN: 978-1-032-58967-1 (pbk)
ISBN: 978-1-003-45237-9 (ebk)

DOI: 10.4324/9781003452379

Typeset in Sabon
by Taylor & Francis Books

CONTENTS

List of illustrations	ix
List of contributors	xi
Series Editor's Preface	xviii
Appendix I: IPES Global Meetings	xxi
Appendix II: IPES Publications	xiv

Introduction Vicente Riccio, Di Jia and Dilip K. Das	1
1 Performance evaluation of integrated public security areas: Application of the PROMETHEE II method in the Brazilian context Marcio Pereira Basilio, Valdecy Pereira, Max William Coelho Moreira de Oliveira and Antonio Fernandes da Costa Neto	10
2 Addressing the challenges of law enforcement higher education in Hungary László Christián	35
3 The formation of the Local Prevention Police Units at the National University of Lanús Daniel Russo and Alejandro Hener	47

4 Community justice and Chinese immigrants: The
   perspective of law enforcement   75
   Jurg Gerber, Di Jia and Charles W. Russo

5 Understanding officer's behavior in a non-traffic situation:
   Why will police officers use force and verbally attack
   citizens during a street stop?   91
   Francis D. Boateng and Michael K. Dzordzormenyoh

6 The determinant factors of religious radicalization: The
   case of Kyrgyzstan   107
   Erlan Bakiev and Zairbek Kozhomberdiev

7 Cameras, community, and police: Possible correlations in
   the evaluation of the body-worn cameras for the Brazilian
   Federal Highway Police   125
   *Otávio Lacerda, Eduardo Magrone, Vicente Riccio and
   Wagner Silveira Rezende*

8 Officer suicide: Agency protocol and prevention strategies   146
   Charles W. Russo, Jarrod Sadulski and Matthew Loux

9 Police suicide in Brazil: What do we know?   173
   Dayse Assunção Miranda and Fernanda Novaes Cruz

10 PTSD: Is it pension worthy   189
   Charles Russo and Stephanie Myers-Hunziker

11 Addictive hypervigilance and uncontrolled police use of
   force   201
   Jesse Cheng

12 The law enforcement workforce crisis: Developing
   targeted recruitment and retention strategies for future
   generations   214
   Nicole Cain

Index   *231*

ILLUSTRATIONS

Figures

1.1	PROMETHEE II complete ranking	24
1.2	PROMETHEE Diamond	28
1.3	Classification of alternatives according to criteria	28
1.4	PROMETHEE Network View	29
1.5	Thermal map of the 39 IPSA distributed in the State of Rio de Janeiro. Brazil	30
1.6	Thermal map of IPSA located in the Capital of the State of Rio de Janeiro	31
2.1	Complementary law enforcement in Hungary	36

Tables

A.1	IPE Global Meetings	xxi
1.1	Division of the state of Rio de Janeiro	17
1.2	Evaluation matrix	19
1.3	Procedure for selecting a preference function	21
1.4	Model parameters	23
1.5	Criteria flow	25
1.6	The PROMETHEE complete ranking	27
1.7	Categorization of law enforcement agencies by their level of efficiency compared	29
5.1	Descriptive statistics of study variables (N =650)	98

5.2	Factors influencing police verbal assault against suspects during street (non-traffic) stops (N =650)	99
5.3	Factors influencing police use of force against suspects during street (non-traffic) stops (N =650)	100
6.1	Convicts on religious extremism and terrorism	112
7.1	Distribution of the 532 answers to the questions that make up the relationship with the community variable	137
7.2	Distribution of the 532 responses to the component questions of the support variable for using cameras	138
7.3	Model summary	139
7.4	ANOVA b	139
7.5	Coefficients ☒	140
9.1	Military and Civil Police suicide from 2017 to 2022	175
9.2	Military and Civil Police homicide on duty from 2017 to 2022	175
10.1	PTSD without physical injury compensation	193
10.2	Workers' compensation coverage category of injuries	195
12.1	Overall satisfaction comparison by generational classification	220
12.2	Impact of leadership style perceptions comparison by generation	220
12.3	Comparison of perceptions of training as being satisfactory in handling stressful policing situations and community relations	221
12.4	Predicting overall satisfaction by motivational factor for millennials	222
12.5.	Predicting overall satisfaction by motivational factor for Generation X	222
12.6	Predicting overall satisfaction by hygiene factors for millennials	223
12.7	Predicting overall satisfaction by hygiene factors for Generation X	223
12.8	Predicting overall satisfaction by motivation and hygiene factors for millennials	224

CONTRIBUTORS

Erlan Bakiev is a retired police officer at Kyrgyz National Police, with more than 23 years of service. Currently he is a Political Affairs Officer at the UN mission in South Sudan. He received his masters degree on Criminal Justice at the University of Cincinnati and his doctorate is from the University of Central Florida (Public Policy). Dr. Bakiev's main research interests are extremism and terrorism, governance and public policy, and collaborative public management. Dr. Bakiev has published widely in areas of management, criminal justice, public administration and policy.

Francis D. Boateng, Ph.D., is an Associate Professor of Criminal Justice and Legal Studies at the University of Mississippi. He received his Master's and Ph.D. from Washington State University, and his teaching and research interests are in Policing, Comparative Criminology, Victimology, Immigration, Crime, and Terrorism.

Marcio Pereira Basilio holds a bachelor's degree in business administration (FRNL/1996); postgraduate studies in human resources administration (1998); systems analysis (UNESA/2000); public security management (FGV/2007); financial management, compliance and auditing (FGV/2012). He holds a master's degree in public administration (EBAPE-FGV/2007), and a PhD in Production Engineering, with an emphasis on decision support systems (UFF/2019). He has worked for 32 years and 8 months as a Military Police Officer in the State of Rio de Janeiro. In this career, he reached the position of Colonel, where, among other duties, he held his last position in active service as Under-Secretary General of the Military Police Secretariat for the period 2019–2021. He is currently coordinator of accountability for legal entities at the Office of the Controller General of the State of Rio de Janeiro.

Nicole Cain is an Assistant Professor with American Public University. She has instructed numerous criminal justice and forensic courses online for 17 years. She has over 23 years of law enforcement experience serving in a variety of capacities to include, patrol operations, uniform crime scene, community-oriented policing (COP), criminal investigations, and felony intake. In 2020, she earned her Doctoral Degree in Education (Ed.D.) from Southeastern University. She attained a B.A. in Political Science from the University of South Florida, a M.S. in Criminal Justice Administration from Saint Leo University, and Police Officer Minimum Standards from Polk State College. She has taken a variety of professional development courses in her fields. She published "Walking the Ethical Line: The Use of Deception by Police Detectives During Investigative Interviews" in The Florida Police Chief Magazine in July 2004 as well as numerous articles in the American Military University Edge blog.

Jesse Cheng is an Assistant Professor in the DePaul University College of Law. His research uses restorative methods to understand and address root causes of violence, with specific application in U.S. criminal law and sentencing.

László Christián is Police Brigadier General, Vice-Rector of Ludovika University of Public Service (Budapest, Hungary) Vice-Rector for Education of Ludovika University of Public Service since 2020, a police brigadier general and a lawyer. László has been the Head of the Department of Private Security and Municipal Policing of the Faculty of Law Enforcement of Ludovika University since 2013. He is a full professor and has been teaching in higher education since 2002. He started his professional career at the Customs and Finance Guard in 2002, then continued at the National Tax and Customs Office in various management positions. Since 2016 he has been a regular member of the Police. He is the Editor-in-Chief of *Magyar Rendészet* (Hungarian Law Enforcement) and the author of two monographies and 150 publications. László Christián is the holder of several awards, he has participated in 30 study trips abroad on several continents, he regularly gives lectures at national and international conferences. His main field of research is public administration, complementary law enforcement, public and private security, municipal policing and higher education in the 21st century.

Antonio Fernandes da Costa Neto holds a degree from the Officer Training Course at the Dom João VI Military Police Academy (2002), a degree in Law from the Cruzeiro do Sul University (2021), a Master's in Public Administration from the Getúlio Vargas Foundation – EBAPE (2022), a Postgraduate Lato Sensu degree in Politics and Management of Public Security from Estácio de Sá (2007), and an Extension and Improvement Course for Officers, with an emphasis on Ethics (2011). He has been for 24 years an officer in the Military Police of the State of Rio de Janeiro. He is currently a Lieutenant Colonel and holds the position of Deputy Coordinator of Strategic Affairs of the Military Police of the State of Rio de Janeiro.

Fernanda Novaes Cruz is a researcher at the Center for the Study of Violence at the University of São Paulo, Brazil (NEV-USP). She is also an associated researcher at the Institute of Research, Prevention, and Studies in Suicide, Brazil (IPPES Brasil). She holds a Ph.D. in Sociology from The Institute of Social and Political Studies at the University of the State of Rio de Janeiro, Brazil (IESP-UERJ). Her research interests cover diverse topics such as police organizations, police legitimacy, and police officers' mental health issues.

Michael Dzordzormenyoh is an Assistant Professor in the Department of Political Science at Kent State University. He received his Ph.D. from the Department of Political Science at the University of South Dakota, Vermillion. He studies comparative social justice and inequality issues using formal theory, quantitative, and qualitative methods. His past and current research examines social justice and inequality issues in areas such as criminal justice, immigration, healthcare, leadership, and elections in the United States, and the global south, i.e., Africa and Brazil. Prior to joining Kent State, he completed a postdoctoral fellowship and a visiting assistant professor position at the Center for Black Studies Research, University of California, Santa Barbara and the Department of Political Science, Oklahoma State University, respectively.

Jurg Gerber is a professor in the Department of Criminal Justice and Criminology and Director of International Initiatives in the College of Criminal Justice at Sam Houston State University. For 20 years he served as Professeur Invité at the University of Lausanne (Lausanne, Switzerland) and he spent a year as a Fulbright Scholar at Kaliningrad State University, in Kaliningrad, Russia. Research interests include white-collar crime, criminology, drug control policy, policing, and international criminal justice issues. He has co-edited two books on drug policy, one on white-collar crime, and has published extensively in all of the above areas.

Alejandro Hener holds a degree in Sociology and PhD in Social Sciences from University of Buenos Aires (UBA). Reasearch Professor at National University of Lanús (UNLa), Argentine. Professor of Criminology, his research topics are focused on security policies, police training and fear of crime. He has directed the research projects "Scope of training in the police practice at the university level. The experience of the Local Police of the Municipality of Lanús at the National University of Lanús" and "The construction of know-how in the police function: from initial training to the production of criteria for daily practices".

Di Jia is Associate Professor in the Department of Criminal Justice and Criminology at MSU Denver. After receiving her Ph.D. from the College of Criminal Justice at Sam Houston State University, Dr. Jia has committed to teaching in criminal justice. As a former law enforcement officer in emergency and crisis policing, she applies her research and working experience to the classroom. Her teaching/research interests include Police Systems and Practices, Crime Analysis, Homeland Security and Crisis Management, and International and Comparative Studies on Criminal Justice Issues.

Zairbek Kozhomberdiev (Police Lieutenant Colonel) has a degree from the Academy of the Ministry of Internal Affairs of the Kyrgyz Republic named after Major General E. Aliyev. Throughout his career, he worked in the internal affairs bodies in various positions, such as Chief Inspector of the General Staff of the Ministry of Internal Affairs of the Kyrgyz Republic, Head of the Department of Public Security Service of the Ministry of Internal Affairs of the Kyrgyz Republic, coordinator of special purpose police battalions in the UN Mission in South Sudan, police adviser in the field office in Bentiu of the UN Mission in South Sudan, Head of the Department for Combating Drug Trafficking at the Department of Internal Affairs of Pervomaisky district of Bishkek, a police adviser at the field office in El Fasher in Darfur of the UN Mission in Northern Sudan, a senior operative of the Drug Trafficking Control Service of the Ministry of Internal Affairs of the Kyrgyz Republic for the Talas department, a senior operative of the Criminal Investigation Department of the Department of Internal Affairs of the Sverdlovsk district of Bishkek, and an investigator of the investigative department of the Sverdlovsk district of Bishkek.

Otávio Lacerda is a criminal lawyer and researcher in Law and Public Security. He graduated in Law from the Federal University of Juiz de Fora in 2019, specialising in Public Security and Citizenship in 2021, and gaining his Master's degree in Law and Innovation in 2023. His expertise is in Law, with an emphasis on Criminal Law and Criminal Procedural Law.

Matthew Loux is an Assistant Professor at American Public University System (APUS). He started his career in law enforcement in 1992 in Missouri and worked in many specialties such as patrol, field training officer, detective, undercover officer, and SWAT team member. He instructs many criminal justice courses in the APUS School of Security and Global Studies. His research focuses on officer stress, retention, training, human trafficking, and online learning.

Eduardo Magrone is a professor of Sociology of Education. He is currently an associate professor at the Federal University of Juiz de Fora-MG (Brazil), with experience in public educational policies. He holds a PhD in Sociology from the University Research Institute of Rio de Janeiro-IUPERJ (Current Institute of Social and Political Studies-IESP). He participates in the research project "Critical analysis of judicial decisions on environmental crimes in the Amazon".

Dayse Assunção Miranda is a professor and researcher at the Institute of Research, Prevention, and Studies in Suicide, Brazil (IPPES Brasil). She holds a PhD in Political Science at the University of the State of São Paulo, Brazil (USP). Her research interests cover diverse topics such as policy on death violence prevention, gender-based violence and police officers' mental health issues.

Stephanie Myers-Hunziker is currently a full professor of Criminal Justice at the American Public University System (APUS). Dr. Hunziker began her research career as a graduate student working with a local police agency in Albany, NY while mining data from their CAD system and helping the agency navigate and implement crime mapping software. Dr. Hunziker went on to supervise data collection for a large scale study of police in the late 1990s (the Project on Policing Neighborhoods). Later, she received a research grant from the National Institute of Justice (NIJ) which funded her dissertation research on police encounters with juvenile suspects which utilized some of those data. She wrote a report for NIJ on the subject and also testified about her findings before a Congressional panel on Juvenile crime. Since then she has worked with local agencies in Central Florida on best practices projects and has most recently collaborated with Dr. Charles Russo on research studying the impacts of PTSD on first responders.

Max William Coelho Moreira de Oliveira holds a degree in Administration from Federal Fluminense University (UFF/2002), a postgraduate degree (MBA) in Big Data and Business Analytics from Getúlio Vargas Foundation (FGV/2022), a master's degree in Production Engineering (UFF/2012) and a PhD in Production

Engineering (UFF/2018). He is currently Coordinator of Strategic Affairs at the State Secretariat of Military Police in the State of Rio de Janeiro for 5 years, Colonel of the Military Police and a member of this police force for 32 years. Internally, works mainly on the following topics: Administration, R&D, Strategic Planning, Criminal Analysis, Data Science and Project Management.

Valdecy Pereira holds a degree in Production Engineering (UERJ/2006), a Master's in Production Engineering (UFF/2008), is specialized in Construction Planning and Assembly (UFF/2008), qualified as Planning and Construction Engineer (PROMINP/2008), with a PhD in Production Engineering (UFF/2012). He is currently Adjunct Professor at the Federal Fluminense University and works mainly on the following topics: Operations Research, Production Planning and Control, Multivariate Data Analysis, Multicriteria Methods, Machine Learning, Deep Machine Learning and Artificial Intelligence.

Wagner Silveira Rezende holds a PhD on Sociology from the Federal University of Juiz de Fora (UFJF) and a PhD on Education from UFJF. He is currently professor at the Graduate Program in Law and Innovation at the Federal University of Juiz de Fora, and the coordinator of the Center for Evaluation of Basic Education (CAED) at the Federal University of Juiz de Fora.

Charles Russo is the Department Chair of Human Justice/Criminal Justice at the American Public University System (APUS). Dr. Russo also serves as the United Nations liaison representing the International Police Executive Symposium. He began his career in law enforcement in 1987 in Central Florida and was involved in all areas of patrol, training, special operations, and investigations before retiring from law enforcement in 2013. Dr. Russo continues to design and instruct courses, as well as act as a consultant for education, government, and industry throughout the world. His recent research and presentations focus on emerging technology and law enforcement applications, officer hiring and retention, post-traumatic stress, agency response to officer suicide, human trafficking, nongovernment intelligence actors, and online learning.

Daniel Russo is a doctor in Community Mental Health, Universidad Nacional de Lanús (UNLa) and a psychologist specializing in Education. He is Associate Professor at the UNLa, Adjunct Professor at the Faculty of Social Sciences of the University of Buenos Aires and Professor at the Cadet School of the Argentine Federal Police. He is author of the book *Cuidar a la fuerza* (La Docta Ignorancia/Edunla, 2020) and has participated in several publications. He was National Director of Training on Addictions (SEDRONAR), Academic Coordinator of the training of the Police Prevention Units of the Municipality of Lanús and in the Police Buenos Aires 2, on behalf of the UNLa.

Jarrod Sadulski is a faculty member at the American Public University System. He has over 20 years of law enforcement experience and conduct in-country research in Central and South America on some of the most pressing issues in criminal justice, including counter narcotics trafficking and counter human trafficking. His research in human trafficking along the Southwest Border led him to testifying before Congress in late 2023 on current trends in human trafficking and smuggling. Dr. Sadulski engages in speaking events nationwide on human trafficking and serves as a consultant on human trafficking and other pressing issues in criminal justice globally.

SERIES EDITOR'S PREFACE

While the literature on police and allied subjects is growing exponentially, its impact on day to-day policing remains small. The two worlds of research and practice of policing remain disconnected, even though cooperation between the two is growing. A major reason is that the two groups speak in different languages. The research work is published in hard-to-access journals and presented in a manner that is difficult for a lay person to comprehend. On the other hand, the police practitioners tend not to mix with researchers and remain secretive about their work. Consequently, there is little dialogue between the two and almost no attempt to learn from one another. Dialogue across the globe among researchers and practitioners situated in different continents is, of course, even more limited.

A police practitioner turned academic, Dilip Das attempted to address this problem by starting the International Police Executive Symposium (IPES) (www.ipes.info), where a common platform has brought the two together. IPES is now in its 30th year. The annual meetings that constitute most of the major annual events of the organization have been hosted in all parts of the world. Several very impressive publications have come out of these deliberations, and a new collaborative community of scholars and police officers has been created whose membership runs into several thousands.

The International Police Executive Symposium has annual meetings throughout the world. All the editors have attended these meetings. They involve a collaboration of practitioners, scholars, and other experts in law enforcement. Ideas are exchanged in a unique way as all at the meeting not only share their research bur also collaborate during social events. This volume brings chapters from the 31st IPES Meeting held in Albany, New York, after two years of the COVID pandemic. It discusses contemporary challenges for the police throughout the globe such as legitimacy, higher education, technology impacts, and officers' well-being. All those issues are interconnected, and the contributions come from different continents such as Asia, Europe, North America, and South America.

At this moment when the police have been facing increasing demands to deal with issues ranging from drug dealing, criminal organizations, domestic violence, among others, and legitimacy concerns in different countries, they have enormous challenges. This uncertain environment requires new competencies for police officers such as technological and interpersonal skills. It makes higher education and training a relevant topic for the improvement of policing. In this context, police officers work under increased pressure from a more critical civil society, new technological control instruments, and budget constraints. As a consequence, officers' well-being is a real problem in many police forces, and the register of stress, demotivation, depression, substance abuse, and suicide are problems that must be addressed by police managers. This book discusses these issues and hopes to contribute to the debates in the field, and to help the practitioners dealing with these problems on a daily basis.

Finally, this work represents the aim of IPES: A global forum that gathers researchers and practitioners with plural and democratic perspectives. It is an important perspective because policing challenges are becoming more global, and their effects can be observed in different places. Thus, there are new frontiers to be explored by researchers and practitioners.

An account of the IPES meetings and publications is included in the next pages. The global influence and service of IPES was recognized by the United Nations and, as a result, IPES is in special consultative status with the United Nations.

Dilip K. Das PhD, Professor. Founding President, International Police Executive Symposium, IPES, www.ipes.info. Founding Editor-in-Chief, Police Practice and Research: An International Journal, PPR, http://www.tandfonline.com/gppr (2000–2020). Editor-in-Chief, Advances in Police Theory and Practice, Book Series. Founding Editor, Journal of Best Practice and Research in Policing (Forthcoming). Human Rights Consultant to the United Nations,. Vicente Riccio, Associate Professor – Federal University of Juiz de Fora (Brazil). IPES Book Editor.

APPENDIX I: IPES GLOBAL MEETINGS

TABLE A.1 IPE Global Meetings

	Country	Theme	Host
1994	Switzerland	Police Challenges and Strategies	Canton Police, Geneva, Switzerland
1995	Spain	Challenges of Policing Democracies	International Institute of the Sociology of Law, Basque Country, Spain
1996	Japan	Organized Crime	Kanagawa University
1997	Austria	International Police Cooperation	Federal Police in Vienna, Austria
1998	The Netherlands	Crime Prevention	Dutch Police, Europol
1999	India	Policing of Public Order	Andhra Pradesh Police, Hyderabad, India
2000	Evanston, Illinois, USA	Traffic Policing	Northwestern University, Center for Public Safety
2001	Poland	Corruption: A Threat to World Order	Police of Poland
2002	Turkey	Police Education and Training	Turkish National Police
2003	Bahrain	Police and Community	Kingdom of Bahrain
2004	Canada	Criminal Exploitation of Women and Children	Abbotsford Police Department, Canadian Police College, Royal Canadian Mounted Police, University College of the Fraser Valley, Vancouver Police Department

Appendix I: IPES Global Meetings

	Country	Theme	Host
2005	The Czech Republic	Challenges of Policing in the 21st Century: A Global Assessment	The Czech Police Academy, The Ministry of the Interior, The Czech Republic
2006	Turkey	Local Linkages to Global Security and Crime: Thinking Locally and Acting Globally	Turkish National Police
2007	Dubai	Urbanization and Security	Dubai Police
2008	USA, Ohio	Police Without Borders: The Fading Distinction Between Local & Global	Cincinnati Police Department & Ohio Association of Chiefs of Police
2009	FYR Macedonia	Policing, the Private Sector, Economic Development & Social Change: Contemporary Global Trends	Ministry of Interior, Republic of Macedonia
2010	Malta	Tourism, Strategic Locations & Major Events: Policing in an Age of Mobility, Mass Movement and Migration	Commissioner John Rizzo and Malta Police
2010	India	Community Policing: Theoretical Problems and Operational Issues	Government of Kerala and the Kerala Police Department
2011	Argentina	Policing Violence, Crime, Disorder, & Discontent: International Perspectives	IPES
2011	Sweden	Contemporary Issues in Public Safety & Security	The Blekinge Technological Institute and the Swedish Police
2012	USA, New York	Economic Development, Armed Violence and Public Safety	In Cooperation with United Nations Dept of Economic & Social Affairs NGO Branch
2013	Hungary	Global Issues in Contemporary Policing	The Ministry of Interior and The Hungarian National Police
2014	India	Policing by Consent: Theoretical Challenges and Operational Issues	Kerala Police Department
2014	Bulgaria	Crime Prevention & Community Resilience: Police Role with Victims, Youth, Ethnic Minorities and Other Partners	IPES and the Bulgarian Ministry of Interior
2015	Thailand	Police Governance and Human Trafficking: Promoting Preventative and Comprehensive Strategies	The Royal Thai Police Association, The Royal Thai Police and Shinawatra University

	Country	Theme	Host
2016	USA, Washington DC	Urban Security: Challenges for 21st Century Global Cities	The George Washington University
2017	England	Organized Crime & Terrorism: Policing Challenges for Local to International level	Liverpool John Moores University
2018	Austria	International Police Cooperation	United Nations Office on Drugs and Crime
2019	Serbia	Contemporary Police Challenges in Light of a New World and New Knowledge	IPES
2022	Albany, New York, USA	Integrating Science, Technology, and Higher Education into Policing: Interdisciplinary & International Perspectives	IPES and University of Albany (Criminal Justice School)
2023	Manaus, Brazil	Policing, Rule of law, Organized Crime, and the Environment	IPES, State University of Amazonas (UEA), and Center for Security Studies in the Amazon (CESAM)

APPENDIX II: IPES PUBLICATIONS

A) Advances in Police Theory and Practice – Routledge

1. *Gender Inclusive Policing*

   Tim Prenzler

2. *International Responses to GenderedBased Domestic: GenderSpecific and SocialCultural Approach*

   Dongling Zhang
   Diana Sharff Peterson

3. *Exploring Contemporary Police Challenges: A Global Perspective*

   Sanja Kutnjak Ivković
   Jon Maskály
   Christopher M. Donner
   Irena Cajner Mraović
   Dilip Das

4. *Translational Criminology in Policing*

   The George Mason Police Research
   David Weisburd

5. *Police Behavior, Hiring, and Crime Fighting: An International View*

   John A. Eterno
   Ben Stickle
   Diana Scharff Peterson
   Dilip K. Das

6. *Women in Policing around the World: Doing Gender and Policing in a Gendered Organization*

   Vanessa Garcia

7. *Policing in France*

   Jacques de Maillard
   Wesley G. Skogan

8. *Policing and Mentally Ill: International Perspectives*

   Duncan Chappell

9. *Civilian Oversight of Police: Advancing Accountability in Law Enforcement*

   Tim Prenzler
   Garth den Heyer

10. *Cold Cases: Evaluation Models with Followup Strategies for Investigators*, second edition

    James M. Adcock
    Sarah L. Stein

11. *Collaborative Policing: Police, Academics, Professionals, and Communities Working Together for Education, Training, and Program Implementation*

    Peter C. Kratcoski
    Maximilian Edelbacher

12. *Community Policing: International Patterns and Comparative Perspectives*

    Dominique Wisler
    Ihekwoaba D. Onwudiwe

13. *Community Policing and Peacekeeping*

    Peter Grabosky

14. *Crime Linkage: Theory, Research, and Practice*

    Jessica Woodhams
    Craig Bennell

15. *Delivering Police Services Effectively*

    Garth den Heyer

16. *Ethics for Police Translators and Interpreters*

    Sedat Mulayim
    Miranda Lai

17. *Honorbased Violence: Policing and Prevention*

    Karl Anton Roberts
    Gerry Campbell
    Glen Lloyd

18. *Los Angeles Police Department Meltdown: The Fall of the Professional Reform Model of Policing*

    James Lasley

19. *Police Corruption: Preventing Misconduct and Maintaining Integrity*

    Tim Prenzler

20. *Police Integrity Management in Australia: Global Lessons for Combating Police Misconduct*

    Louise Porter
    Tim Prenzler

21. *Police Investigative Interviews and Interpreting: Context, Challenges and Strategies*

    Sedat Mulayim
    Miranda Lai
    Caroline Norma

22. *Police Performance Appraisals: A Comparative Perspective*

    Serdar Kenan Gul
    Paul O'Connell

23. *Police Organized Crime: Intelligence Strategy Implementation*

    Petter Gottschalk

24. *Policing Terrorism: Research Studies into Police Counterterrorism Investigations*

    David Lowe

25. *Policing Whitecollar Crime: Characteristics of Whitecollar Criminals*

    Petter Gottschalk

26. *Policing in Hong Kong: History and Reform*

    Kam C. Wong

27. *Policing in Israel: Studying Crime Control, Community, and Counterterrorism*

    Tal JonathanZamir
    David Weisburd
    Badi Hasisi

28. *Security Governance, Policing, and Local Capacity*

    Jan Froestad
    Clifford Shearing

29. *The International Trafficking of Human Organs: A Multidisciplinary Perspective*

    Leonard Territo
    Rande Matteson

30. *Police and Society in Brazil*

    Vicente Riccio
    Wesley G. Skogan

31. *Police Reform in China*

    Kam C. Wong

32. *Cold Cases: An Evaluation Model with Followup Strategies for Investigators*

    James M. Adcock
    Sarah L. Stein

33. *The Crime Numbers Game: Management by Manipulation*

   John A. Eterno
   Eli B. Silverman

34. *Mission-based Policing*

   John P. Crank
   Dawn M. Irlbeck
   Rebecca K. Murray
   Mark Sundermeier

35. *The New Khaki: The Evolving Nature of Policing in India* Arvind Verma

B) Copublications – Routledge/Taylor & Francis

1. *Change and Reform in Law Enforcement: Old and New Efforts from Across the Globe*

   Scott W. Phillips
   Dilip K. Das

2. *Contemporary Issues in Law Enforcement and Policing*

   Andrew Millie
   Dilip K. Das

3. *Criminal Abuse of Women and Children: An International Perspective*

   Obi N.I. Ebbe
   Dilip K. Das

4. *Economic Development, Crime, and Policing: Global Perspectives*

   Frederic Lemieux
   Garth den Heyer
   Dilip K. Das

5. *Effective Crime Reduction Strategies: International Perspectives*

   James F. Albrecht
   Dilip K. Das

6. *Examining Political Violence: Studies of Terrorisms, Counterterrorism, and International War*

   David Lowe
   Austin Turk

Dilip K. Das

7. *Global Community Policing: Problems and Challenges*

   Arvind Verma
   Dilip K. Das
   Manoj Abraham

8. *Global Environment of Policing*

   Darren Palmer
   Michal M. Berlin
   Dilip K. Das

9. *Global Issues in Contemporary Policing*

   John Eterno
   Arvind Verma
   Aiedeo Mintie Das
   Dilip K. Das

10. *Global Perspectives on Crime Prevention and Community Resilience*

    Diana Scharff Peterson
    Dilip K. Das

11. *Global Trafficking in Women and Children*

    Obi N.I. Ebbe
    Dilip K. Das

12. *Police Without Borders: The Fading Distinction Between Local and Global*

    Cliff Roberson
    Dilip K. Das
    Jennie K. Singer

13. *Policing Global Movement: Tourism, Migration, Human Trafficking and Terrorism*

    (A) S. Caroline Taylor
    (B) Daniel Joseph Torpy
    (C) Dilip K. Das

14. *The Evolution of Policing: Worldwide Innovations and Insights*

    Melchor C. de Guzman
    Aiedeo Mintie Das

Dilip K. Das

15. *Urbanization, Policing and Security: Global Perspectives*

    Gary Cordner
    AnnMarie Cordner
    Dilip K. Das

16. *Policing Major Events: Perspectives from around the World*

    James F. Albrecht
    Martha Christine Dow
    Darryl Plecas
    Dilip K. Das

17. *Strategies and Responses to Crime: Thinking Locally, Acting Globally*Melchor de Guzman
    Aiedeo Mintie Das
    Dilip K. Das

C) Interviews with Global Leaders in Policing, Courts and Prisons – Routledge

1. *Trends in the Judiciary: Interviews with Judges across the Globe*, volume four

    Wendell C. Wallace
    Michael M. Berlin
    Dilip K. Das

2. *Trends in Policing: Interviews with Police Leaders across the Globe*, volume six

    Bruce F. Baker
    Dilip K. Das

3. *Trends in Corrections: Interviews with Corrections Leaders around the World*, volume two

    Martha Henderson Hurley
    Dilip K. Das

4. *Trends in Corrections: Interviews with Corrections Leaders around the World*, volume one

    Jennie K. Singer
    Dilip K. Das

Eileen Ahlin

5. *Trends in Legal Advocacy: Interviews with Prosecutors and Criminal Defense Lawyers across the Globe*, volume one

   Jane Goodman Delahunty
   Dilip K. Das

6. *Trends in Policing: Interviews with Police Leaders across the Globe*, volume five

   Bruce F. Baker
   Dilip K. Das

7. *Trends in Policing: Interviews with Police Leaders across the Globe*, volume four

   Bruce F. Baker
   Dilip K. Das

8. *Trends in the Judiciary: Interviews with Judges across the Globe*, volume one

   Dilip K. Das
   Cliff Roberson

9. *Trends in the Judiciary: Interviews with Judges across the Globe*, volume three

   David Lowe
   Dilip K. Das

10. *Trends in the Judiciary: Interviews with Judges across the Globe*, volume two

    David Lowe
    Dilip K. Das

11. *Trends in Corrections: Interviews with Corrections Leaders around the World*, volume three

    Dilip K. Das
    Philip Birch

12. *Trends in Policing: Interviews with Police Leaders across the Globe*, volume two

    Dilip K. Das
    Otwin Marenin

13. *Trends in Policing: Interviews with Police Leaders across the Globe*, volume three

   Otwin Marenin
   Dilip K. Das

INTRODUCTION

Vicente Riccio, Di Jia and Dilip K. Das

The police are the state institution with the most prominent social visibility. They can be observed daily when patrolling the streets on foot or in vehicles, as well as in the protection of public spaces such as schools, hospitals, and public buildings. In addition to these traditional spaces, the police are constantly portrayed in media (television, radio, newspapers, and social media) or through cultural products such as films, journals, or books. The presence of the police in our daily lives is deeply rooted in the society.

The modern police that emerged in the United Kingdom in 1829 with the action of Robert Peel placed the role of maintaining order and repressing crime in the hands of the State (Ignatieff 2005). The power to ensure order would no longer be defined *ad hoc* or by the action of individuals occasionally deployed to resolve problems of this nature. The evolution of the police from the 19th century to the present day has undergone several changes and criticisms.

The literature on the police, mostly from the Anglo-Saxon world, has pointed out the relationship between changes in society and the way in which policing models are constituted. Additionally, another important topic is addressed by such studies: the relationship between police and society (Skogan 2006). Therefore, the analysis of the police in the contemporary world must consider changes since the end of the 20th century because their environment has become more complex and uncertain (Moore 1992). The contemporary world is characterized by the expansion of democracies, and it impacts on policing. Democracies are based on constitutional systems that ensure human, social, and diverse rights, that are not simple to fulfill.

DOI: 10.4324/9781003452379-1

Moreover, real-time communication allows sharing experiences regardless of where one is physically present (Thompson 1995). The impactful and highly mediatized criminal event generates revolt and anxiety in spaces different from those in which it occurs (Innes 2014). The killing of young black man Michael Brown by white police officer Darren Wilson in Ferguson, a suburb of Saint Louis, Mississippi, led to protests in the city and gained worldwide press attention. Wilson was later acquitted, and a new wave of protests occurred in the city. The impact on American and global public opinion was so powerful that President Barack Obama, after Ferguson, created a task force to discuss the relationship between the police and society in the United States. Six years later, George Floyd's murder recorded on video sparked protests in a global scale.

Police activity is increasingly demanded by a public that seeks security and at the same time distrusts state institutions, due to a reality in which the State does not control social processes on a global scale exclusively based on its positive law (Bayley and Shearing 2005) and having its action increasingly impacted by technological innovations. Hence, the following issues impact police action on a global scale: 1) legitimacy, 2) technological innovations, 3) higher education and police training, and 4) officers' well-being. They reflect the daily challenges of the police, taking into account the police relations with the society, the visibility and control of police action brought about by the development of communication technologies, the education offered to police officers to deal with this complex reality, and the impacts on officers' well-being. Regarding the last aspect, officers' health problems occur in different countries across the globe.

Therefore, the way in which the institutions of the justice system apply the law is a relevant issue from the point of view of the problem of legitimacy (Tonry 2009). In the case of the police, the characteristics of their work are central to understanding the way in which the State agents act directly in everyday life (Lipsky 1980; Oberweis and Musheno 2001; Roché 2021).

Research in the United States shows that black people are more likely to be stopped and searched than white people. Residents of poorer neighborhoods experience greater abuse from police than residents of wealthier areas. For instance, the vast majority of people killed in confrontations with the police in Brazil are poor, black young people (Skogan and Riccio 2018). Such problems cast doubts regarding the legitimacy of the judicial system as perceived by the people of a developed or developing country (Dammert and Alda 2023). Why is legitimacy important for the police work? It is important because in all societies the Law and the institutions depends on the acceptance of the communities in which they operate (Tyler and Wakslack 2004).

In relation to the second issue, the application of new technologies has always been present in the development of modern policing. It covers a vast panorama comprising instruments ranging from weapons, motor vehicles, radios, audio recorders, cameras, computers, and software of the most varied types. As an example, images are central to contemporary life and the technical means to record them are ever present in our daily lives. Surveillance cameras, smartphones, computers, and other technological devices record everyday events and interactions. In this way, the image recorded on video constitutes a new variable in the law enforcement realm due to its capacity to produce evidence.

Regarding the police, the most recurrent events refer to excessive violence or corruption which tend to be hidden behind the blue wall of silence (Bittner 1990). Smartphones and cameras eroded this barrier and became new modes of control outside the traditional police and judicial institutions (Goldsmith 2010). The expansion of police surveillance through video monitoring technologies has implications for its culture and daily behavior (Campeau 2015; Constantinou and Kokkinos 2023).

The third theme of the book is the police education. This is a topic discussed in the literature, as there is a question about its impact on everyday practice. In this way, the studies cover different fields of interest such as identity aspects (Paes-Machado 2009), the emphasis on militarized elements (Riccio et al. 2013), the socialization processes existing in the Police Academy (Conti 2009), and the impacts of higher education on police practice (Paoline and Terrill 2007; Roberg and Bonn 2004), among other topics. Education is central to improving the police officer ability to deal with their daily complex tasks.

Finally, the last topic is officer well-being. In this complex context, the pressure on police officers has increased considerably, and health issues are a reality. Problems such as substance abuse, depression, stress, and suicide have been registered in different countries. Despite the occurrence of illness among police officers, few policies are drafted to curb it.

To deal with all these issues, this book is organized in three sections. The first is science, education, and technology in global policing. The second is the global challenge of police legitimacy, and the third is officer's well-being.

The chapter by Marcio Basilio, Valdecy Pereira, Max William, and Antonio Costa Neto titled "Performance evaluation of integrated public security areas: Application of the PROMETHEE II method in the Brazilian context" discusses the model (Multi Criteria Data Analysis – MCDA) to measure the performance of operational and logistical variables in Rio de Janeiro through a multicriteria method. The applied method is PROMETHEE II with the aid of the Visual PROMETHEE software. It has emulated the systematized data in the impact matrix and produced the final ordering of the most efficient police agencies in equalizing the operational, logistical, financial, and human resources applied in fighting crime and reducing criminal rates.

The results confirmed that the resources made available to the police agencies located in different municipalities in the metropolitan region of the state of Rio de Janeiro (Brazil) are better applied by managers compared to police units in the capital of Rio de Janeiro. From the research, it can be inferred that the use of multicriteria methods in modeling problems in public security can contribute to the rationalization of the use of available resources to fight crime in large cities. Research has shown that multicriteria methodology is able to determine which agencies make better use of the available resources, especially in the context of fiscal restraint as observed in Rio de Janeiro.

The chapter by László Christián, titled "Addressing the challenges of law enforcement education in Hungary", discusses the new strategies required for law enforcement education in a context of uncertainty. In Hungary, police training within the framework of higher education has been practiced for over 50 years. To perform this task, Ludovika University of Public Service (LUPS) developed a Creative Learning Program and a Research Center. The chapter focuses on the reform efforts to implement the new approach at LUPS.

Despite the existence of a higher education degree for a long time in the Hungarian Police, some initiatives have been implemented to comply with the new contemporary context, such as the elaboration of the Methodology Handbook, prizes for outstanding scholars, a new curriculum, and the measurement of results by the application of surveys. The paper concludes that LUPS has been able to promote changes in its training program.

The chapter by Daniel Russo and Alejandro Hener titled "The formation of the *Local Prevention Police Units* at the National University of Lanús" deals with a policy in the Province of Buenos Aires (Argentina) aimed at improving the quality of service through a partnership with the National University of Lanús (Universidad Nacional de Lanús – UNLA). The idea emerged due to the creation of the Local Prevention Police Units (Unidades Policiales de Prevención Local – UPPL by its Spanish acronym), which was expected to implement a new security policy more focused on the interaction with the community. The objective was to train these new police forces with the University's support. Each municipality in the Province of Buenos Aires was responsible for selecting the candidates, the instructors, and for the training itself. The administrator responsible for the project was appointed by the Mayor with the approval of political authorities. It resulted in a political conflict between the Governor's office and the municipal chiefs.

This led to the failure of the experiment and raised questions about the need for institutional cooperation between the University, the Police, and the political actors when drafting policies for implementing new projects and training methodologies. Thus, the chapter keeps open a relevant question for the police studies: Are the basic training programs able to transform the culture of police institutions? In this context marked by a constant economic crisis, low legitimacy, and social disparities, the change of police culture is a hard task.

The second section discusses the issue of legitimacy, and the chapter titled "Community justice and Chinese immigrants: The perspective of law enforcement" by Jurg Gerber, Di Jia, and Charles Russo deals with a relevant topic: Community justice, that is linked to legitimacy. Thus, a huge body of research has highlighted the significance of collaboration between criminal justice professionals and civilian populations to enhance the quality of life in the community (Tyler and Wakslack 2004). However, there is little research on the practitioners' perspective from the community justice model.

Based on the data collected from law enforcement agencies in three cities in the U.S., the chapter is a pilot study exploring the impacts of community justice on the new Chinese immigrant groups. The research found a gap in the existing body of literature that deals with the relationship between police officers and the Chinese immigrants in the 21st century. The study was implemented in four cities: New York, Houston, Daytona Beach, and Denver. The current research findings shed light on the variety of policing strategies in immigrant communities. In general, there is a positive relationship between the police and Chinese immigrants. The immigrants have positive views toward American police officers and describe them as positive and fair. In the same way, the officers consider the Chinese immigrants as hard-working and trustworthy people. It is important to note that this paper is part of a broader research project aimed at understanding the relationship between the police and migrants in China and in the United States.

The chapter by Francis Boateng and Michael Dzordzormenyoh titled "Understanding officer's behavior in a non-traffic situation: Why will police officers use force and verbally attack citizens during a street stop?" discusses the interactions between police officers and citizens during street stops. The study of non-traffic street stops has received limited research attention, and because of that, less is known about the nature and dynamics of such contacts. Several important questions related to officers' decision-making processes, attitudes, and behaviors remain unanswered. To answer some of these questions, the authors analysed self-reported data from citizens to explain police citizen interactions during non-traffic situations. Specifically, the authors examined the factors that influence police use of force during non-traffic street stops as well as assessing the effects of variables predicting police verbal attacks against citizens. Results from the regression models suggest that in verbal assaults against officers, gender and race are variables that predict whether officers will verbally attack a citizen or not. Additionally, the findings revealed that verbal assault against an officer, the officer's race, and suspect characteristics such as gender and income influence officers' decision to use force. The findings have serious implications for developing policies and enhancing the relationship between citizens and their local police departments.

The chapter by Erlan Bakiev and Zairbek Kozhomberdiev titled "The determinant factors of religious radicalization: The case of Kyrgyzstan" deals with a relevant topic: The reasons that drive citizens to terrorist and extremist organizations in Kyrgyzstan. They discuss why young people leave their native countries and join those organizations. The study was carried out with inmates serving a term in Kyrgyz prisons. The data was collected through the analysis of the opensource information and on field observations of Kyrgyz citizens who returned from the conflict zones. The research focused on (1) data collection from open sources and on field observations, (2) classification, and (3) observation and reconstruction of life stories of subjects who were recruited by terrorist organizations (Jihadists).

The results indicate that the majority of the inmates surveyed were between 22 and 30 years old, and it shows that extremist and terrorist organizations target relatively younger individuals. Most of them had enough resources for their livelihood before leaving for war zones. One of the main reasons they join Jihadi groups is the ideology which originates in religious illiteracy. Moreover, social networks and new information technologies played a significant role in the radicalization process of the respondents. In this sense, the police forces have been impacted by the appropriation of technological apparatuses by terrorist organizations. The authors conclude that the Kyrgyz government must be a prevailing actor in containing violence from extremist groups. Measures to protect society must contain the security problems and control those connected with economic development.

The chapter by Otavio Lacerda, Eduardo Magrone, Vicente Riccio, and Wagner Silveira Rezende titled "Camera, community, and police: Possible correlations in the evaluation of the body-worn cameras for the Brazilian Federal Highway Police" discusses the perceptions of Federal Highway Police Officers in Brazil about the use of body-worn cameras (BWC) and community relations. The Brazilian Federal Highway Police (Polícia Rodoviária Federal – PRF) are responsible for patrolling the federal highways in the country. This is a force of 12,000 officers working throughout the Brazilian territory. This study is based on a web survey conducted by the Federal University of Juiz de Fora (Universidade Federal de Juiz de Fora – UFJF) in partnership with the PRF. Through a simple linear regression, the study has shown a correlation between support for BWCs and favorable attitudes towards community policing.

The third section of the book discusses officers' well-being. This topic is important for understanding the effects of everyday problems on officers' health and the need for policies to deal with it (Griffin and Sun 2023). The chapter by Charles Russo, Jarrod Sadulski, and Matthew Loux titled "Officer suicide: Agency protocol and prevention strategies" presents the problem of agency protocols and prevention strategies in cases of officers' suicide. It explores issues such as family safety, access to firearms, substance abuse, and domestic violence that are related to the occurrence of suicide among officers. The authors analyse how agencies can curb suicide through pre-employment screening and positive practices. They conclude that there are no simple solutions for the suicide problem of officers, and that any solutions must involve colleagues, family, and other kinds of support for those with suicidal tendencies.

The chapter by Dayse Miranda and Fernanda Cruz analyses the problem of police officers' suicide in Brazil titled "Police suicide in Brazil: What do we know about?" This is a newly developing field of research in the country. The authors describe how the available suicide data from the Brazilian Death Certificates provided by forensic pathologists are limited. The forms are not properly filled in, and there is a misclassification of the causes of death. This information is processed by the Ministry of Health, that provides the data for studying violent deaths in Brazil.

According to the authors, there are four dimensions to consider when studying officers' suicide: (1) organizational, (2) situational, (3) social, and (4) individual. All these dimensions are interdependent and interactional. This qualitative study focuses on Military Police Officers, Civil Police Officers, and Firefighters from the State of Espírito Santo in Brazil. Some 19 active personnel were interviewed in this sample. They found an integration of individual, social, organizational, and situational risk factors associated with suicide.

The chapter by Charles Russo and Stephanie Myers-Hunziker titled "PTSD: Is it pension worthy" analyses whether posttraumatic stress disorder (PTSD) impacts officers in returning to work. The chapter discusses whether officers can get disability pensions and compensation benefits. Law enforcement personnel deal constantly with stressful situations. These moments affect them, and in general they suffer in silence. Pensions or benefits are a possibility for those who suffer from a physical disability but are not in sight for those who pass through PTSD. In some cases, police officers have profound psychological damage and must return to work without an improvement in their health condition.

The chapter by Jesse Cheng titled "Addictive hypervigilance and uncontrolled police use of force" discusses the problem of hypervigilance addiction among police officers. From a contemporary framework of behavioral addiction, the author analyses the relationship between an uncontrolled use of force and hypervigilance. This addiction can lead to a compulsion for the rush of a reactive, fight-or-flight physiological state that impairs rational deliberation and the accurate perception of threats. In this sense, the fear-based and on-guard mentality that is part of the police mentality should be modulated through the cultivation of other professional roles. The development of these new competencies requires new training programs and a strong incentive for accountability structures.

The chapter by Nicole Cain titled "The law enforcement workforce crisis: Developing targeted recruitment and retention strategies for future generations" discusses the law enforcement workforce crisis from a generational perspective. The United States has faced a decrease in law enforcement professionals of 4.6% from 1996 to 2018, and there are vacant positions in many agencies. Additionally, the resignation rate is growing each year. This situation leads to overworked personnel, resulting in more stress and health problems. Therefore, there is an increase in the overuse of sick time, accidental on-duty injuries, and the number of citizen complaints.

In this context, it is not simple for law enforcement agencies to attract and retain skilled personnel. It is problematic when dealing with millennials who do not remain in the same job or profession in their life and prefer satisfaction over gains. The research found that millennials consider the motivational factor and sense of mission as the most important satisfaction component related to the decision to pursue a career in law enforcement.

As previously noted, this book discusses how policing is affected in a context of great complexity. In this sense, the problems of legitimacy, the impact of new technologies, and the need to readapt police training and education are related. Furthermore, the impact on police officers' well-being is extremely relevant and deserves to be explored in greater depth. This book will contribute in this direction by integrating all these themes into common axes based on works built in different countries.

References

Bayley, D and Shearing, C. 2005. The future of policing. In T. Newburn, (ed.). *Policing: Key Readings*, 715–732, Devon: Willan.

Bittner, Egon. 1990. *Aspects of Police Work*. Boston: Northeastern University Press.

Campeau, H. 2015. Police cultures at work: Making sense of police oversight. *British Journal of Criminology*. January, 55 (4).

Constantinou, A. and Kokkinos, M. 2023. The forthcoming of body-worn police cameras in Cyprus: A blessing, a curse or something in the middle? In S. Kutnjak, I. Maskaly, C. Donner, I. C. Mraovic, D. K. Das, (eds.). *Exploring Contemporary Police Challenges: A Global Perspective*, 152–166, Routledge, New York and London.

Conti, N. 2009. A Visigoth system: shame, honor and police socialization. *Journal of Contemporary Ethnography*, 38, 409–432.

Dammert, L. and Alda, E. 2023. Police legitimacy in Chile. In S. Kutnjak, I. Maskaly, C. Donner, I. C. Mraovic, D. K. Das, (eds.). *Exploring Contemporary Police Challenges: A Global Perspective*, 34–47, Routledge, New York and London.

Goldsmith, A. J. 2010. Policing's new visibility, *British Journal of Criminology*, 50, 914–934.

Griffin, J. D. and Sun, I. Y. 2023. A qualitative study of the impacts of work-family conflict on police officer stress. In S. Kutnjak, I. Maskaly, C. Donner, I. C. Mraovic, D. K. Das, (eds.). *Exploring Contemporary Police Challenges: A Global Perspective*, 347–357, Routledge, New York and London.

Ignatieff, M. 2005. Police and people: The birth of Mr. Peel's 'blue locusts'. In T. Newburn, (ed.). *Policing: Key Readings*, 25–30. Devon: Willan.

Innes, M. 2014. *Signal Crimes: Social Reactions to Crime, Disorder, and Control*. Oxford: Oxford University Press.

Lipsky, M. 1980. *Street-level Bureaucracies: Dilemmas of the Individual in the Public Service*. New York: Russel Sage Foundation.

Moore, Mark. 1992. Problem-solving and community policing. In M. Tonry and N. Morris, (eds.). *Modern Policing, Crime and Justice: A Review of Literature*, v.15, 99–158. Chicago: Chicago University Press.

Oberweis, T. and Musheno, M. 2001. *Knowing Rights: State Actors' Stories of Power, Identity and Morality*. Aldershot: Ashgate.

Paes-Machado, E. and Albuquerque, C. L. 2006. The family curriculum, socialization process, family networks and the negotiation of police identities. *The Australian and New Zealand Journal of Criminology*, 39 (2), 248–267.

Paoline, E. and Terrill, W. 2007. Police, education, experience and the use of force. *Criminal Justice and Behavior*, 34 (2), 179–196.

Riccio, V., Miranda, M. Rys and Müller, A. 2013. Professionalizing the Amazonas military police through training. *Police Practice and Research*, 14 (4), 295–307.

Roberg, R. and Bonn, S. 2004. Higher education and policing: where are we now? *Policing*, 27 (4), 469–486.

Roché, S. 2021. Police and the public in France. In J. Maillard and W. Skogan, (eds.) *Policing in France*, 269–292, New York and London: Routledge.

Skogan, W. 2006. *Police and Community in Chicago: A Tale of Three Cities*. Oxford: Oxford University Press.

Skogan, W. and Riccio, V. 2018. Police and society in Brazil. In V. Riccio and W. Skogan, (eds.) *Police and Society in Brazil*, 1–24, New York and London: Routledge.

Thompson, J. B. 1995. *The Media and the modernity: a social theory of the media*. Stanford, Stanford University Press.

Tonry, M. 2009. Preface. In T. Tyler, (ed.) *Legitimacy and Criminal Justice*, 3–8, New York: Russel Sage.

Tyler, T. and Wakslack, C. 2004. Profiling and the legitimacy of the police: Procedural justice, attribution of motive, and the acceptance of social authority. *Criminology*, 42 (2), 13–42.

1
PERFORMANCE EVALUATION OF INTEGRATED PUBLIC SECURITY AREAS

Application of the PROMETHEE II method in the Brazilian context

Marcio Pereira Basilio, Valdecy Pereira, Max William Coelho Moreira de Oliveira and Antonio Fernandes da Costa Neto

1 Introduction

Maintaining public order is one of the central collective assets of modern society. Fighting crime is a crucial role of the state in contemporary societies. In addition to providing healthcare, education, and other social welfare services, the state should ensure the preservation of citizens' assets and physical integrity. Social conflicts arising out of deviant behavior are managed in modern societies by public organizations specialized in implementing mechanisms of social control. From an institutional standpoint, contemporary democratic states seek to maintain order through obedience to various legal institutions, which establish the parameters of their power to act. Thus, as stated by (Sapori, 2007; Basilio, 2009; Basilio, 2010a; Basilio and Riccio, 2017), under this view, in a democratic state of law, the highest order is enforced by law.

Because the fight against crime has been nationalized, the state is responsible for crime prevention through proactive policing, investigating and collecting evidence against potential perpetrators of crimes through the trial of those individuals with the goal of finding the truth and exacting punishment by imprisoning those found guilty and duly convicted. Hence, the institutional arrangement of public security is a complex organizational and legal system, which in turn is divided into subsystems with their own unique characteristics, albeit coordinated by the division of labor and the complementarity of functions. In general, this system encompasses the Police,

DOI: 10.4324/9781003452379-2

the judicial subsystem, and the prison subsystem (Sapori, 2007; Basilio, 2010b). However, this complex structure requires human, logistical, and financial resources to carry out its activities. On the other hand, National States have limited resources arising from taxes charged to citizens. From this perspective, common to several countries around the globe, the study of the performance of police agencies becomes paramount to the optimization of their available resources used to fight crime and disorder in a different way in general.

The performance of police organizations is in the interest of not only the police administrators but also the citizens (Akdogan, 2012). The efficiency of police organizations in a neighborhood can be a measure of success for the organization and the department's administrators, but it means more to the citizens living in that neighborhood. It means a safer place to live for them and a quality of life. However, it is hard to measure the performance of police departments because police officers do a variety of tasks. Although police officers are supposed to prevent and investigate crimes, they have many other duties. These tasks are the hidden part of the iceberg for police organizations in many countries, including Brazil.

Asmild et al. (2012) assert that productivity measurement is as important in the public sector as it is in the private sector since it can highlight strengths and weaknesses in current practices, show potential and directions for improvements, and ultimately may lead to better utilization of the resources spent on providing public services. In this chapter, we consider the police services delivery in a city with a population of several million. Police services are characterized by being multidimensional, consisting of many different functions that are difficult to quantify, are measured in different ways, and for which objective and well-defined prices are not given. This makes defining and estimating the productivity of police work difficult.

Generally, Data Envelopment Analysis (DEA) has been used to measure the productivity of police units in a number of studies (Thanassoulis, 1995; Carrington et al., 1997; Nyhan and Martin, 1999; Sun, 2002; Diez-Ticio and Mancebon, 2002; Drake and Simper, 2000, 2001, 2002, 2003a,b, 2004, 2005a, b; Barros ,2006, 2007; Verma and Gavirneni, 2006; Goltz, 2008; Gorman and Ruggiero, 2008; García-Sánchez, 2007, 2009; Wu et al., 2010; Asmild et al., 2012). However, the purpose of this chapter is to use a multicriteria method (Basilio, 2019; Basilio et al., 2022) to order police agencies based on specific criteria, which include variables that measure operational, logistical, financial, and human resources. We believe that the result of the ordering indicates the agencies that best equalize the available resources.

The present study was conducted from 2019 to 2020 and examined the public security context of Rio de Janeiro, Brazil. Since 2009, the state has subdivided its territory into 39 integrated public security areas (IPSA)

(Basilio et al., 2018; Basilio and Pereira, 2020a). The territorial division is heterogeneous, and some IPSA are responsible for law enforcement in one or several cities. Conversely, IPSA correspond to one or several neighborhoods in the state capital. Police activity is complex and diverse, as stated by (Basilio and Riccio, 2017; Riccio and Skogan, 2018; Basilio and Pereira, 2020b). Therefore, considering the diverse contexts of each of the 39 IPSA, the authors sought to answer the following question: How can the Government identify the police agencies that best use the resources available to fight local crime? In this sense, a model was developed based on the decision analysis of multiple criteria, introducing 13 criteria corresponding to variables that measure the operational, logistical, financial, and human resources. Therefore, 39 IPSA were used as alternatives. The data matrix inserted in the model was generated from data collection in the open database of the Public Security Institute (Instituto de Segurança Pública – ISP). The method used, PROMETHEE II, ranked the 39 IPSA in Visual PROMETHEE software. The result reveals that the police units with the best performance are those in the State of Rio de Janeiro interior. In the state capital, the opposite occurs, as illustrated in the thermal map. The results can influence the local Government's decision-making in allocating resources and offer economic sectors information relevant to local development.

This research study is divided into five sections. The first section is the introduction, in which the research problem, objective, and method summaries are applied, and partial findings are presented. The second section is the literature review. The third section describes the method. The fourth section describes the numerical application of the model. The fifth section covers the discussion of results and final considerations.

2 An overview of studies that address efficiency in police structures

Efficiency is an important and desired term in the corporate world. In a complex world with scarcity of resources, being efficient occupies a relevant position in managers' minds because being efficient is synonymous with survival. In the context of public administration, being efficient means that public resources, which have their genesis in the payment of taxes by the citizen, are being converted into public services and policies for the citizen's welfare. In this scenario, we have the police agencies concerned with an overview of guaranteeing life, the right to come and go, and people's assets. Thus, measuring the efficiency of police agencies is important and has an impact on society. Over the past few years, numerous researchers have researched this topic, as we will see below.

Akdogan (2012) reported that in 1991 researchers measured the efficiency of road maintenance patrols in Ontario, Canada. In Ontario, 244 patrols were working on highways, and each patrol was responsible from their province, which was scattered to some fixed number of lane kilometers. The authors used seven variables to assess efficiency: 1) area served factor; 2) average traffic served; 3) pavement rating change factor; 4) accident prevention factor; 5) maintenance expenditures; 6) capital expenditures; and 7) climatic factor.

Thanassoulis (1995) applied DEA to measure the performance of police forces in England and Wales. Violent crimes, burglaries, other crimes, and officers were used as inputs. He employed violent crime clear-up rate, burglary clear-up rate, and other crime clear-up rates as outputs. The researcher then compared those efficient units with other inefficient units and showed the possible improvement areas for those weak units.

Carrington et al. (1997) assessed the performance of police services in New South Wales (NSW). They used a two-staged study; in the first stage, they measured the efficiency of all police patrols and then used Tobit regression to analyze external factors affecting the variation in technical efficiencies across patrols. In the first stage, where they used DEA, police officers, civilian employees, and police cars were used as inputs, whereas offences, arrests, summons, major car accidents, and kilometers traveled by police cars were used as outputs. Based on the results of the study, the authors recommended that NSW police districts reduce input usage by 13.5 percent.

Barros (2006) used panel data from the Portuguese Public Security Police on 33 precincts for the years 2000, 2001, and 2002 to estimate the productivity change in terms of technical efficiency and technological efficiency. The author used 14 variables in the measurement process, as follows: the number of police officers, cost of labor, cars, other costs, theft, burglaries, car robberies, and drug-related crimes were employed as inputs; outputs were set as clear-ups of thefts and burglaries, clear-ups of car robberies, clear-ups of drug-related crimes, search operations, traffic-stop operations, and minor offenses.

Akdogan (2012) developed his research in Turkey based on his study of the Turkish National Police organization. The researcher used ten variables to measure the efficiency of police stations in Ankara: the number of personnel, the number of police vehicles, the population of the precinct, the area of the precinct (meter square), the number of critical entities in the precinct (such as schools, hospitals), the number of incoming documents (both judicial and managerial), the number of incidents that occurred in the precinct, the number of processed judicial and managerial documents, the number of outgoing documents, the number of solved incidents. The results showed that ten out of 19 police stations in Ankara were efficient.

In their research work, Asmild et al. (2012) developed a model for evaluating police units. Asmild et al. (2012) conducted interviews with senior police officers, which led to the division of the variables used in the model into three distinct groups: law enforcement, answer for emergencies, and crime prevention. In preliminary analyses, the authors considered the variable workforce or number of personnel assigned to each function as a common variable in each model. Then, they listed the specific variables related to enforcement law: the number of arrests, the number of other cases worked, and the rate of resolution. For the answer to the emergency model, the variables are the percentage of time available, the number of answered calls, and the inverse of the response time (or the response speed). The crime prevention model initially considered the inverse of the crime rate, the percentage of time on patrol, and the number of times people are stopped and interviewed.

Asif et al. (2018) made use of DEA to measure police efficiency in the city of Lahore, which is a large metropolitan city of Pakistan. The researchers used eight variables: number of investigators, total staff, number of police vehicles, operating expenditures, average response rate to reported crimes/emergencies, crime clearance rate, number of processed judicial and managerial documents, and staff serving at critical entities.

DEA has been very popular in measuring police efficiency worldwide; see, e.g., in the UK (Drake and Howcroft, 1994; Drake and Simper, 2004, 2005), Portugal (Barros, 2007), Slovenia (Aristovnik et al., 2013), Guatemala (Alda, 2014), Mexico (Alda, 2017), Peru (Alda and Dammert, 2019), Israel (Hadad et al., 2015), the USA (Gyimah-Brempong, 1987; Gorman and Ruggiero, 2008), India (Verma and Gavirneni, 2006), and Spain (Diez-Ticio and Mancebon, 2002), among many others. The mentioned studies are only representative and all use DEA. We differentiate our study from others by developing a structured structure based on various measures of efficiency to provide valuable information on the measurement of police performance using a multicriteria method.

3 Methodology

To solve the proposed problem and classify police units by the management of their inputs with a focus on reducing crime in their districts, we turned to the field of Operational Research (OR). We applied a multicriteria method as an alternative to the traditional Data Envelopment Analysis (DEA) method. This methodology consists of five stages, described below:

Step 1 – Identification of the alternatives to be introduced in the model:
In this study, we use 39 police agencies that are responsible for the execution of the radio patrol service throughout the State of Rio de Janeiro.

Step 2 – Identification of the criteria: At this stage, managers identified thirteen criteria related to logistical and operational variables for evaluating local police agencies.

Step 3 – Obtaining the matrix of evaluation of alternatives versus criteria: After identifying the criteria and alternatives, the researchers collected the data between April 20 and May 15 2020 on the public security institute's open database (https: //www.ispvisualizacao.rj.gov.br:4434/).

Step 4 – Application of the PROMETHEE II method:

Step 4.1 – Determination of deviations based on pair-wise comparisons

$$d_j(a,b) = g_j(a) - g_j(b) \tag{1}$$

Where $d_j(a,b)$ denotes the difference between the evaluations of a and b on each criterion.

Step 4.2 – Application of the preference function

$$P_j(a,b) = F_j[d_j(a,b)] \qquad j = 1,\ldots,k \tag{2}$$

Where $P_j(a,b)$ denotes the preference of alternative a concerning alternative b on each criterion as a function of $d_j(a,b)$

Step 4.3 – Calculation of an overall or global preference index

$$\forall a,b \in A, \pi(a,b) = \sum_{j=1}^{k} P_j(a,b)w_j \tag{3}$$

Where $\pi(a,b)$ of a ober b is defined as the weighted sum $P_j(a,b)$ of for each criterion and is the weight associated with the jth criterion.

Step 4.4 – Calculation of outranking flows/ The PROMETHEE II partial ranking

And $\varphi^+(a) = \sum_{x \in A} \pi(a,b)$
$\varphi^-(a) = \sum_{x \in A} \pi(b,a)$

Where $\varphi^+(a)$ and $\varphi^-(a)$ denotes the positive outranking and negative outranking flow for each alternative, respectively.

Step 4.5 – Calculation of net outranking flow/The PROMETHEE II complete ranking

$$\varphi(a) = \varphi^+(a) - \varphi^-(a) \qquad (6)$$

Where $\varphi(a)$ denotes the net outranking flow for each alternative.

Step 5 – Construction of the thermal efficiency map:

After obtaining the solution to the model using the PROMETHEE II method, a georeferenced heat map will be built on which managers, the Government, and society will be able to observe the police units that show signs of inefficiency directly. The heat map will be divided into four colours: red for units considered highly inefficient, orange for moderately weak; light green for moderately efficient; and dark green for highly efficient. This classification is based on the Quartile statistical measure.

4 Numerical application to the actual case

The research was developed in Rio de Janeiro, a southeast region of Brazil. The state has an estimated population of 17,264,943 inhabitants spread across an area of 43,696 km², which results in a population density of 395 inhabitants/km². It is subdivided into 92 municipalities. The state's main economic activities are industry, tourism, services, and mineral extraction (petroleum). These activities generate a gross domestic product of BRL 659.137 billion, which generates a per capita income of BRL 39,826. The Human Development Index (HDI) of the state is 0.761.

Based on public security data reported by the ISP in 2019, in Rio de Janeiro, there is a rate of 23 intentional homicides per 100,000 inhabitants. The rate of motor vehicle theft is 541 vehicles per 100,000 people. The pedestrian robbery rate per 100,000 inhabitants is 702. The ISP monitors a portfolio of 43 types of police occurrences.

The police force responsible for proactive policing is allocated to 39 integrated public security areas, as described in (Basilio et al., 2020a,b; Basilio et al., 2021). The current in public security policy of Rio de Janeiro is focused on reducing three strategic indices: the violent death index, the street robbery index, and the motor vehicle theft index. In contrast to the American model, in which each police institution performs both proactive policing and criminal investigation work, the model is split in Brazil. Article 144 of the Federal Constitution of 1988 listed the institutions active in public security and indicated their competencies. Accordingly, the Military Police are responsible for proactive policing in states and federal districts, while the investigation service is the responsibility of the Civil Police (Riccio and Skogan, 2018). Since January 4, 2019, the Military Police of the State of Rio de Janeiro have been elevated to the status of Secretary of State, becoming the Secretaria de Estado de Polícia Militar – SEPM, which has given more autonomy for managers to formulate and conduct public policy in terms of protecting people's lives and assets. In 2020, the Military Police of the State of Rio de Janeiro executed a budget of approximately 5.7 billion BRL (1.15 billion US$) to maintain 44,653 police officers and a fleet of 4,472 radio patrols.

After an overview of the situation studied, we began to apply the methodology and obtain the results. Below, we will detail the stages of the methodological process with the use of the data obtained.

Step 1: Identification of alternatives for introduction in the model

This stage identifies the alternatives to be inserted in the proposed model. In this study, we will use 39 police agencies that are responsible for the execution of the radio patrol service throughout the State of Rio de Janeiro. Basilio et al. (2019) recorded that the territory of the State of Rio de Janeiro is divided into integrated public security regions (IPSRs). IPSRs are subdivided into IPSA (integrated public security areas), as illustrated in Table 1.1. IPSA operate in the tactical-operational field and apply physical boundaries corresponding to a Military Police Battalion and may involve at least two and at most six Police Departments (PD).

TABLE 1.1 Division of the state of Rio de Janeiro

IPSR	Region	PMERJ	PCERJ	IPSA
1st IPSR	Capital (the south and center and part of the northern zone)	1st APC	1st APD	1, 2, 3, 4, 5, 6, 13, 16, 17, 19, 22, 23
2nd IPSR	Capital (the west and part of the northern zone)	2nd APC	2nd APD	9, 14, 18, 27, 31, 39
3rd IPSR	Baixada Fluminense	3rd APC	3rd APD	15, 20, 21, 24, 34, 40
4th IPSR	Niteroi and Região dos Lagos	4th APC	4th APD	7, 12, 25, 35
5th IPSR	Sul Fluminense	5th APC	5th APD	10, 28, 33, 37
6th IPSR	Norte Fluminense	6th APC	6th APD	8, 29, 32, 36
7th IPSR	Região Serrana	7th APC	7th APD	11, 26, 30, 38

Note: Polícia Militar do Estado do Rio de Janeiro (PMERJ); Polícia Civil do Estado do Rio de Janeiro (PCERJ); Area Police Command (APC); and Area Police Department (APD).

In this sense, as alternatives to the developed model, we will use the set of 39 IPSA, which are decision-making units (DMU) that we will identify as follows: $A_1^n = \{a_1,\ldots,a_n\} \rightarrow A_1^{39} = \{a_1,\ldots,a_{39}\} \rightarrow A_1^{39} = \{IPSA_2, IPSA_3, IPSA_4, IPSA_5, IPSA_6, IPSA_7, IPSA_8, IPSA_9, IPSA_{10}, IPSA_{11}, IPSA_{12}, IPSA_{13}, IPSA_{14}, IPSA_{15}, IPSA_{16}, IPSA_{17}, IPSA_{18}, IPSA_{19}, IPSA_{20}, IPSA_{21}, IPSA_{22}, IPSA_{23}, IPSA_{24}, IPSA_{25}, IPSA_{26}, IPSA_{27}, IPSA_{28}, IPSA_{29}, IPSA_{30}, IPSA_{31}, IPSA_{32}, IPSA_{33}, IPSA_{34}, IPSA_{35}, IPSA_{36}, IPSA_{37}, IPSA_{38}, IPSA_{39}, IPSA_{40}, IPSA_{41}\}$. It is worth explaining that the police agencies identified as $IPSA_1$ and $IPSA_{13}$ are not part of the list, as they were disabled by the command of the Military Police of the State of Rio de Janeiro for more than ten years, and the policing areas corresponding to these agencies were integrated into other surrounding areas. As well, their denominations, for local cultural reasons, were no longer implemented.

Step 2: Identification of criteria

At this stage, based on the literature review, we identified 13 criteria for introducing the proposed model to order police agencies by efficiency. We categorize the criteria into two groups: operational and logistic. The operational group included criteria related to criminal indices, such as intentional lethal crimes (C1), cargo theft (C2), street theft (C3), and vehicle theft (C4). In the logistical group, variables related to the resources made available to each police agency in 2019 were included, such as annual payroll value (C5), annual fuel consumption (C6), percentage of police contingent applied to operational activity (C7), annual cost of food for the police contingent (C8), police contingent rate 100 thousand/inhabitant (C9), police contingent rate in conditions of immediate employment (C10), number of police operations carried out (C11), number of vehicles (C12); amount of ammunition available (C13).

Step 3: Construction of the matrix to evaluate alternatives versus criteria

At this stage, after identifying the criteria and alternatives, the researchers collected, from April 20 to May 15, 2020, data on the open base of the public security institute https://www.ispvisualizacao.rj.gov.br:4434/) and built Table 1.2, which corresponds to the evaluation matrix that will be used in the construction of this model.

Step 4: Application of the PROMETHEE II method

In this step, the data referring to the actions described in step 1, the criteria registered in step 2, and the decision matrix inserted in Table 1.2 will be introduced in Visual PROMETHEE software version 1.4.0.0. At this moment, two questions need to be modeled by the decision-maker:

TABLE 1.2 Evaluation matrix

Alternative	C1	C2	C3	C4	C5	C6	C7	C8	C9	C10	C11	C12	C13
IPSA2	4	11	963	138	31,150,157	195,156	0.65815	446,584	163,51	107.62	14	35	379
IPSA3	18	50	1,151	366	42,006,748	290.560	0.65609	472,356	104,57	68.61	151	50	11,685
IPSA4	26	57	1,752	341	45,979,903	255.315	0.65991	432,765	376,34	248.35	4	43	3,642
IPSA5	32	38	4,249	165	40,854,215	222.026	0.71995	402,416	665,05	478.8	3	45	2,245
IPSA6	7	17	933	226	60,979,111	234.127	0.65082	455,931	114,81	74.72	9	38	4,779
IPSA7	26	129	1,012	429	30,556,956	367.407	0.66087	451,421	79,08	52.26	737	64	26,086
IPSA8	31	5	189	25	60,200,782	464.932	0.71819	496,141	154,47	110,94	35	84	512
IPSA9	22	43	1,677	507	86,405,035	236.947	0.6115	329,378	111,62	68,26	163	36	5,874
IPSA10	10	6	20	3	69,202,405	350.047	0.70775	283,111	240,18	169,99	45	87	188
IPSA11	13	3	50	6	41,465,931	205.231	0.71326	347,670	166,23	118,56	1	57	786
IPSA12	25	26	580	223	70,779,078	444.650	0.72284	434,483	133,96	96,83	349	81	10,392
IPSA14	27	87	1,064	403	54,135,433	286,817	0.56987	338,941	99,35	56,62	198	36	9,265
IPSA15	32	106	1,050	389	24,785,277	284,438	0.73205	472,006	95,72	70,07	266	64	10,170
IPSA16	18	86	789	274	27,563,270	175,823	0.69259	401,484	89,47	61,96	46	37	21,804
IPSA17	8	15	370	53	34,788,375	135,039	0.61848	273,836	139,76	86,44	23	26	2,784
IPSA18	15	18	609	120	58,291,111	316,800	0.70563	375,584	106,77	75,34	59	62	20,059
IPSA19	6	1	814	10	35,113,707	134,537	0.69227	417,855	187,66	129,91	0	24	1,576
IPSA20	31	35	979	319	25,508,189	233,773	0.674	424,292	79,01	53,25	247	105	6,272
IPSA21	24	114	1,046	484	49,203,338	114,159	0.60519	397,733	91,89	55,61	73	50	5,119
IPSA22	25	76	1,359	238	71,309,022	199,096	0.63947	355,914	146,93	93,96	81	48	31,009

Alternative	C1	C2	C3	C4	C5	C6	C7	C8	C9	C10	C11	C12	C13
IPSA23	10	1	537	40	35,072,193	201,751	0.65257	524,703	205,95	134,39	0	43	3,480
IPSA24	32	23	471	139	35,019,414	232,659	0.65307	295,541	93,85	61,29	230	46	9,223
IPSA25	38	6	285	52	41,373,558	371,148	0.64819	288,547	130,14	84,36	53	98	8,985
IPSA26	8	7	59	8	40,912,305	182,796	0.70927	219,391	123,41	87,53	107	43	210
IPSA27	10	14	293	60	69,772,648	205,271	0.66667	294,630	67,22	44,81	32	33	132
IPSA28	28	5	114	22	67,254,214	240,585	0.7108	346,765	144,78	102,91	49	62	1,274
IPSA29	14	2	26	2	30,551,480	317,360	0.73862	357,725	350,2	258,67	338	60	116
IPSA30	9	2	28	3	30,692,460	189,085	0.72035	336,806	169,04	121,77	5	52	60
IPSA31	15	10	740	143	53,556,122	190,142	0.58993	348,669	164,88	97,27	0	56	293
IPSA32	30	7	332	52	33,261,290	331,754	0.74739	486,035	142,07	106,18	120	77	1,959
IPSA33	43	22	131	67	41,725,205	209,881	0.68841	543,726	166,07	114,32	19	55	8,501
IPSA34	32	14	335	79	59,014,406	269,799	0.73844	233,262	115,85	85,55	20	32	1,653
IPSA35	36	29	464	187	39,683,712	277,904	0.70504	306,271	107,96	76,11	63	54	6,046
IPSA36	20	2	13	10	29,550,998	203,235	0.67864	265,902	383,05	259,95	13	42	128
IPSA37	24	2	80	12	29,983,303	180,550	0.66086	388,656	184,99	122,25	70	40	344
IPSA38	34	8	30	11	36,804,431	113,573	0.76232	404,965	228,37	174,09	32	39	157
IPSA39	41	49	609	509	39,265,730	114,148	0.66115	309,464	75,7	50,05	92	53	10,758
IPSA40	10	34	394	193	29,598,214	160,112	0.53708	457,549	57,2	30,72	23	34	523
IPSA41	12	129	1,291	760	31,875,619	251,437	0.6568	420,716	103,78	68,16	174	55	27,296

the first refers to the weight to be applied to each criterion. The second refers to the preference function to be used in each criterion, as recorded in Table 1.3. Regarding the weight of the criteria, the researchers assigned different weights for each criterion, depending on the evaluation of the decision makers of the studied police agency, as recorded in Table 1.4. Regarding the preference function, the choice of a good preference function depends on the scale of the underlying criterion, as stated (Mareschal, 2018). In this sense, the literature considers three types of cases: a) a continuous numerical scale (real numbers), b) the discrete numerical scale (small integer numbers), and c) a qualitative scale (few ordered levels). Mareschal (2018) presents a protocol to identify the most appropriate preference function, according to Table 1.3.

According to the procedures for choosing the preference function discussed in Table 1.3 and considering that the evaluation matrix inserted in Table 1.2, the researchers adopted the Type III V-shape preference function for the criteria {C1, ..., C4}, and the Linear Type V preference function for criteria {C5, ..., C13}, as shown in Table 1.4.

TABLE 1.3 Procedure for selecting a preference function

Case	Convention	Preference function suggestion
If the criterion has a continuous numerical scale.	If you want to introduce an indifference threshold (and thus neglect very small differences).	Consider using a Type V linear preference function.
	If you want that even very small differences play some role in the PROMETHEE computation.	Consider using a Type III V-shape preference function.
If the criterion has a discrete numerical scale or a qualitative scale.	If the number of possible values is small (<= 5) and if the values are perceived as quite different from each other.	Consider using a Type I usual preference function.
	If the number of possible values is larger or if you want to have a weaker degree of preference for smaller differences.	Consider using a Type IV level preference function.

Source: Adapted from (Mareschal, 2018).

Note: This procedure does not include the Type II (U-shape) and Type VI (Gaussian) preference functions. In practice, the Type II preference function is seldom used. Type VI can be an alternative to the Type V preference function.

After identifying the preference function for each criterion, the data related to criteria and actions were entered in Visual PROMETHEE Software, according to Tables 1.2 and 1.4. After inserting the data, Equations (1) to (6) were applied, as shown in Figure 1.1. Emulating the data, Visual PROMETHEE Software produced the following outputs as results: Table 1.5 records the synthesis of the flows for each according to each of the criteria used in the model.

Then, Table 1.6 presents a complete ranking. Using formula 4, the positive flow was obtained and recorded in the fourth column. Likewise, with the implementation of formula 5, the negative flow, represented in the fifth column, was obtained. The partial ranking result was obtained with positive and negative flows, as shown in Figure 1.1. Applying formula 6 resulted in the complete flow. It is registered in the third column of Table 1.6 and illustrated in Figure 1.2. As a result, we have IPSA29 as the first in the ranking, followed by IPSA30, in third place by IPSA26. Figure 1.3 clearly illustrates how the classification is distributed and records the criteria by which police agencies perform better or worse compared to one agency or another. The IPSA29 in 92.3% of the criteria was better than the other 38 agencies analyzed. They obtained only a negative result in criterion C13. Both IPSA30 and IPSA26 were efficient in 53.84% of the evaluated criteria. Figure 1.4 clearly illustrates how many criteria had a positive flow in the evaluation, alongside the other police agencies, and registers the criteria that had a negative flow; other agencies surpassed that in the peer comparison. Figure 1.3 also shows the direct relationship between the weight of each criterion and the result. Figure 1.4 illustrates the existing relationship between evaluated police agencies, considering the parameters used. It is also observed that IPSA29 stands out in isolation from the others.

Step 5: Construction of the thermal efficiency map

After identifying the ranking of police agencies based on the 13 proposed criteria. the classification was made into four subgroups. For this grouping. the Quartile statistical measure applied to the final flow constant in the third column of Table 1.6 was used. After identifying the segmentation points. the police agencies were grouped and assigned a specific color. which will be used to identify the agencies in the thermal map of Figures 4.5 and 4.6. The classification colors are as follows: red for units considered to be highly inefficient. orange to moderately inefficient. light green to moderately efficient. and dark green for strongly efficient. The data resulting from this step are recorded in Table 1.7.

5 Discussion of results and final remarks

The activities that orbit the area of public security. more precisely. the police agencies. which are charged with enforcing the law. are complex and challenging.

TABLE 1.4 Model parameters

Parameters	C1	C2	C3	C4	C5	C6	C7	C8	C9	C10	C11	C12	C13
Objective	min	min	min	min	min	max	max	min	max	max	max	max	max
Weight	7	5	2	3	7	5	9	7	2	2	5	2	3
Unit	Scalar	Scalar	Scalar	Scalar	Scalar	Scalar	Scalar	Scalar	Scalar	Scalar	Scalar	Scalar	Scalar
Scale	R	R	R	R	R	R	R	R	R	R	R	R	R
Preference function	V-Shape	V-Shape	V-Shape	V-Shape	Linear	Linear	Linear	Linear	Linear	Linear	Linear	Linear	Linear
Thresholds	Absolute	Absolute	Absolute	Absolute	Absolute	Absolute	Absolute	Absolute	Absolute	Absolute	Absolute	Absolute	Absolute
Q: Indifference	n/a	n/a	n/a	n/a	13,740,898	73,294	0.04304	170,171	124	89	153	17	8,224
P: Preference	21	75	1,510	2,622	31,105,026	167,356	0.09909	301,073	225	162	281	38	16,496
S: Gaussian	n/a	n/a	n/a	n/a	n/a	n/a	n/a	n/a	n/a	n/a	n/a	n/a	n/a

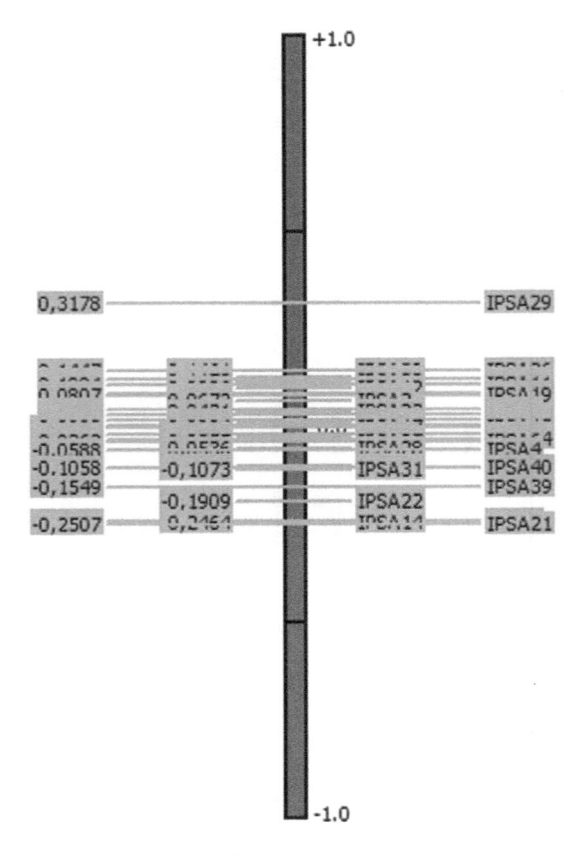

FIGURE 1.1 PROMETHEE II complete ranking

Decisions made in this field of knowledge directly impact the lives of thousands of people in large or small cities around the world. Given the complexity. many public policies lead managers focus on final results. such as reducing crime rates. However. a police agency is no different than any other organization. They need input so that their activities can be developed. Resources are finite and need to be managed efficiently and optimally. This issue has led researchers and managers to research the subject. as noted in Section 2.

In Basilio et al. (2018) the integrated goal system model was discussed from the perspective of the multicriteria methodology. The integrated target system assesses the operational performance of the IPSA based on three strategic indicators. However. it does not infer how managers equate and apply the resources available to achieve the goals established by the Government through the Institute of Public Security. The decision

Performance evaluation of integrated public security areas Brazil 25

TABLE 1.5 Criteria flow

Uni-criterion flows	C1	C2	C3	C4	C5	C6	C7	C8	C9	C10	C11	C12	C13
IPSA2	0.7155	0.2544	-0.2169	0.0169	0.2825	-0.1852	-0.0887	-0.0228	-0.0907	-0.0897	-0.1365	-0.2456	-0.1642
IPSA3	0.1729	-0.2347	-0.3414	-0.0723	0.1447	0.1644	-0.1061	-0.0529	-0.1085	-0.1155	-0.0426	-0.1078	0.0845
IPSA4	-0.2093	-0.3277	-0.7059	-0.0625	0.0546	0.0096	-0.0738	-0.0146	0.7997	0.7189	-0.148	-0.1654	-0.1313
IPSA5	-0.4687	-0.0793	-1	0.0064	0.165	-0.0947	0.2885	-0.0026	1	1	-0.1493	-0.1454	-0.1364
IPSA6	0.6228	0.1811	-0.197	-0.0175	-0.4531	-0.0573	-0.1489	-0.0308	-0.1057	-0.1111	-0.1419	-0.208	-0.1277
IPSA7	-0.2093	-0.9028	-0.2493	-0.097	0.2897	0.6006	-0.0657	-0.0267	-0.1226	-0.1272	1	0.1566	0.88
IPSA8	-0.4323	0.3239	0.2948	0.0612	-0.4257	0.8984	0.2764	-0.0985	-0.0969	-0.0861	-0.1178	0.6729	-0.1612
IPSA9	-0.015	-0.1439	-0.6702	-0.1275	-0.865	-0.0478	-0.4658	0.0139	-0.1066	-0.1157	-0.0257	-0.2318	-0.1224
IPSA10	0.5201	0.3123	0.4012	0.0698	-0.6473	0.5007	0.2022	0.0567	0.0663	0.09	-0.1096	0.7318	-0.1687
IPSA11	0.3972	0.347	0.3824	0.0686	0.1546	-0.1521	0.2414	0.0066	-0.0886	-0.0779	-0.1517	-0.0063	-0.1552
IPSA12	-0.1617	0.0705	0.0368	-0.0163	-0.6777	0.8558	0.308	-0.0153	-0.103	-0.1011	0.7296	0.6065	-0.0066
IPSA14	-0.2569	-0.6982	-0.2838	-0.0868	-0.1966	0.1456	-0.7904	0.0101	-0.1112	-0.1241	0.0831	-0.2318	-0.07
IPSA15	-0.4687	-0.8161	-0.2745	-0.0813	0.366	0.1336	0.3732	-0.0524	-0.1131	-0.1144	0.4245	0.1566	-0.0207
IPSA16	0.1729	-0.6902	-0.1017	-0.0363	0.3217	-0.241	0.1168	-0.0024	-0.1163	-0.1202	-0.109	-0.2193	0.7682
IPSA17	0.589	0.2056	0.1758	0.0502	0.2423	-0.3811	-0.4069	0.0737	-0.1015	-0.1051	-0.1277	-0.411	-0.1337
IPSA18	0.3095	0.1688	0.0175	0.024	-0.3579	0.2992	0.1873	0	-0.1078	-0.1106	-0.1005	0.1053	0.6925
IPSA19	0.6554	0.3702	-0.1182	0.067	0.2388	-0.383	0.1155	-0.0086	-0.0702	-0.0621	-0.153	-0.4574	-0.1437
IPSA20	-0.4323	-0.0414	-0.2275	-0.0539	0.3528	-0.0585	0.0301	-0.0112	-0.1226	-0.1265	0.3178	0.8972	-0.1199
IPSA21	-0.1128	-0.8519	-0.2719	-0.1185	-0.0324	-0.483	-0.5197	-0.0016	-0.115	-0.1248	-0.088	-0.1078	-0.1266
IPSA22	-0.1617	-0.5877	-0.4791	-0.0222	-0.6866	-0.1727	-0.2433	0.0035	-0.0996	-0.1024	-0.0806	-0.1228	0.9065

Uni-criterion flows	C1	C2	C3	C4	C5	C6	C7	C8	C9	C10	C11	C12	C13
IPSA23	0.5201	0.3702	0.0652	0.0553	0.2393	-0.1641	-0.135	-0.1709	-0.0438	-0.0555	-0.153	-0.1654	-0.1316
IPSA24	-0.4687	0.1074	0.1089	0.0165	0.2398	-0.062	-0.131	0.0403	-0.114	-0.1207	0.2274	-0.1378	-0.072
IPSA25	-0.6667	0.3123	0.2321	0.0506	0.1562	0.6208	-0.171	0.0488	-0.104	-0.1055	-0.1046	0.8584	-0.0833
IPSA26	0.589	0.3007	0.3767	0.0678	0.164	-0.223	0.2129	0.2239	-0.1053	-0.1047	-0.0619	-0.1654	-0.1682
IPSA27	0.5201	0.2179	0.2268	0.0475	-0.6585	-0.152	-0.0179	0.0414	-0.1318	-0.1327	-0.1203	-0.2757	-0.1702
IPSA28	-0.3033	0.3239	0.3422	0.0623	-0.6089	-0.0356	0.2241	0.0069	-0.1002	-0.0948	-0.1071	0.1053	-0.1475
IPSA29	0.3534	0.3586	0.3974	0.0702	0.2898	0.3024	0.4254	0.0032	0.7066	0.7671	0.7076	0.0551	-0.1706
IPSA30	0.5551	0.3586	0.3962	0.0698	0.2881	-0.2056	0.2911	0.011	-0.0865	-0.0738	-0.1468	-0.0865	-0.172
IPSA31	0.3095	0.266	-0.0692	0.015	-0.1764	-0.202	-0.6485	0.0062	-0.0897	-0.1008	-0.153	-0.0251	-0.1661
IPSA32	-0.391	0.3007	0.201	0.0506	0.2585	0.3887	0.4954	-0.0781	-0.1009	-0.0912	-0.0553	0.5063	-0.1389
IPSA33	-0.8045	0.1196	0.3315	0.0447	0.1498	-0.1355	0.0999	-0.2331	-0.0888	-0.0825	-0.1314	-0.0426	-0.1027
IPSA34	-0.4687	0.2179	0.199	0.04	-0.3837	0.0631	0.424	0.1763	-0.1055	-0.1053	-0.1303	-0.2932	-0.1427
IPSA35	-0.6065	0.0337	0.1136	-0.0023	0.185	0.0997	0.1831	0.0291	-0.1075	-0.1101	-0.0972	-0.0589	-0.1213
IPSA36	0.0802	0.3586	0.4056	0.067	0.3014	-0.1591	0.0553	0.0896	0.8179	0.7726	-0.1375	-0.1742	-0.1703
IPSA37	-0.1128	0.3586	0.3635	0.0662	0.2967	-0.2284	-0.0658	0	-0.0729	-0.0731	-0.0911	-0.1905	-0.165
IPSA38	-0.5401	0.2891	0.3949	0.0666	0.2219	-0.4861	0.609	-0.0034	0.0167	0.114	-0.1203	-0.1992	-0.1695
IPSA39	-0.7519	-0.2218	0.0175	-0.1283	0.192	-0.4831	-0.0634	0.0265	-0.1252	-0.1288	-0.0715	-0.0739	0.0176
IPSA40	0.5201	-0.0288	0.1599	-0.0046	0.3009	-0.287	-0.9175	-0.0324	-0.1425	-0.153	-0.1277	-0.2607	-0.161
IPSA41	0.4398	-0.9028	-0.4341	-0.2265	0.2737	-0.0028	-0.1001	-0.0097	-0.1089	-0.1158	0.0006	-0.0426	0.8919

TABLE 1.6 The PROMETHEE complete ranking

Multicriteria flows	Rank	Phi	Phi+	Phi-
IPSA29	1	0.2359	0.3116	0.0758
IPSA30	2	0.1399	0.1847	0.0448
IPSA26	3	0.1397	0.1838	0.0441
IPSA32	4	0.1152	0.1938	0.0786
IPSA11	5	0.107	0.1542	0.0472
IPSA10	6	0.1069	0.2069	0.1
IPSA12	7	0.0993	0.2349	0.1356
IPSA18	8	0.0896	0.1709	0.0813
IPSA7	9	0.0883	0.2382	0.1499
IPSA19	10	0.0805	0.1566	0.0761
IPSA2	11	0.0685	0.1496	0.0811
IPSA8	12	0.0487	0.181	0.1323
IPSA38	13	0.0387	0.1625	0.1238
IPSA23	14	0.0355	0.1347	0.0992
IPSA20	15	0.0298	0.1437	0.114
IPSA25	16	0.0251	0.1495	0.1244
IPSA36	17	0.0213	0.1811	0.1597
IPSA16	18	0.0189	0.143	0.1241
IPSA37	19	0.0164	0.1088	0.0924
IPSA15	20	0.0138	0.17	0.1562
IPSA41	21	0.0119	0.1524	0.1405
IPSA17	22	0.009	0.1381	0.129
IPSA34	23	-0.0043	0.1354	0.1396
IPSA3	24	-0.0044	0.1058	0.1102
IPSA35	25	-0.0129	0.0985	0.1115
IPSA24	26	-0.0164	0.1024	0.1188
IPSA27	27	-0.0167	0.1212	0.138
IPSA6	28	-0.0225	0.1124	0.1348
IPSA28	29	-0.0382	0.1015	0.1397
IPSA40	30	-0.081	0.1249	0.2059
IPSA33	31	-0.0819	0.0768	0.1587
IPSA31	32	-0.0938	0.0859	0.1797
IPSA5	33	-0.1029	0.1394	0.2424
IPSA39	34	-0.1245	0.0683	0.1928
IPSA4	35	-0.1463	0.101	0.2474
IPSA22	36	-0.1619	0.0806	0.2425
IPSA9	37	-0.2077	0.0544	0.2621
IPSA14	38	-0.2106	0.0574	0.268
IPSA21	39	-0.2138	0.0418	0.2556

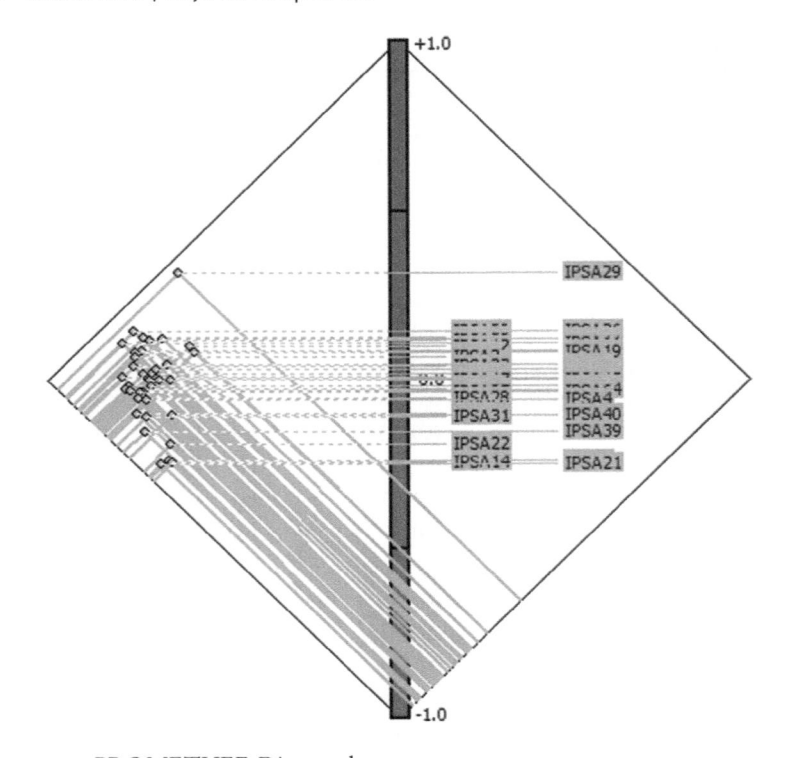

FIGURE 1.2 PROMETHEE Diamond

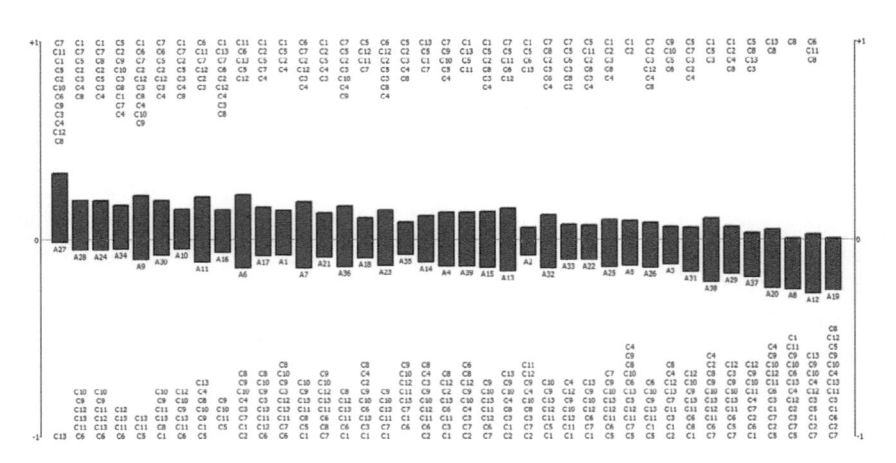

FIGURE 1.3 Classification of alternatives according to criteria

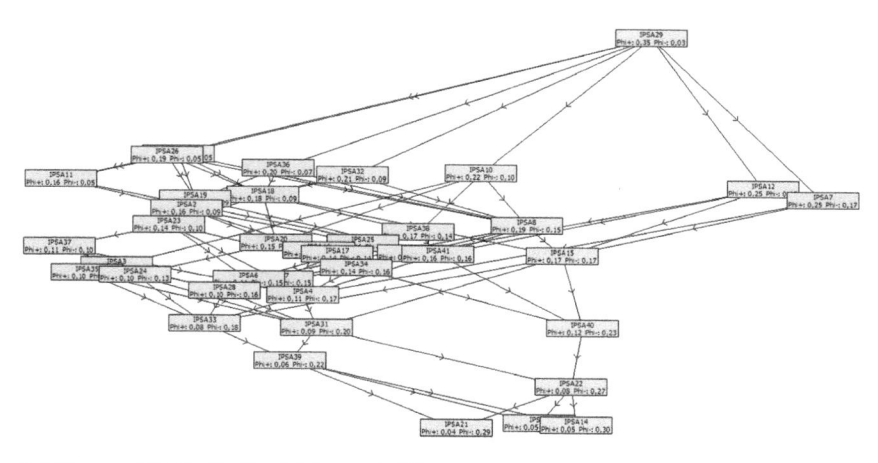

FIGURE 1.4 PROMETHEE Network View

TABLE 1.7 Categorization of law enforcement agencies by their level of efficiency compared

Cluster	Quartile	Interval Phi	Police Agencies	Thermal color
Strongly Efficient	4&	(0.2359. ....0.0745)	{IPSA29; IPSA30; IPSA26; IPSA32; IPSA11; IPSA10; IPSA12; IPSA18; IPSA7; IPSA19}	
moderately efficient	3&	(0.0745. ....0.0138)	{IPSA2; IPSA8; IPSA38; IPSA23; IPSA20; IPSA25; IPSA36; IPSA16; IPSA37; IPSA15}	
moderately inefficient	2&	(0.0138..... -0.0596)	{IPSA41; IPSA17; IPSA34; IPSA3; IPSA35; IPSA24; IPSA27; IPSA6; IPSA28}	
highly inefficient	1&	(-0.0596. ....-0.2138)	{IPSA40; IPSA33; IPSA31; IPSA5; IPSA39; IPSA4; IPSA22; IPSA9; IPSA14; IPSA21}	

maker responsible for an IPSA must be able to equate the logistical and operational variables. The proposed model was emulated with 13 criteria. including operational variables that are measured and used in the integrated system of goals and logistical variables that represent the main inputs available to IPSA managers.

Table 1.6 records the ranking of the 39 IPSA. and Figure 1.4 illustrates the relationships between police agencies arising from the application of the PROMETHEE II method. In the first moment. we identified the IPSA29 (1st). IPSA30 (2nd). and IPSA26 (3rd) as the first three placed in the ranking. In the last three positions. we have IPSA9 (37°). IPSA14 (38°). and IPSA21 (39°). This information shows us the thermal map illustrated in Figures 1.5 and 1.6. Figure 1.5 represents the geographical distribution of the 39 IPSA in the territory of the State of Rio de Janeiro. Figure 1.6 shows the state capital and its metropolitan region. Looking at Figure 1.5 immediately. the ranking result reveals that the IPSA mostly located in the interior of the State of Rio de Janeiro. was categorized as strongly efficient or moderately efficient. This was the case with the first three placed. The exception were IPSA28. IPSA33. IPSA34 and IPSA35. When we look at Figure 1.6. we have an opposite situation. In the state capital. where most of the population is concentrated. police agencies are categorized as highly inefficient and moderately inefficient. as in the case of the last three positions of the ranking. However. we can also observe exceptions such as IPSA02. IPSA19. and IPSA23. which correspond to an area of high purchasing power and tourism in the city. which corresponds to the neighborhoods of Copacabana. Botafogo. and Leblon. Another exception is IPSA18. which is isolated among other surrounding agencies. In the first analysis. the result of the proposed model presents the Government with a systemic view of how IPSA decision-makers manage the resources made available in the face of local operational problems. Considering the results presented. we can say that the

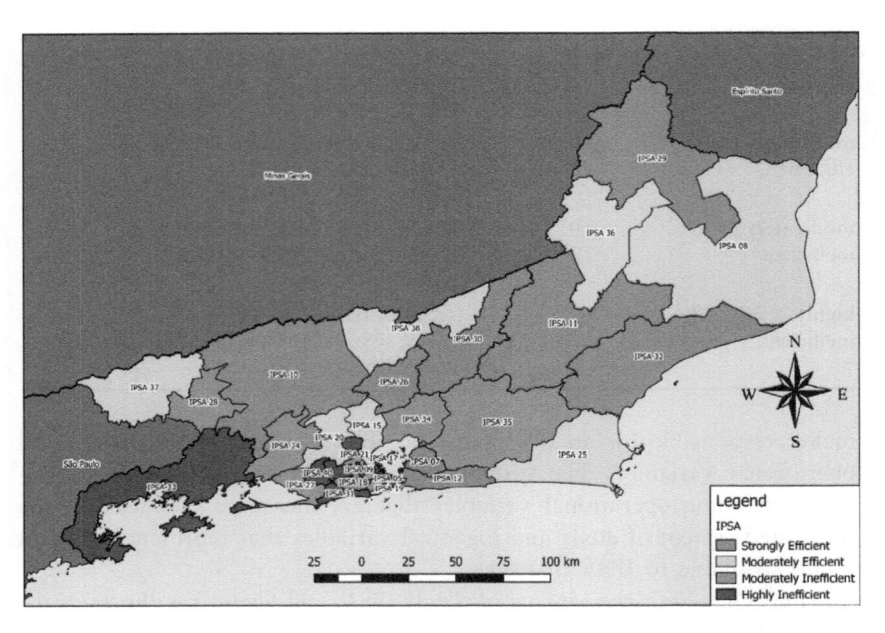

FIGURE 1.5 Thermal map of the 39 IPSA distributed in the State of Rio de Janeiro. Brazil

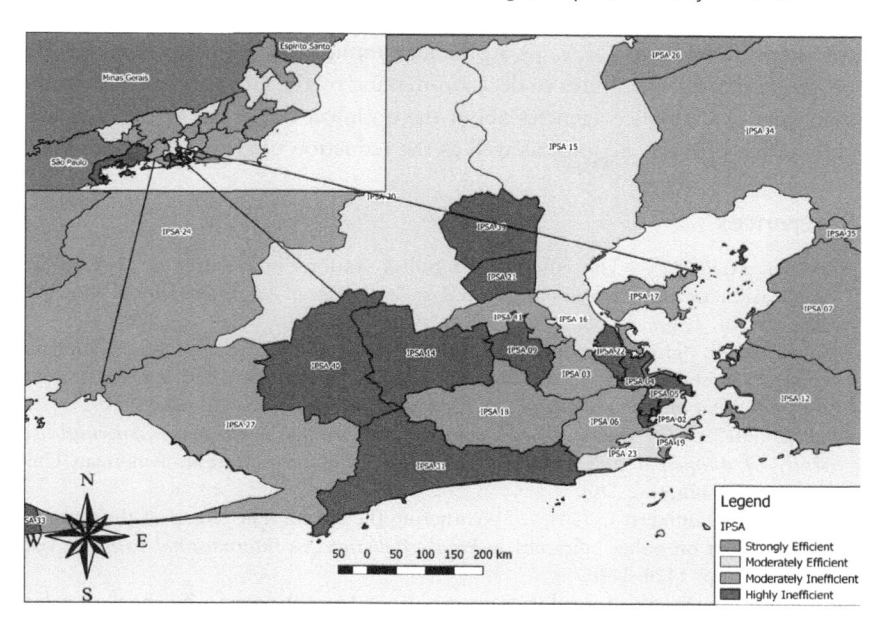

FIGURE 1.6 Thermal map of IPSA located in the Capital of the State of Rio de Janeiro

resources made available to police agencies in the state's interior are better equalized compared to the police units operating in the state capital. as shown in Figure 1.6. In this sense. the information produced in the proposed model can help the Government better assess the reallocation of available resources. On the other hand. the improvement in public security provides an improvement in the quality of life of the citizens and in the local economic development. Thus. we can infer that the results can also contribute to decision-making in other sectors. such as tourism. the economic sector. real estate. and the insurance sector because in places where police agencies are more efficient. the trend is that criminal rates are also lower compared to 100.000/inhabitants.

As a contribution to new research. we can indicate the realization of qualitative research with the decision makers of the police agencies to identify the best practices. such as what the IPSA18 manager did that differentiates it from the bordering IPSA managers. Or what factors contribute to the fact that police units in the state's interior stand out concerning those in the capital. Or even conduct a comparative study between the economic development of the areas where the agencies are more efficient and the inefficient ones.

In this sense. we believe that the proposed model answers the research problem and presents practical contributions to the scientific community. From the methodological point of view. ordering the IPSA by means of a multicriteria method proved to be viable since. regarding the efficiency theme. the most commonly used is the DEA. As a practical implication, we can assert that the proposed model contributes to decision-making by the Government and by the managers of the police agencies about the optimization of the resources available to face criminal actions, as well as the reduction of criminal indicators.

References

Akdogan. H. (2012). "The efficiency of police stations in the city of Ankara: an application of data envelopment analysis". *Policing: An International Journal*. Vol. 35 No. 1, pp. 25–38.

Alda. E. (2014). "How are police doing in combating crime? An exploratory study of efficiency analysis of the Policía Nacional Civil in Guatemala". *Policing: An International Journal of Police Strategies & Management*. Vol. 37 No. 1. pp. 87–107.

Alda. E. (2017). *"The impact of exogenous factors on police efficiency: An empirical study of municipal police forces in Mexico"*. PhD dissertation. American University. Washington. DC.

Alda. E. and Dammert. L. (2019). "Weathering the storm! The effects of the external environment on police efficiency in Peru". *Policing: An International Journal*. Vol. 42 No. 6. pp. 1124–1140.

Aristovnik. A., Seljak. J. and Mencinger. J. (2013). "Relative efficiency of police directorates in Slovenia: A non-parametric analysis". *Expert Systems with Applications*. Vol. 40 No. 2. pp. 820–827.

Asif. M., Shahzad. M., Awan. M.U. and Akdogan. H. (2018). "Developing a structured framework for measuring police efficiency". *International Journal of Quality & Reliability Management*. Vol. 35 No. 10. pp. 2119–2135.

Asmild. M., Paradi. J.C. and Pastor. J.T. (2012). "DEA based models for reallocations of police personnel". *OR Spectrum*. Vol. 34. pp. 921–941. doi:10.1007/s00291-011-0243-6.

Barros. C.P. (2006). "Productivity growth in the Lisbon Police Force". *Public Organization Review*. Vol. 6. pp. 21–35.

Barros. C.P. (2007). "The city and the police force: analysing relative efficiency in city police precincts with data envelopment analysis". *International Journal of Police Science & Management*. Vol. 9 No. 2. pp. 164–182.

Basilio. M.P. (2009). "O desafio da formação do policial militar do estado do Rio de Janeiro: utopia ou realidade possível?". *Gestão & Sociedade*. Vol. 2 No. 3. doi: https://doi.org/10.21171/ges.v2i3.552.

Basilio. M.P. (2010a). "Tempos líquido". *Sociologias*. Vol. 23. pp. 438–449. doi:10.1590/S1517-45222010000100016.

Basilio. M.P. (2010b). "O desafio da formação do policial militar do Estado do Rio de Janeiro: entre o modelo reativo eo contingencial". *Administración and Desarrollo*. Vol. 38 No. 52. pp. 71–96.

Basilio. M.P. (2019). "O modelo multicritéio de ordenação de estratégias de policiamento: uma aplicação dos métodos da família ELECTRE". *Niteroí. RJ. Brazil: Universidade Federal Fluminense*. http://app.uff.br/riuff/handle/1/29865.

Basilio. M.P. and Pereira. V. (2020a). "Estudo sobre a premiação das áreas de segurança pública no Rio de Janeiro via método multicritério: uma aplicação do método Electre

III[Study on the award of public safety areas in Rio de Janeiro via multicriteria method: an application of the ElectreIII]". *Exacta*. Vol. 18 No. 1. pp. 130–164.

Basilio. M.P. and Pereira. V. (2020b). "Operational research applied in the field of public security: the ordering of policing strategies such as the ELECTRE IV". *Journal of Modelling in Management*. doi:https://doi.org/10.1108/JM2-02-2019-0034.

Basilio. M.P. and Riccio. V. (2017). "The challenge of military police training in Rio de Janeiro: Utopia or real possibility?". *Universal Journal of Management*. Vol. 5 No. 12. pp. 570–580.

Basilio. M.P., Pereira. V. and Costa. H.G. (2018). "Classifying the integrated public safety areas (IPSAs): a multicriteria based approach". *Journal of Modelling in Management*. pp. 106–133.

Basilio. M.P., Pereira. V. and Brum. G. (2019). "Identification of operational demand in law enforcement agencies: An application based on a probabilistic model of topics". Data Technologies and Applications. Vol. 53 No. 3. pp. 333–372. doi:10.1108/DTA-12-2018-0109

Basilio. M.P.Pereira. V. and Oliveira. M.W.C.M.d. (2021). "Knowledge discovery in research on policing strategies: an overview of the past fifty years". *Journal of Modelling in Management*. https://doi.org/10.1108/JM2-10-2020-0268.

Basilio. M.P., Brum. G.S. and Pereira. V. (2020a). "A model of policing strategy choice: The integration of the Latent Dirichlet Allocation (LDA) method with ELECTRE I". *Journal of Modelling in Management*. doi:10.1108/JM2-10-2018-0166.

Basilio. M.P., Pereira. V., Oliveira. M.W.C.d. and Costa Neto. A.F.d. (2020b). "Ranking policing strategies as a function of criminal complaints: application of the PROMETHEE II method in the Brazilian context". *Journal of Modelling in Management*. https://doi.org/10.1108/JM2-05-2020-0122.

Basilio. M.P., Pereira. V., Costa. H.G.Santos. M. and Ghosh. A.A. (2022). "Systematic review of the applications of multi-criteria decision aid methods (1977–2022)". *Electronics*. Vol. 11 No. 11. p.1720. doi:10.3390/electronics11111720.

Carrington. R., Puthucheary. N., Rose. D. and Yaisawarng. S. (1997). "Performance measurement in government service provision: the case of police services in New South Wales". *Journal of Productivity Analysis*. Vol. 8 No. 4. pp. 415–430.

Diez-Ticio. A. and Mancebon. M.J. (2002). "The efficiency of the Spanish police service: An application of the multiactivity DEA model". *Applied Economics*. Vol. 34. pp. 351–362.

Drake. L. and Howcroft. B. (1994). "Relative efficiency in the branch network of a UK bank: an empirical study". *Omega*. Vol. 22 No. 1. pp. 83–90.

Drake. L.M. and Simper. R. (2000). "Productivity estimation and the size-efficiency relationship in English and Welsh police forces: an application of data envelopment analysis and multiple discriminant analysis". International Review of Law and Economics. Vol. 20 No. 1. pp. 53–57.

Drake. L.M. and Simper. R. (2001). "The economic evaluation of policing activity: an application of a hybrid methodology". *European Journal of Law and Economics*. Vol. 12. pp.173–192.

Drake. L.M. and Simper. R. (2002). "X-inefficiency and scale economic in policing: a comparative study using the distribution free approach DEA". *Applied Economics*. Vol. 34. pp. 1859–1870.

Drake. L.M. and Simper. R. (2003a). "The measurement of English and Welsh police forces: a comparison of distance function models". European Journal of Operational Research. Vol. 147 No. 1. pp. 165–186.

Drake. L.M. and Simper. R. (2003b). "An evaluation in the choice of inputs and outputs in the efficiency measurement of police forces". *Journal of Socio-Economics.* Vol. 32. pp. 701–710.

Drake. L.M. and Simper. R. (2004). "The economics of managerialism and the drive for efficiency in policing". *Managerial and Decision Economics.* Vol. 25 No. 8. pp. 509–523.

Drake. L.M. and Simper. R. (2005a). "The measurement of police force efficiency: An assessment of UK Home Office policy". *Contemporary Economic Policy.* Vol. 23 No. 4. pp. 465–482.

Drake. L.M. and Simper. R. (2005b). "Police efficiency in offences cleared: an analysis of English 'Basic Command Units'". *International Review of Law and Economics.* Vol. 25 No. 2. pp. 186–208.

García-Sánchez. I.M. (2007). "Evaluating the effectiveness of the Spanish police force through data envelopment analysis". *European Journal of Law and Economics.* Vol. 23 No. 1. pp. 43–57.

García-Sánchez. I.M. (2009). "Measuring the efficiency of local police force". *European Journal of Law and Economics.* Vol. 27 No. 1. pp. 59–77.

Goltz. J.W. (2008). "Determinants of performance of police organisations in the state of Florida: an evidence based confirmatory approach". *International Journal of Public Policy.* Vol. 3 No. 5–6. pp. 419–429.

Gorman. M.F. and Ruggiero. J. (2008). "Evaluating US state police performance using data envelopment analysis". *International Journal of Production Economics.* Vol. 113 No. 2. pp. 1031–1037.

Gyimah-Brempong. K. (1987). "Economies of scale in municipal police departments: The case of Florida". *The Review of Economics and Statistics.* Vol. 69 No. 2. pp. 352–356.

Hadad. Y.Keren. B. and Hanani. M.Z. (2015). "Combining data envelopment analysis and Malmquist Index for evaluating police station efficiency and effectiveness". *Police Practice and Research.* Vol. 16 No. 1. pp. 5–21.

Mareschal. B. (2018). "Preference functions and thresholds". Fonte: http://www.promethee-gaia.net/FR/assets/preffunctions.pdf.

Nyhan. R.C.. and Martin. L.L. (1999). "Assessing the performance of municipal police services using data envelopment analysis: an exploratory study". *State Government Review* . Vol. 31 No. 1. 18–30.

Riccio. V. and Skogan. W.G. (2018). *Police and society in Brazil.* New York: Taylor and Francis.

Sapori. L.F. (2007). *Segurança pública no Brasil: desafios e perspectivas.* Rio de Janeiro: Editora FGV.

Sun. S. (2002). "Measuring the relative efficiency of police precincts using data envelopment analysis". *Socio-Economic Planning Sciences.* Vol. 36. pp. 51–57.

Thanassoulis. E. (1995). "Assessing police forces in England and Wales using data envelopment analysis". *European Journal of Operational Research.* Vol. 87 No. 3. pp. 641–657.

Verma. A. and Gavirneni. S. (2006). "Measuring police efficiency in India: an application of data envelopment analysis". *Policing: An International Journal.* Vol. 29 No. 1. pp. 125–145.

Wu. T-H., Chen. M-S. and Yeh. J-Y. (2010). "Measuring the performance of police forces in Taiwan using data envelopment analysis". *Evaluation and Program Plannning.* Vol. 33 No. 3. pp. 246–254.

2

ADDRESSING THE CHALLENGES OF LAW ENFORCEMENT HIGHER EDUCATION IN HUNGARY[1]

László Christián[2]

Introduction to the Hungarian law enforcement system and its current challenges

Law enforcement is a part of public administration and its mission is to maintain the internal order of the State, preserve public order and security, to protect the members of society and their fundamental values by preventing, deterring, and disrupting offences that violate or threaten them, even by the legitimate use of physical force. This is an extremely complex and multifaceted task which no single public body, in this case the police, can be expected to carry out exclusively. Fulfilling the mission of policing, of creating security, is the result of social cooperation and collective endeavor, in which, in addition to law enforcement agencies and the bodies responsible for law enforcement, local authorities, private security companies, and civilian self-defense organizations also play an important role. These additional bodies can be described as a complementary law enforcement system, in which the activities of state bodies are complemented, supported, and assisted by commercial and civil organizations (Christián, 2018).

Since 1994, the police organization has been regulated by a discrete act of Parliament. In Hungary, law enforcement services are provided by the National Police force, which is under the command of the Ministry of Interior and includes the border police force (Leyrer, 2013). The law enforcement system is based on the following state law enforcement agencies: the Police Force, the Disaster Management Service, the Civil Security Organization, and the Prison Service, but there are other institutions that play an

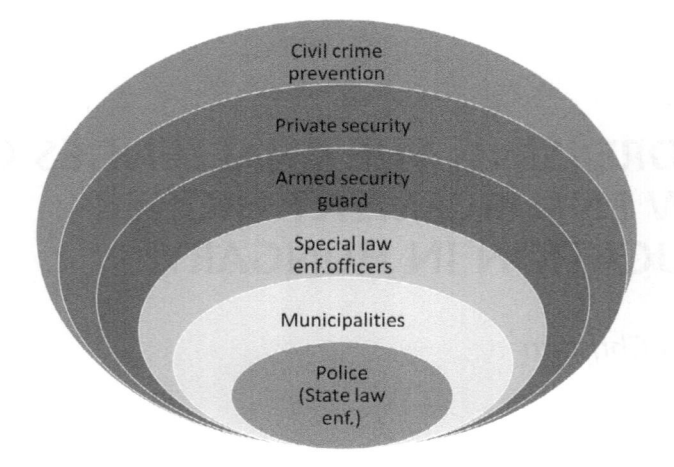

FIGURE 2.1 Complementary law enforcement in Hungary (Christián, 2022)

important complementary role: the National Tax and Customs Administration service, municipal law enforcement agencies, civil volunteer security organizations and the private security sector. Private security enterprises and social crime prevention organizations (in Hungary, the unique Nationwide Civil Self-Defense Organization) also play a complementary role in providing security. As a major institution in the Hungarian law enforcement system, the principle function of the National Tax and Customs Administration is financial control and taxation, alongside which they also have law enforcement functions. This is a special organization, which includes the former public order body, the Customs and Finance Guard.

Challenges in law enforcement

In recent years, global challenges have significantly affected Hungary, its law enforcement agencies, and their activities.

Illegal migration

In 2015, an explosive illegal migration wave reached Hungary and Europe as a whole. In Hungary in 2015, border law enforcement agencies apprehended 2,500–30,000 illegal immigrants each week. In 2023, these numbers were between 2,000–5,000 persons.[3] The increased border protection at the southern border section resulted in many additional tasks for the police that required the involvement of thousands police officers and soldiers from all over the country. In 2022, special border search units were established to carry out these tasks. The handling of the above mentioned situation required not only border police but significant numbers of immigration police, also administrative and other measures had to be carried out throughout the country. The process of illegal migration still represents a significant additional task for the police force as a whole, and not just at the border.

The COVID-19 pandemic

In Hungary, the protection of state and social order, legal compliance, crime prevention and the elimination of infringements, along with the restoration of any violated legal order is primarily carried out by public administration organizations (state administration and local governmental bodies) within the framework of law enforcement activities. As a state administration organization, the police force is responsible for maintaining public safety, public order and the ordered conditions of the state border. The municipal law enforcement organization supports the activities of the police and contributes to the maintenance of public safety locally. The measures introduced in response to the COVID-19 pandemic transferred significant additional tasks to these organizations. The scope of their duties as laid down in legislation was extended, and other organizations were also involved. The police (including the border policing branch) were primarily involved in managing the COVID-19 pandemic: they acted predominantly on the front line in the public space.

However, the National Tax and Customs Administration service, the Nationwide Civil Self-Defense Organization, and the Hungarian Defense Forces also played significant roles in relieving the police, which was ensured by legal mandate (*Act CLXV of 2011; Act CXXII of 2010; Government Decree 410/2020*). The government established the hospital command system, which included police officers, soldiers, and disaster management officers to whom health institutions were assigned to carry out epidemiological protection tasks. On 30 March 2020, 109 hospital commanders in 108 health institutions took up their roles. There were 29 police officers, 29 disaster management agency officials, 51 Hungarian Armed Forces personnel who became hospital commanders. The Hungarian police had to enforce stay-at-home orders between 28 March and 17 June, 2020 under the relative legislation (*Government Decree 71/2020*), which meant more than 1,000,000 quarantine checks (Lobnikar et al., 2023).

The Ukrainian–Russian war

Over the last year and a half, the Ukrainian–Russian war has also created a very significant additional workload for the entire public administration system, including all law enforcement agencies. Since the outbreak of the war (February 2022), more than 1,300,000 Ukrainian refugees have entered Hungary. The majority of these refugees moved to Western Europe, however, huge forces had to be mobilized to transport, take care of, and accommodate these people, mostly women and children, in addition to carrying out immigration enforcement procedures. A significant part of this additional workload was carried out by the Alien Police as the newest part of the Hungarian Police (formerly the independent Immigration and Citizenship Agency).

In conclusion, it can be stated that law enforcement, and law enforcement bodies in particular, faced global challenges in managing all these problems, which required both huge financial and human resources and for other basic tasks to be deferred.

Workforce crisis

The American Police Executive Research Forum points out that currently, the police profession is facing a workforce crisis because in recent years fewer people are choosing to join the police force, and increasingly officers are leaving the field after just a few years (Police Executive Research Forum, 2019).

Wilson and Grammich drew attention to the fact that the two biggest challenges facing law enforcement agencies in the 21st century may be recruitment and retention; they also stated that these challenges will be sharpened by the retirement of the baby-boom generation, the bottleneck in budgetary resources, the competition for skilled and qualified applicants, as well as the new attitude to work among the younger generation (Wilson, Grammich, 2009).

The United States Department of Justice's comprehensive assessment of the situation (Office of Community Oriented Policing Services, 2020) highlighted the professional and social factors that make it difficult for law enforcement agencies to recruit. Their summary indicates that law enforcement agencies are forced to face such challenges as:

- Competition between organizations in relation to the recruitment of new employees
- Length of service, overtime, burnout
- Specific organizational culture
- Negative social attitudes affecting some law enforcement sectors; procedures and policies limiting the recruitment of women
- Drug use policy (Morison, 2017)

- Lack of a recruitment strategy and branding aimed at the new generation with a realistic presentation of the activities of the given law enforcement agency
- Lack of partnership with the communities served by law enforcement agencies
- Length of the application processes based on outdated concepts and technology

In 2019, the average number of police officers per capita in the European Union was 334/100,000 citizens, while in Hungary it was 386 police officers/100,000 citizens. This number is lowest in Scandinavian countries, where it falls below 200, and highest in Mediterranean countries, where it rises to over 400 (Eurostat, 2019). Currently, the most intense staff shortage in Hungary is experienced in the staff of executive police officers (around 5,000 police officers). Moreover, the average age of Hungarian police officers has increased by more than three years in the past decade, in 2020 it was 38.5 years (HCSO, 2019).

Background of law enforcement higher education in Hungary

Higher education in Hungary

As the excellent Hungarian Nobel Prize scientist Albert Szent-Györgyi once said, "It is the school's job to teach us how to learn, to arouse our appetite for knowledge, to teach us the joy of a job well done, and the excitement of creation, to teach us to love what we do and to help us find what we love to do."

Higher education in Hungary has a long history, dating back to the 14th century with the country's first university being founded in Pécs in 1367. Recently, due to the expansion of higher education in the past two decades, both the number of enrolled students and the capacity of the institutions have increased considerably. Between 1990 and 2010, the population of students in higher education more than quadrupled, from 90,000 to almost 400,000; currently the number is ca. 280,000 across the 64 universities operating in Hungary today. Hungary participates in the Bologna Process, in which EU member states have voluntarily undertaken to coordinate their higher education systems. The Bologna Process has brought unprecedented change to European higher education and has fundamentally defined the recent history of Hungarian higher education. As a result, the higher education system of Hungary has become (or will become) part of a large European system, the European Higher Education Area.

The Ludovika University of Public Service

In Hungary, law enforcement higher education has a tradition of more than half a century, as the police college was founded in 1971. After the millennium, the idea was of restructuring military and law enforcement higher education, professional, cost-saving considerations and the concentration of resources. The structure of Hungarian higher education as a whole at that time did not sufficiently reflect the accepted European standards, and Hungary had many more higher education institutions than it needed. The creation of LUPS was a part of this complex process.

LUPS was created out of the recognition that within the public service, the training of law enforcement personnel, civil administration, national defense and national security services rests on common foundations. In this context, the strengthening of common professional awareness and expertise requires coordinated and planned refresher training, which can be implemented efficiently and cost-effectively within the organizational framework of a university.

LUPS was founded in 2011, with the primary aim of offering the higher-level training of the present and future workforce in public administration, law enforcement, national defense and national security services at Bachelor, Master, and Doctoral levels. LUPS is a place that provides for the unique, special training and development needs of the Hungarian government, so this university has developed a comprehensive approach in the field of public service education that will enable mobility and cross-career pathways between civil, military and law enforcement services in the future.

The Faculty of Law Enforcement

The mission of the Faculty of Law Enforcement is to provide training for the future mid- and high-level leaders of the Hungarian law enforcement agencies, including the Hungarian National Police force, the National Tax and Customs Office, the Prison Service, the National Directorate-General for Alien Policing and the Counter Terrorism Centre.

Being a good police officer is becoming increasingly difficult in the 21st century or perhaps more challenging today, but it is not impossible. But to do this, we need a new approach and a new toolbox, which is what I present in the next section.

Creative Learning Program at the Ludovika – University of Public Service

The university management has recognized that higher education as a whole, including law enforcement education, faces a number of global challenges, one of the most exciting and burning of which is the replacement of frontal, theoretical education with practice-oriented, experience-based, student-centered training (Hegedűs et al., 2022). To promote this pedagogical turnaround a Creative Learning Program (CLP) and Research Centre was established at the university. The planned education reform is based on a stable assessment of the situation, to which end a thorough student satisfaction and needs survey (*studium* program) and our own research (student competence test and motivation measurement) were conducted at the Faculty of Law Enforcement with the involvement of an independent external actor, as well as our own research.

In this chapter, I highlight university-level reform efforts that focus on the effective development and assessment of student skills, mentoring of individual learning pathways, and support for person-centered interaction and professional communities. The reform of law enforcement training is already able to show a number of innovations. The joint public service exercise, which has been carried out several times in recent years with the participation of hundreds of students and teachers from all four faculties at LUPS, shows how to deal with a dangerous disaster situation, where professional systems (law enforcement, defense, civil administration) work intensively to solve a serious challenge. Here, cooperation, communication and problem-solving skills are developed simultaneously.

CLP aims to implement a pedagogical turnaround that sees the essence of education as "the effective development and assessment of the students' skills, the mentoring of individual learning pathways, and the cultivation of personality-based, active creative professional communities" (Christián et al., 2023: 19). In this context, the following objectives have been set:

1. Community learning – creation – individual development
2. The ideal type of teacher who guides collaborative learning and mentors individual creative work
3. Small group training instead of mass education
4. Assessment of students' knowledge on the basis of the collaborative and/or individual creative work during the semester
5. Development of key competences rather than drilling.

(Christián et al., 2023)

In the spring semester of the academic year 2019/2020, CLP started with a comprehensive review of the recommended curricula, followed by the collection of pedagogical good practice that can be applied and adapted either in a specific subject area or in other fields of education. We systematically collect good practices and share them with the university community through workshops and open lectures, while a mentoring network is also being developed for both students and lecturers to be able to engage effectively in the program. We aim to share them in different ways, for example, by organizing professional days where university instructors can participate in such development programs to expand their teaching methodology repertoire. The two-day events focus on different creative methods, online platforms, and good practice. Interested teachers have the opportunity to learn about methods and techniques that can be applied in the development of education, such as the role of the Moodle system in creative learning; tutorial learning; the use of VR in the development of soft skills; the use of PedTech in education; motivation, gamification as a new dimension of education; innovative, intellectual creation techniques in education; presentation with digital tools, etc.

Further assistance is provided to the citizens of the University through the organization of a Methodology Tea Party once a month, where teachers and students have the opportunity to participate in an informal discussion on the process of the reform pedagogy at LUPS. The topics covered so far are:

1. "Classical knowledge and creative learning? Friends or enemies?"
2. Presentation of the teachers who received the most votes in the "Teacher of the Year" poll
3. "Assessment and testing"
4. "Presentation of the LUPS educational portfolio"
5. In the autumn term: "Board games in education".

The collection of good practice gave us the idea of creating a methodology handbook (Korpics et al., 2023) from which we can draw ideas and suggestions to use in everyday teaching. This is the main purpose of this handbook, but it also supports the ongoing pedagogical/teaching methodological process and transformation that started at the University in 2019. In compiling this handbook, we have taken into account the fact that the University is essentially taught by non-teaching staff, so there are three chapters that contain didactic principles with many practical examples and guidelines. The other chapters contain methodologies that can be applied and adapted in teaching, whatever the subject. As mentioned above, the pandemic brought our digital difficulties into focus (Dominek et al., 2023), so a chapter is devoted to this topic (Botos et al., 2023).

To further motivate the teachers at the University, the Vice Rector for Education launched within the framework of CLP a call for applications for the Innovative Department Award 2021 for teachers working in departments at LUPS. It has spectacularly encouraged our professional communities to incorporate excellent new practices into the university's bloodstream. The Award provides an opportunity for methodological innovation, while at the same time offering students the experience of and opportunity to develop a constructive learning environment. The aim of the Award is to recognize departments that are actively involved in the implementation of CLP, supporting the paradigm shift in teaching methodology at the University. Eligibility and commitments of the department awarded the Prize are as follows:

1. The department and its teachers may use the logo of the Award.
2. The department and its teachers can participate in the expansion of the CLP Service Basket courses, which includes training for teachers and teaching methodology.

In 2022, the winners at the Faculty of Law Enforcement were the Department of Public Safety. In 2021, the winners at the Faculty of Law Enforcement were The Department of Languages for Specific Purposes (Ürmösné et al., 2022). Special Prize: 1. The Department of Behavioural Sciences and Law Enforcement; 2. The Department of Customs and Finance Guard.

In 2022, the full-time curriculum of the BA in International Management was transformed according to the principles of creative teaching methodologies. Feedback was received from the first year students on the practical implementation of the 2nd semester. The focus of the questionnaire (11 questions) was on the measurement of its effectiveness. According to the optional responses, there are very well-organized subject areas that use a variety of methodological tools and support students' activities. Students highlighted the excellent teaching skills, professional knowledge, and the teachers' positive student-friendly attitude. In terms of professional development, deeper knowledge acquisition was emphasized several times, and English lessons promoted the use of English for specific purposes (ESP) language. In addition, feedback was also received on the development of general skills. The interactive sessions, group work, student presentation, debates, argumentation exercises and field exercises were all found to be useful and enjoyable.

Last but not least, CLP-related research activities are coordinated by the members of the Creative Learning Research Workshop, which has planned its research over a four-year period. A part of the research can be considered to be action research that accompanies each development and provides feedback on the usefulness of each development within a short time. Research papers have been written and published in national volumes and journals. In addition, various CLP-related research activities are being conducted in the context of the Thematic Excellence Programme (TEP) 2021.

In 2022, three major empirical research projects were carried out by the researchers. The first one was entitled "The state of education after the pandemic". The second one measured the digital competences of the teachers at LUPS through a questionnaire survey. The third one dealt with the pedagogical competences of the teachers at LUPS. Research Workshop staff are also working with experts and doctoral students on a mentoring concept and a mentoring handbook for the University's mentoring system.

Heutagogy and transformative learning in law enforcement education

The evolution of law enforcement higher education in Hungary, particularly the establishment and development of Ludovika – University of Public Service (LUPS), offers valuable insights and lessons for police educators worldwide. First and foremost, the recognition of the interconnectedness of public service training is crucial. The creation of LUPS stems from the acknowledgment that the training of law enforcement personnel, civil administration staff, national defense, and national security services share common foundations. This understanding underscores the importance of coordinated and planned refresher training to enhance common professional awareness and expertise efficiently. International police educators can learn from Hungary's experience in consolidating resources and restructuring higher education to meet contemporary standards.

Moreover, the Hungarian example highlights the significance of adaptability and responsiveness to global challenges in law enforcement education. The establishment of the Creative Learning Program (CLP) at LUPS reflects a commitment to move away from traditional, theoretical education towards practice-oriented, experience-based, and student-centered training. This pedagogical shift emphasizes the effective development and assessment of student skills, individualized learning pathways, and the cultivation of active, creative professional communities. Police educators worldwide can draw inspiration from this approach, recognizing the need to prepare future law enforcement leaders with the practical skills, problem-solving abilities, and collaborative mindset required in the 21st century.

The LUPS journey toward a Creative Learning Program embodies principles of heutagogy, emphasizing self-directed learning and the empowerment of learners in shaping their educational experiences. The CLP's objectives, such as community learning, small group training, and the development of key competences, align with the essence of heutagogy. This approach challenges the traditional teacher-centered model and fosters a more personalized and engaging learning environment. The emphasis on individual development and the assessment of collaborative and creative work during the semester reflects a transformative approach to education, encouraging students to take ownership of their learning journey.

Furthermore, the CLP's commitment to sharing good practice, organizing workshops, and establishing a mentoring network for both students and lecturers contributes to the creation of a dynamic, learner-centric ecosystem. The methodology handbook created by LUPS serves as a valuable resource for educators, seeking to globally implement heutagogical principles in their curricula. By prioritizing continuous research, assessment, and adaptation of teaching methodologies, LUPS showcases a commitment to staying abreast of educational advancements. International police educators can draw on these heutagogical principles to cultivate a learning environment that not only imparts knowledge but also empowers law enforcement professionals to be flexible critical thinkers capable of addressing the complex challenges of their roles.

Notes

1 I would like to thank my great colleagues Nóra Barnucz, Márton Demeter and Gergő Háló for their excellent support in putting into final format this chapter.
2 Professor Dr. László Christián, Habil, Police Brigadier General, Vice Director (Rector) of the Ludovika – University of Public Service, Hungary. E-mail: Christian.Laszlo@uni-nke.hu
3 Hungarian Police data: https://www.police.hu/hu/hirek-es-informaciok/hatarinfo/illegalis-migracio-alakulasa

References

Botos A., Botos V., Barnucz N. (2023): Sárkány ellen sárkányfű, avagy alternatív oktatási módszerek a tanítás-tanulás folyamatának támogatására az IKT eszközök használatával [Dragon flowers against dragons, or alternative teaching methods to support the teaching-learning process using ICT tools]. In: Korpics M., Méhes T., DomokosK.: *Módszertani kézikönyv* [Methodology Handbook] (under publication). 219–234.

Christián L. (2018): Rendészeti szervek. In: Jakab A., Fekete B. (eds): *Internetes Jogtudományi Enciklopédia* [Internet Law Encyclopedia] (Constitutional Law Column, ed.: Bodnár E., JakabA.), https://ijoten.hu/szocikk/rendeszeti-szervek, date of download: 14/12/2021.

Christián L. (2022): *Komplementer rendészet* [Complementary Law Enforcement], Ludovika Egyetemi Kiadó. 66.

Christián L., Korpics M., Botos V. (2023): Kreatív Tanulás Program a Nemzeti Közszolgálati Egyetemen [Creative Learning Programme at the National University of Public Service]. In: Korpics M., Méhes T., Domokos K. (eds): *Módszertani kézikönyv* [Methodology Handbook]. 9–20. (under publication).

Dominek D.L., Barnucz N., Uricska E., Christián L. (2023): Experiences of digital education from the students' perspective. *Információs Társadalom*, Vol. 23. No. 2. 9–24.

Eurostat (2019): Government expenditure on public order and safety – Statistics explained (europa.eu) https://ec.europa.eu/eurostat/statistics-explained/index.php?title=Government_expenditure_on_public_order_and_safety&oldid=628842

Office of Community Oriented Policing Services (2020): Deliberative and pre-decisional: Chapter 2. *Law Enforcement Recruitment and Training*, United States Department of Justice.
HCSO (2019): *Statistical Yearbook of Hungary*. Hungarian Central Statistical Office.
Hegedűs J., Matlári A., Barnucz N. (2022): Kihívások a pandémia idején a rendészeti felsőoktatásban [Challenges in law enforcement higher education during a pandemic]. In: Kattein-Pornói R., Mrázik J., Pogátsnik M. (eds). *Tanuló Társadalom Oktatáskutatás járvány idején* [Learning Society Educational Research during an Epidemic]. HERA Évkönyvek IX. Debreceni Egyetemi Kiadó. Magyar Nevelés és Oktatáskutatók Egyesülete. Budapest – Debrecen.
Korpics M., Méhes T., Domokos K. (2023): *Módszertani kézikönyv* [*Methodology Handbook*]. (under publication).
Leyrer, R. (2013). Finding the right path of policing in Hungary. In: Meško G., Fields C.B., Lobnikar B., & Sotlar A. (eds), *Handbook on Policing in Central and Eastern Europe*, 115–128. Springer.
Lobnikar B., Christián L., Balla J., Kalmár Á., Mraović Cajner I., Borovec K., Sotlar A. (2023): Police and other plural policing institutions in Central and Eastern Europe facing COVID-19 pandemic. In: Den Boer M., Bervoets E., Hak L. (eds) *Plural Policing, Security and the COVID Crisis: Comparative European Perspectives*. Cham, Switzerland: Springer-Verlag, 116.
Morison K.P. (2017): *Hiring for the 21st Century Law Enforcement Officer: Challenges, Opportunities, and Strategies for Success*. Washington, D.C.: Office of Community Oriented Policing Services, 15.
Police Executive Research Forum (September 2019): *The Workforce Crisis, and What Police Agencies Are Doing About It*. Washington D.C., p 7. https://www.policeforum.org/assets/WorkforceCrisis.pdf
Ürmösné S.G., Barnucz N., Kudar M. (2022): Út az Innovatív Tanszék első helyezett díja felé [The Road to the Innovative Department First Prize]. *Belügyi Szemle*, Vol. 70. No. 10. pp. 2113–2133.
Wilson J.M., Grammich C.A. (2009): *Police Recruitment and Retention in the Contemporary Urban Environment*. Santa Monica, CA: RAND Corporation. 3.

3

THE FORMATION OF THE LOCAL PREVENTION POLICE UNITS AT THE NATIONAL UNIVERSITY OF LANÚS[1]

Daniel Russo[2] and Alejandro Hener[3]

Introduction

The creation of the Local Prevention Police Units (Unidades Policiales de Prevención Local, UPPL by its Spanish acronym) constituted one more chapter of the eclectic set of actions taken by the Province of Buenos Aires in its security policies. The virtual shut-down of this institutional project so close to its inception is one more case of good intentions falling through; this had also happened to the Policía de Buenos Aires 2 a decade earlier with Arslanian at the head of the Buenos Aires Ministry of Security.

We take this failed experience in the Municipality of Lanús as an opportunity to reflect on the potential to transform the institutional matrix of the police from the field of training, as well as the effects of the Public University as a central actor in the production of police personnel.

To this end, we will first analyze the process of creating the UPPL in the context of Governor Daniel Scioli's Presidential candidature. Secondly, we will study the implementation of this Plan in the Municipality of Lanús, and the configuration of a multiple training matrix in which the National University of Lanús had a significant role. Finally, we will see the perspective of the police officers involved in the UPPL Lanús.

1 The formulation of the UPPL in the context of the 2015 national election

The creation of Local Police Departments in the province of Buenos Aires must be analyzed in light of the presidential aspirations of Daniel Scioli, who was governor at the time. His nomination as candidate to succeed Cristina Fernández de Kirchner in the 2015 elections generated controversy amongst the power players of the ruling coalition. During the step preceding the PASO,[4] the Frente para la Victoria itself questioned his position with sectors of the opposition from the government he represented. The core of the criticism pointed out the shortcomings of Scioli's administration at the head of the provincial government. In particular, his security policies became the primary target of criticism from both the opposition parties and similarly aligned political sectors. In this context, the creation of the UPPLs constituted one of the main bets towards consolidating his image as president-like.

1.1 Daniel Scioli's governments in the province of Buenos Aires (2007–2011 and 2011–2015)

The ruling party's victory in the national elections of 2007 brought about a rearrangement of the political scene. On a national level, it reaffirmed the path traced by President Néstor Carlos Kirchner (2003–2007). The result obtained by the party headed by his wife Cristina Fernández de Kirchner was categorical.[5] This pattern replicated itself in the new composition of the map of provincial governments. The Frente para la Victoria had imposed itself in most electoral districts and achieved a majority in both legislative chambers.[6]

The election in the province of Buenos Aires showed a similar composition in the percentages obtained on a national level.[7] In his inauguration speech, Scioli reaffirmed his full agreement to the political powers of the national government. His message was clear: he intended to accompany *the project to which Cristina Fernández de Kirchner is calling us* Nevertheless, this definition of harmony with the national government quickly gave way to the emergence of differences in the very understanding of political action.[8]

From the very first act of government, Scioli sought to differentiate himself from his predecessor Felipe Solá, who came from the same coalition. The major point of divide would come to be security policy. León Arslanian's replacement as Minister of Provincial Security was the prosecutor Carlos Stornelli, whose profile was diametrically opposed to his forerunner. Stornelli would void the main initiatives intended in the *Plan de reformas de las policías 2004–2007* [9]: the coup de grace came with the closure of the institution leadership by a citizen from outside the force and the restitution of leadership to a uniformed officer. At the inauguration ceremony, the governor himself announced to the press the name of the Superintendent Daniel Salcedo as the new Chief of Police of the province.[10]

The result of the 2011 elections marked a rift in the relationship between the national and provincial governments.

After a setback in the 2009 midterm elections, the victory of the ruling party in 2011 was categorical. With 54.11% of votes in its favour, the Cristina Fernández de Kirchner–Amado Boudou formula took over 37 points of advantage over the Binner–Morandini (16.81%) binomial and almost 43 over Alfonsín–González Fraga. Likewise, they won in 21 out of 24 districts. In the province of Buenos Aires, Governor Daniel Scioli was reelected with 55.18% of the votes getting nearly 40 points over the "Unión para el Desarrollo" formula.

Once again, what could have been interpreted as an opportunity to align the guidelines of the National and the Buenos Aires governments turned into a progressive and growing tension. At the same time as the polling closed, the race for the presidential succession in 2015 was at stake.

Scioli's willingness to be the Frente para la Victoria's candidate collided with the political timetable managed by the president. The early anointing of a successor would take away his ability to lead for the rest of the term. A new chapter of political tensions was then beginning in which the governor would try to accumulate the necessary power to be considered the natural successor of his ruling party. To this end, he would take security as his banner and the creation of local police forces as his main bet.

2 Implementation of the UPPL of the Municipality of Lanús

The link between the Local Police project and electoral urgencies can be seen in the fact that its implementation was brought forward to the last quarter of 2014, while it was originally planned for January of 2015. The municipalities that adhered early to the project to create the UPPL had to assume the budgetary and organizational costs, since the provincial management areas did not yet have the regulatory instruments to support these initiatives. For example, the province undertook to standardize the initial stage of training carried out by each municipality before 2015.

Although the Municipality of Lanús was among the first jurisdictions to adhere to the UPPL proposal, the decision of Mayor Darío Díaz Pérez can be interpreted as an obligatory response to the initiative taken by his neighboring peers in Avellaneda and Lomas de Zamora, who had anticipated its implementation.

One of his boldest decisions was to call on the National University of Lanús (UNLa) to become actively involved in the training of future UPPL personnel. Amongst the main arguments for this decision was the experience of the Citizen Security career since the year 2004. The starting point included already formed teaching teams, with research and experience in the management of initial training courses for police officers, as had been the case with the Buenos Aires 2 Police Force between 2005 and 2008. Thus, in August 2014, a working team was formed that would be responsible for carrying out the process at the university level.[11]

Once the basic agreements had been reached to advance the proposal, the spokesperson designated by the municipality agreed to a meeting with the heads of the provincial Ministry of Security, to which the academic responsible proposed by the University[12] was invited. In this first meeting, the provincial government's technical teams indicated that they would only consider as valid interlocutors the representatives of the municipalities with which the implementation agreements were signed. Nevertheless, they decided to hold this first meeting as a sign of goodwill for the progress of the formalization of the course.[13]

The flowing relationship between the members of the municipal and university teams allowed the former to request assistance in the design of the pedagogical proposal and in the relationship with the provincial officials assigned to monitor the implementation of the first phases of the work. The original scenario was drastically inverted: from the initial exclusion of third parties that were not contemplated, a direct request for collaboration was made to carry out the pedagogical and organizational adjustments of the training proposal.

From the first meeting at the end of August until the start of the training activities in October, the provincial Ministry of Security had three consecutive interlocutors, who changed the working perspectives of the previous area manager. Something similar happened with the municipal teams, which changed operational managers but kept the main interlocutor throughout the work process.

The participation of the UNLa in the formation of the UPPL of Lanús might be described through the graphic image of the Gaussian distribution bell. At the beginning of the project, its institutional responsibility was limited to the teaching of a series of subjects through its own staff. However, the vacancies that arose among those who were to lead the implementation of the training, both at provincial and municipal level, meant that this originally unforeseen actor ended up influencing decision-making at both municipal and provincial levels. This centrality achieved by the university representatives in the initial stages of the course was limited when the Director of the Local Police School in Lanús took up the post of Director of the Local Police School in Lanús.

The process of consolidation of the new police force contemplated the creation of a specific training school for the UPPL in each municipality, which would be responsible for the selection of applicants, the formation of teaching teams and the development of the training cycle. Its director was to be appointed by the mayor and submitted for consideration to the provincial ministry authorities.

At this point, tensions arose that highlighted one of the main latent conflicts in the creation of this new police force: the political relationship between the governor's office and the municipal chiefs. Mayor Díaz Pérez submitted a first appointment proposal to the ministerial authorities, which was rejected. The promotion of a second candidate chosen by the municipality met the same fate. Following the negative evaluation of the two candidates, the provincial authorities recommended the appointment of a commissioner who had been stationed in Lanús during his police career. In this case it did not seem to matter that he did not have experience in the field of police training, as the two rejected candidates did.

This new institutional figure on the scene meant a first moment of crisis.

From the first day of classes, the UNLa promoted the inclusion of applicants under the same conditions as other regular students: access to the use of the university's facilities and services (physical spaces, library, computer rooms, registration of the course and students in the SIU-Guaraní vocational system) and the same regime of coexistence on campus. For the police authorities of the Ministry, and for the new Director of the School, the applicants had to be differentiated from the rest of the student body. The implicit argument was that a police officer should not be trained within university parameters. The pressure started with the most obvious: making it compulsory to wear black trousers and a white shirt. This requirement put a strain on the perspective of those coordinating the course from the university. Uniformity accentuated the notion of differentiation of the police officer from the community in which he or she would serve. It also made the rest of the students perceive them as a foreign population and not as social actors with the right to be educated in a public university.

The discrepancies between the new UPPL authorities and the UNLa coordination escalated over time. The highest point was reached when the students expressed that the police authorities considered what they had studied in the academic sphere to be useless and called for the centrality of practical knowledge to be considered when defining future practices.

Although the applicants considered the university to be a serious, organized, and reliable institution, to their police instructors they complained about its lack of rigour. At the same time, at the university, they complained about the improvisation and lack of rigour of the design of the activities in the police training spaces. The UNLa organized a day of activities for each of the three cohorts that passed through its classrooms. The first one focused on Community Participation in Security. In addition to the invited panelists, the presence of members of "La casita de los pibes",[14] a community work organization from the city of La Plata, was highlighted. For the other two cohorts, meetings were held with graduates of the UNLa's Citizen Security program with professional police experience. In both cases, the focus was on the transition from the last day as an aspirant to the first day as a police officer. As a sign of the willingness to integrate academic knowledge with that of the police, the UNLa coordination team invited the Director of the School of the UPPL Lanús, who joined as a panelist to tell the story of what his first steps as a police officer had meant to him. After the presentations, each commission worked in plenary sessions with teachers on the elaboration of their own anxieties and fantasies regarding the change of status.

The general elections were approaching. In order to anticipate criticism, especially those who linked the length of the course with the fragility of the results, the provincial government instituted an integrative[15] exam at the end of each cohort. In these tests, problem situations were presented which each candidate had to solve by integrating procedural content and theoretical knowledge. The 227 applicants who completed the course of subjects taught at the National University of Lanús passed the integrative instance, with the UPPL of Lanús being the best qualified in the whole province.

The elections marked a change of political direction in the nation, the province and the municipality. As of December 2015, the formation of the UPPL was entirely in the hands of the new municipal authorities.

3 Being a Local Police officer in the Municipality of Lanús

Police work is qualitatively different from the tasks carried out by other actors in society as a whole. In the democratic system, the police are the only officials authorized to restrict citizens' freedom of movement and, eventually, to use physical force against third parties to the point of lethality. Each uniformed officer thus has the power to influence substantive aspects of his or her community and the biography of those who make it up, which implies a high degree of personal, institutional and social responsibility.

A second degree of differentiation between the police and the members of the community to which they belong is given by their particular work regime and the consequences that derive from it. Although police personnel are included in the universe of public workers responsible for providing essential services, the work statutes, traditions and a particular institutional culture place them on a level of differentiation that promotes the production of certain "marks" that have the effect of distancing them from the social group as a whole. These marks are produced and reproduced not only during the training period, but also in the daily interactions they establish with other individuals during the development of their functions.

The participation of the National University of Lanús in the basic training of the Local Police of the Municipality provided a golden opportunity to study the convergence of representations in the production of police identity. To this end, we analyzed their appropriation of the contents, definitions and procedural matrices developed during the months of initial training. The following are some of the advances made in the research "Alcances en la práctica policial de la formación en el ámbito universitario. La experiencia de la Policía Local del Municipio de Lanús en la Universidad Nacional de Lanús".[16] The testimonies belong to officers who graduated from the cohorts that completed their training in the classrooms of the UNLa.

3.1 Characterization of daily work from the perspective of Local Police officers in Lanús

An attempt was made to establish how the interviewees characterize police work. To this end, we asked for a description of the usual tasks and situations that a Local Police officer in Lanús might encounter during the course of a working day. The initial responses show a monotonous and routine record, as if it were a mere administrative task.

"You do the 8 hours, they come and pick you up and that's it".

"In six or eight hours of service there is a control from the headquarters or not, beyond the one they have on the subject of the cameras of the municipality and then nothing..."

"In an ordinary neighbourhood there is usually not much... much to do, that is to say, it is more than anything else to make an act of presence, security, that is to say, to show security through presence".

"The usual thing is the control of that... of the street, that no illicit acts are committed, and nothing goes against the law...".

Some testimonies highlight presence in the territory as the main reason justifying the deployment of officers. Staying on the streets is not, at first sight, related to traditional police functions. On the contrary, the exchanges that take place between neighbours and uniformed officers do not seem to be any different from those with other citizens who carry out their work in public spaces (newspaper vendors, florists, etc.).

"Nothing... you come across people.... They ask you which street is this, you are more of a GPS sometimes than a help, I mean, you are the one who knows what time it is, where there is a pharmacy open, you have the kiosk in front of you, but they come and ask the policeman if that kiosk recharges the Sube, instead of ringing the doorbell, and asking 'do they recharge Sube?'"

However, police presence is not a minor factor when it comes to measuring the impact of the work of the police forces, and even more so in the case of *proximity assignments*. [17] This impact is not necessarily related to an effective reduction in crime in the area, but rather to a certain proven effect on the population's subjective experience of insecurity. When asked about the day-to-day interventions that are closest to the specific function of the police, the interviewees identified two main fields of action. On the one hand, the matrix of assistance to people appears in a wide range of registers: "health emergencies", "people who have an accident, who faint, who have health problems", "attending a birth". On the other hand, the actions to be taken in the territory will be determined by the directives established at the management level:

"A boss gets up and says 'today, please, I need a statistic on... drugs'. Then, vehicles, motorbikes, people on foot are stopped, they are asked for their documents, and nothing, they are invited to open their wallets, or else they are searched, a general search is carried out to see if they have any drugs in their clothes".

Low-profile procedures, such as motorbike checks and seizures of small quantities of illegal substances, take up a significant part of officers' working time on a daily basis; even if from their own perspective this direction of effort is perceived as insignificant. Police work must demonstrate measurable marks of effectiveness. These will be set by the political officials in the area, or by members of the judiciary. They also tend to be shaped more directly by what the commissioner in charge deems most effective at the time to show "something is being done" in his or her jurisdiction. This changes what should be a crime statistics register from one that "records what happens" to one that "goes after what is needed/required". The squandering of energy in this type of operation is nothing more than a means of protection against potential claims from opposing political sectors and, especially, from demands coming from the judiciary.

The production of police statistics becomes relevant as a technical matrix that allows the crystallization of a certain brand of actions that will be taken as objective measures for the evaluation of institutional effectiveness. This quantification of police work not only presents the theoretical and methodological difficulties involved in translating the criminal issue into numbers, but also, and mainly, the fact that its use is taken as the main input for the elaboration of public policies in this area (Kessler, 2007; Kaminsky and Galeano, 2007; Sozzo, 2003).

The register of this operational cadence coexists with the certainty of the unforeseen change of scenery. The interviewees point out that the smooth routine changes radically in a matter of seconds, which is why passivity is never a full state. With a delicate tone of humour, one of the interviewees associates the occurrence of complex situations with a certain moment in the service: closing time.

> "You always have conflicts at one o'clock in the afternoon, always, always one, one minus ten, two minus ten… it's always when you leave, never before, if it's before, it's for gender violence or mobile phone snatching. But the big things always happen almost at the end of the service, when you relax the most".

Each intervention represents a kind of "Pandora's box", the contents of which always entails the initiation of a course of unwanted actions, even in scenes that do not appear to hold any risk. Every officer perceives that he or she must be prepared to contain the situation if there is a sudden change of direction. Even when the situation appears to be under control, there remains a register of an uncertain scenario that does not allow the state of alarm to cease. It is the uncertainty about the potential consequences that shapes, in a certain sense, the register of the other as a bearer of danger, a threat. Regardless of whether it is the policeman himself who initiates the sequence of exchange with a citizen, each encounter activates significant amounts of stress and anxiety.

When it comes to characterizing the different services that can be provided in the municipality, the interviewees differentiate between central commercial areas and predominantly residential areas. Central areas require a higher level of attention, as they are a scenario of multiple circulations and risks, as one of the interviewees characterizes: "we work more with passing issues". The dangerous figures are pickpockets, snatchers and shoplifters. Interventions are therefore aimed at hindering their actions by means of spontaneous interceptions for the purpose of investigating possible legal requirements. In this sense, the collaboration between the UPPL police and the shopkeepers in the area becomes a central aspect.

The testimonies naturally refer to the direct accompaniment at the opening and closing times of the premises, to the presence as a guard at the doors of the premises and at the entrance in the presence of people who pose some level of threat. In exchange for this quasi-personalized attention, officials are guaranteed refreshments, places to rest or shelter when inclement weather requires it.

> "I mean, now I go to the shop and since I already know them, because I've always been walking around, it's a 'hello, how are you?'. I already know how many times they have been robbed… I know everything."

The work in residential areas involves a differentiated record on two levels. While interventions tend to be more sporadic than in commercial areas, when they do occur they are of higher critical intensities, such as break-ins and car theft. Also, as the daily dynamics of neighbourhoods are calmer than in commercial residential areas, the sustained presence of police in a specific area allows for greater knowledge of the people who live there, of those who circulate regularly even if they are not residents, and of the typical situations that occur on a daily basis.

> "Because if you've been in a place for five months, you know the people who come in, the time they come, the time they leave, you know all the faces. In a place where you don't know anyone, you start to register the familiar faces, don't you? In other words, who enters this house, who is the neighbour, as the days go by, who is a regular in the area, even if they live there or not, who always passes by".
>
> "You talk to the neighbours, you see, you learn about the movement, you see known and unknown people, you ask for information… you take some ID cards".

This register of regularity makes it possible, by contrast, to intervene in the presence of the atypical. An unfamiliar face, clothing that does not coincide with the usual, a hesitant way of moving. Any of these signs enables action to be taken to identify the meaning of this person in a space that does not recognise them as their own. The main intervention consists of requesting identity documents and, at the same time as requesting information about possible arrest warrants, enquiries are made about the reasons for the presence in that place.

When asked about the usual reactions to the request for personal identification, the answers coincide in pointing out a differentiated reaction according to the social class of the subject in question.

> "Ordinary people, let's say, from middle class and upwards, are reluctant to do this because they are not used to being stopped and asked for documentation. So they get hostile towards us, they scold us as to why

we do it, with what justification. In the lower sectors, in my experience, they are more used to it, so there is no reaction. Unless they feel they might be in danger of being imprisoned."

Each police intervention is structured around two dimensions: the territorial and the institutional. The first organizes the space into segments where some subjects are considered natural, while others are considered outsiders. When it comes to intervention, the territory marks specific possibilities and limits. The institutional dimension, on the other hand, refers to the concrete demands that police authorities and judicial officials make on police personnel. In the decision-making process, the uniformed officer sets in motion a complex system of situational interpretation (Russo, 2020).

3.2 Neighbourhood proximity and compulsive rotations

The relationship between the Local Police and the neighbours is one of the central aspects of the work of the UPPL. Therefore, the constancy in the operational destinations represents a differential value compared to other ways of moving through the territory, such as patrolling on motorbikes or in cars. The differential value of a police force that established as one of its main objectives the integration with the residents of the neighbourhood in which it operates depends on the fact that the operational destinations are maintained for sufficient periods of time to allow for this mutual knowledge between officers and residents. To this end, the institution's initial strategy was to establish a binomial per zone and, if necessary, to arrange the transfer of only one of the members. In this way, members gaining more operational experience could be promoted to more complex sectors of the municipal jurisdiction, while maintaining a stable presence capable of introducing the replacement to the relationships built with neighbours. However, interviewees report that this strategy of proximity deployed during the first year of the UPPL Lanús led to changes in strategy, the results of which are negatively evaluated.

> "In the first year, I had almost all the same assignment... I spent six, seven months in the same assignment. In the second year, most of us stayed there for at least three or four months, then they rotated us, because they wanted us to get to know everything Lanús had to offer."
>
> "The lie that they instilled in you about what you were going to do, you yourself are already realizing that nothing is happening, they are moving you from one side to the other and you don't end up having any contact. You know what happens? It's not because of us, because I have the predisposition to go and meet people and get to know them. People

get tired of having to meet a new official every day and people don't feel like talking to them."

Regarding the origin of the community and community policing models, Cristian Varela (2008) traces continuity with the experiences of the mental health field in Great Britain after the Second World War. The urgent needs posed by that context had forced the construction of creative responses with the scarce material resources available, giving rise to a practice of centrality in the networks of social relations. The strategy of transposing this matrix to the field of security responds, in the author's perspective, more to the search for solutions based on existing experiences than to the critical evaluation of these proposals. Taken as defined objects in themselves, the models of community policing and community policing constitute more of a question mark for the actors in the system themselves than a clear definition of identity and meaning.

Ultimately, the dilemma remains as expressed by Ferret (2004:181):

> before any evaluation, it is advisable to review the practical definition of the police strategy to be evaluated, taking a precise account of the professional techniques actually implemented. This implies for the evaluator to go beyond the classical representations, particularly those of community policing professionals. Indeed, police officers tend to value, in the most natural way, a supposedly "real police work" (repression of criminal acts) and devalue a "false police work" (prevention, "social").

Although in discursive terms the appeal to community or proximity policing shows the intention of bringing police action closer to the direct collaboration of citizens, on the practical level of the daily actions of each uniformed officer these definitions remain subsidiary to the central tensions that they carry.

3.3 Intervention on the exceptional

During the interviews, members of the UPPL Lanús were asked about the most atypical and exceptional situations in which they had had to intervene. The answers referred to violent and unexpected situations, reaffirming that police work does not allow for relaxation. The crystallization of an unexpected scene requires the ability to change the attentional and cognitive register dramatically in an instant, since the irruption of the unexpected is not accompanied by a coherent explanation that allows the course of events to be understood. The following testimony clearly reflects this abrupt change of state and the need to act with little information about what is happening.

"It was a day like today, midday, the children playing there in the little square, the birds singing, a normal, ordinary day, suddenly a van turns around, shouting, ... 'grab him, grab him, that's him'... and we were left.... That's who? It's a matter of milliseconds. We went out running after him, at this point, people were chasing him down. We didn't know what was going on [...]. As we were passing through the children who were playing, the kids, the parents... we grabbed our gun to wield it but we didn't take it out, so as not to scare the children. When we passed the kids there, we drew our gun and shouted: 'drop down, drop down, stop'. The people who had been running after him told us that he had killed one of them. We kept running. Another one of the people who had been following him said: 'watch out, he has a gun'. The situation changes again... well, he has a gun, yes, but maybe it doesn't work, so you look and see that he has ammunition and you say 'well, maybe he's already shot them all'. No, he had one left. Then you start to think back on everything, he could have shot me, my partner, the kids who were playing in the back...".

It is not necessary to reproduce the record of all the exceptional situations referred to because, as one of the interviewees said, "it is that millions of things can happen to you out of the ordinary... because the police do everything, everything".

The breadth of the daily work of a street policeman presents such a wide range of potential operations that in a day's work a newly trained officer may need to intervene in situations of interpersonal tension, be the first barrier of assistance in a road accident or in a situation of acute intoxication due to the consumption of psychoactive substances, contain a victim of aggression or use a lethal weapon to stop an aggression that puts his life or that of third parties at risk.

Based on the idea that a police officer may find himself obliged to resolve the most diverse and complex scenes, we investigated the process of constructing criteria for professional action. What are the sources from which the officers of the UPPL Lanús draw when it comes to intervening in this range of possibilities?

In the specific case of the object of this research, we find that the complexity is multiplied by the number of actors and training spaces present in the construction of this new institutional identity. What is usually produced as an endogamic identity matrix in police institutes is presented here as a space of confluence, tensions and disputes of meaning that act on the same horizon of production.

"The matter suddenly comes to mind when we studied, when we went to the industrial estate and we were told that the theoretical and the practical had little to do with each other, the matter of the street".

"Everything we learned was useful to me, which is all theory... because you get practice in the street but I think that practice ends up beating theory a little later on. You learn to handle yourself in situations that theory doesn't tell you about, you learn from experience...".

The differentiation between the field of theoretical knowledge, provided mainly by the training proposal developed by the UNLa, and the practical knowledge offered by the traditional educational spaces of the police institution is only the first link in the chain of divorce between the basic training process and the transition to the construction of know-how once you are a police officer. As one of the interviewees pointed out: "the manual is one thing and the street is another... when you go out on the street you find yourself in situations that are not in the manual". The process of appropriating the theoretical and practical knowledge of policing is seen as a necessary but insufficient step.

"It would have been good, more emphasis on the more practical part, not so much on the theoretical part".

"It should work more from the practice itself and build a base beyond the legal part, beyond the purely book part, shouldn't it?"

Nor is there any lack of criticism of how the content was distributed and organized in the different training spaces: "what happened is that we had it at the UNLA, we had it at school, but there were so many different theories that the police officer was dizzy". The differences in criteria for approaching the same subject matter according to the frames of reference established in each of the training spaces may have contributed to the perception of distance between the instances of classroom transit and the subsequent demands that would be required in daily practice. In this respect, one of the testimonies clearly illustrated the partial divorce between the academic proposal and the daily experience: "Human Rights was unnecessary, of course...".

The distance between the training area and the production of specific know-how is not, as might be supposed, limited to the university. On the contrary, many testimonies highlight this distance in the field of learning the subject of "police operations", considered to be the hard core of teaching the basic skills that police life will require.

"They tell you, well take it, tell her to get on her knees, to give you her hands. Take the handcuffs, put them on both the same, cuff one, then cuff the other. It's very textbook and even when you practice it with your partner, even if he gets rebellious, let's say to make it a bit more hostile, it doesn't even reach 2% of what it can be like to handcuff someone in the street".

> "You have people who may be upset by nerves, by drugs, who resist because they are bigger or because they are smaller and female, and you have to handcuff them anyway. How do you manage to exert force without breaking them?"
>
> "When police personnel act on the streets, they make mistakes and there is no one who can guide them [...] there is a kind of suspicion and a real Academy is not transmitted as it should be, as it used to be in the old days in a police station."

The differential perception between theory and practice leaves, however, a space of recognition for the knowledge produced from the academic world, to the point of recognizing its usefulness when making decisions in the midst of complex scenes in progress: "The thinking part of the brain automatically leads you to search in 2014 and that is where we find that which tells you 'ah no, stop, we have to do this'... and there we apply the part of the University".

The university appears as a valued space, especially for its training in tools for non-violent conflict resolution. Its brand is identified as a valid reference institution, whose actors and contents are taken into consideration by the current members of the UPPPL Lanús. One of the hypotheses used in this work is that the formative matrix of the institution itself bases its effectiveness on two pillars: the first lies in the identification of this space as their own. The second lies in the recognition of the validity of what is presented there as a vision of reality.

> "The first instance of our intervention is dialogue, to see what happens, how we solve it without entering into a more physical conflict".
>
> "These are little things that automatically bring the brain back to the present day, and on many occasions I had to put them into practice, and I automatically remember the faces of the teachers and what they were saying to us at that time".

In relation to the first term, the National University of Lanús was recognized by the applicants to the Local Police as an organized space, with clear processes and objectives. By considering themselves as recipients of this institutional relationship matrix, the entrants carried out a process of double attribution: both of valuation towards themselves, knowing that they were recipients of this relational matrix, and also of esteem towards the institution.

As for the validity of the knowledge presented by the university, the recognition responds to what the actors themselves define as the periphery of police work: the non-violent containment of situations of tension. This opens one of the most significant chapters in the discussion on the scope of university intervention in initial police training processes. More than an answer, the field is shaped by a question: what does a police officer do?

3.4 Meeting the real policemen

For the members of the Local Police, the representation of police know-how and police being is embodied in the members of the traditional provincial police force. Bearers of the experience necessary to carry out their daily work, their members showed a repertoire of welcome to their new local colleagues that ranged from initial rejection to subsequent sponsorship.

The various testimonies point to a process that begins with the distrust of the province's police officers when they had to coordinate their work with a new security force that was identified on the basis of its limited training,[18] at the same time as confusion was generated regarding the police status of its members and their institutional dependence.

> "The first contact was complicated, because we were like distant cousins who show up one day for a little visit: 'hello, I'm coming here to your house'... and they looked at us strangely...".
>
> "When the local police went out on the streets, nobody sent a paper to the police station saying 'look, there are going to be police personnel who are police from the province of Buenos Aires but work for a new superintendence which is the local prevention police'... so the old police personnel, who were in blue, from the old school, thought they were a type with immediate local jurisdiction but municipal, and we were like that for a year. I explained to the people that no, that it was the police of the province of Buenos Aires, that we worked in a branch that was the superintendence of the local police."

This initial resistance on the part of the provincial police can be explained by an initial negative assessment of the status and capabilities of the newcomers. However, in the opinion of some interviewees, the ultimate reason for the rejection was due to a latent fear that the "newcomers" would expose the faults and mistakes of their old colleagues: "if we did things perfectly and well, many faults that existed elsewhere would be exposed". The testimonies make reference to the fact that in the retraining cycles, Local Police officers obtained better marks than their PBA peers. The explanation given by some interviewees for this phenomenon is that they have "fresher knowledge", or in the more conspicuous version: "because we apply it more".

As time went by, this friction turned into collaboration. The interviewees point out that as the new graduates of the UPPL were incorporated and their presence in the territory was consolidated, the initial anxieties gave way to closeness and trust: "now we have a very good relationship in general with everyone, from the police station, the Community Patrol Command, the people from citizen protection".

The progressive integration of the UPPL into the institutional system of public security is sealed by the attitudes of the old cops, and their concomitant recognition and appreciation of experience as an essential matrix for becoming a true policeman.

> "I've worked many times with police officers from Buenos Aires... and you learn a lot of things because you come across police officers who have 10, 15 years of service and have a lot of experience on their backs that I won't have in three years. In a situation that would have driven me crazy... he got down and in two seconds he solved it, because of his experience...".

The implementation of the Local Police opened a significant chapter in the conception of police proximity and the way in which this is registered and translated by the actors themselves. The image of these new police officers walking the streets of the neighbourhood and getting to know its inhabitants marks a contrast with the usual perception of members of the PBA going about their squares without getting out of their patrol cars, or receiving complaints at the police stations. The immediacy of contact is reminiscent of the figures of the "corner watchman", a direct helper of his neighbours in the most diverse situations.

> "What I've learned over the three years from the experience of seeing how people behave, how people change with us because they like the situation of us being there. People remember the old watchman from ages past, who was there, who was always in the neighbourhood".

However, those interviewed recognise that the general discrediting of the security forces in general and the provincial police in particular, reaches them even when there have been no significant events to justify this reticence. The perception of those who were until recently neighbours in the same neighbourhoods they now walk through in their uniforms keeps the general population's rejection and distrust of their police fresh in their minds.

> "The security forces are frowned upon, I mean, they are necessary, people need them, but they want them and they don't want them... and it's more

that they don't want them than that. If they want them it's because they know that if there is a policeman there they won't be robbed, but if you are there a lot they also complain, complain because you are not somewhere else doing your job".

The general discrediting of the uniformed police becomes a particularity in the case of the UPPL: the predominant colour of their clothing is light blue.[19] This distinctive sign was immediately translated into the nickname "Smurfs", alluding to the tiny elves from a cartoon series popularized in Argentina during the 1980s. The origin of this nickname has no precise source, although it was adopted by both neighbours in general and members of the PBA.

"We were bad with the previous colour we had, which was turquoise. Everyone called us Smurfs".

"I think the suspicion comes from the traditional police: here come the Smurfs, they don't understand anything."

Some Local Police dealt with this disadvantageous nomination position by overcompensation mechanisms in the procedures, especially if those who suffered derogatory treatment were women.

"once a guy said to me: 'ehh, smurfette'. Yes, this smurf can fill your chest with lead, so don't bust my balls."

"There's the typical one, as he's robust, giant... he comes up to me... and I tell him 'look, stay still because I'm really shifty', I'll shoot you, you move once more I'll shoot you' and that's how they stay still...".

"When I put the hooks on you and take you to the police station, you can tell me later if I'm a real cop."

In order to carry out their function, police officers need to dominate the scene and impose their authority. This particular system of exchanges with others is centred on the concept of 'respect', an issue that has already been addressed in other research on police function and identity (Garriga Zucal, 2013a, 2013b). Paradoxically, one of the most significant situations in terms of police status is the view that members of the force themselves have of their colleagues. In this sense, there is a singular phenomenon: each interviewee presents a disqualifying view of the rest of their colleagues.

"People who didn't even have a job joined the local police, without knowing what it was, without checking out what the force was, I won't say all of them, but seventy percent did".

"They lacked a little bit of instruction... they are afraid, they are hesitant, they don't have the Academy".

"You have this image of the policeman who goes and solves everything and who can do everything and who is allowed to put the prisoner in jail and goes back home happy and content, that is, this idyllic image... of fantasy...".

The production of differences has, in the case of the UPPL Lanús, a specific dividing line marked between those of the "old" and the "new" management. This differentiation responds to the distribution of those who entered between 2014 and 2015, during the governments of Daniel Scioli and Darío Díaz Pérez, and received their theoretical training at the university. On the contrary, those who joined from 2016 onwards, under the administrations of María Eugenia Vidal and Néstor Grindetti in the province and municipality respectively, received all their training at the UPPL School.

Regarding the effects of the change of management on the daily work of the Local Police, the testimonies point to the commotion caused by the massive incorporation of new members, who doubled the number of existing officers. The process of assimilation between old and new members was marked by two very significant elements: although in the new municipal administration the link with the UNLa was discontinued and the educational profile was considered as a change of course, the authorities of the Police School incorporated some teachers who had been part of the previous training process. The second noteworthy element was the assignment of Local Police officers from the first promotion, who had minimal experience as civil servants, to central management and coordination positions in the training cycle of the incoming promotions.

"The preparation was the same, the teaching staff changed a bit... many lawyers were incorporated... many of them belonging to the police institution".

"[...] the fourth graduating class was not totally homogeneous, they had many different teachers, many of the courses did not have teachers until the last minute in some subjects. They have a lot of gaps... with so many people... it's like they didn't polish certain details".

The change of direction proposed by the new municipal authorities for the operational management of the UPPL was well received by the first promotions of Local Police, as it was identified as an explicit expansion of the operational capacities in the territory.

"With the change in the boss's management... since the boss comes from another, more operative side... with more of a forward-looking approach... so he gave us more leeway to act... it was good for us because it took us out of that lethargy we had of just being tour guides, so to speak...".

"Even though we got to know the street little by little, but we stayed there, we stagnated... because the first administration did not allow us to do more, did not get us involved in more complex procedures".

Regardless of the management in question, the interviewees' overall assessment of the role of the municipality as the political leadership of their own local police is, to say the least, poor.

"It leaves me with nothing because I suffered it when we were 80, 90 guys locked in a room where we had no physical space to change and nobody came out to tell us 'guys, look, we're going to do this, this and this', they always lied to us with a bonus, which I remember perfectly, they lied to us with a lot of things. I have a lot of respect for the municipality, the mayor, and whoever is in charge, but they don't understand anything, the municipality doesn't understand anything...".

By way of conclusions

We have presented here one of the attempts made in recent years to produce police training outside traditional identity matrices. Although this is not a pioneering experience, there are not many precedents in our country and in the region in which a public university has been set up as a field of study for those aspiring to join a police force.

The need to break the inertia of police isolation and self-government was a reflex that the political class identified belatedly after the return to democracy in 1983. And it can be argued that this identification was driven more by the operational, economic and legal difficulties that this self-government generates than by the conviction that it is really possible to build a democratic and professional institution.

Beyond the opportune media and/or electoral functions, a large part of the political power is usually indifferent to the governance and direction of the police forces. This indifference towards a central actor in the maintenance of the social system explains, in part, why since the middle of the last century only two attempts at reform have succeeded in the most populous of Argentina's provinces: that of Lieutenant Colonel Adolfo Marsillach between 1946 and 1951, during the government of Alfredo Mercante, and the two processes carried out by León Carlos Arslanian, between 1998 and 1999, and between 2004 and 2008, during the governments of Eduardo Duhalde and Felipe Solá, respectively.

The creation of a police force managed by local governments was not a decision that came from within the provincial executive branch, but rather from actors from other political spheres. The UPPL project is an analysis of how the design and execution of security policies end up constituting, above all, a scenario linked to obtaining some kind of political-electoral advantage. It is enough to observe how some of the original promoters of the idea became opponents when they came up against the government's initiative, while other sectors close to the government saw their intentions diluted behind a proposal that did not take their contributions into account.

One of the direct consequences of the diagram of a new police force that emerged from the urgencies of the political context was the improvisation with which substantive aspects were resolved, such as the tensions derived from a double command: on the one hand, the organic dependence of the UPPL on the provincial police and the functional-operational dependence on the security plan of each municipality; on the other, the competencies of each jurisdiction to define the basic training model for its officers.

The need of the then Mayor Darío Díaz Pérez to join the provincial government's plans opened the scene to a unique situation among the municipalities that adhered to the UPPL project: the participation of a public university as a central actor in the process. At the same time, the lack of experience of local government representatives in police training enabled a progressive interference of the representatives appointed by the UNLa at various levels of decision-making, both in the pedagogical dimension and in aspects of operational definition. However, the active presence of academics triggered disputes with members of the provincial police belonging to the management of the Ministry of Security, as well as with those appointed to run the UPPL School in the municipality.

The significant differences in the consideration of the implications of the police function gave rise to numerous tensions between the perspectives that each institution presented to the students: on the side of the authorities of the UPPL School this ranged from the demand for the use of a common dress code in the university environment to the reproduction of military classroom formalities. On the side of the University representatives, there was an attempt to incorporate the aspirants into the common experience of UNLa students (responsibility for their own training process, self-regulation of conduct, among others). In the middle, were the students, constructing their own identity matrix through the modulation of their responses to the expectations of their eventual interlocutors.

The training experience of the UPPL at the National University of Lanús raises a question that recurs in every attempt to transform the training matrix of the police: are the basic training processes powerful enough to transform the identity matrices of police institutions? Of course, the answer is not simple. Transformations of such complexity cannot be satisfied only with isolated (good) intentions, nor can they be nourished only by theoretical declarations or programmatic proposals that are disconnected from reality. The effective implementation presents obstacles related to political situations, the capacities and traditions of the institutions involved, and the accumulation or lack of experience of the actors involved.

The traditional police training model continues to be the point of reference even for new generations who have had no contact with the existing historical systems. Theoretical training is, in the first level of interviewees' records, confined to questions of law regulating police activity. The so-called "social" subjects are seen as enriching general knowledge, but not anchored in the specific day-to-day function.

The contents related to conflict mediation are highlighted as useful, as it is recognized that a substantial part of the work involves intervention in interpersonal tensions between neighbours and within families.

In relation to the training received in diverse educational spaces and with very different institutional logics, the overall assessment is positive. The UNLa is recognized as an enriching experience in the personal human dimension but decoupled from the practical needs required in professional practice. Strikingly, the training spaces closest to the core of police operations receive a similar evaluation. The simulated practices are significantly distant from the real competencies required once on the street.

Police know-how is something that is necessarily acquired in the exercise of the function. The initial training process received is perceived as insufficient, if not obtuse. The construction of being a police officer takes place in the opposite direction to what is learnt in the months of training. One of the slogans with which the rookies are received urges them to forget everything they have learnt up to that point in order to make room for real knowledge.

This does not necessarily mean that institutional efforts are useless. On the contrary, strategies should be developed that creatively link the basic training processes with the first steps in the function (professional internships, internships, on-site tutoring, among other options). In order to adequately orientate resources to strengthen the transition from trainee to officer, the process of knowledge construction by police officers with work experience should be investigated.

Firstly, it is imperative to acknowledge that identifying the limitations in the institutional efforts described in this work does not necessarily imply deeming them ineffective. On the contrary, it is essential to do so in order to conceive innovative strategies that establish creative connections between basic training processes and early stages in police function, such as professional practices, internships, and destination-based mentoring. These options not only enrich theoretical learning but also afford aspirants the opportunity to apply their knowledge in real-world situations, thus fostering a more comprehensive and contextualized learning experience.

Secondly, to effectively direct resources aimed at strengthening the transition from aspirant to officer, it is imperative to conduct detailed research on the knowledge-building process among police officers with work experience. Understanding how knowledge is constructed and solidified in the daily practice of the profession will aid in the identification of areas for improvement and the adjustment of training programs accordingly. Research focused on knowledge construction can also unveil successful practices within the police force that could be systematically integrated into training curriculum.

Lastly, the establishment of a more effective police training system necessitates a deepened collaboration between specific training areas of the police institution and universities with expertise and curriculum development in the field. The implementation of feedback mechanisms between professional practices and curriculum designs, along with the regular updating of study programs, constitutes essential elements to ensure improvement in training processes. In this way, the continuous evolution of the police training system can actively respond to emerging challenges and contribute to the development of professional officers.

Notes

1 This work is part of the Amilcar Herrera Research Project entitled "Alcances en la práctica policial de la formación en el ámbito universitario. La experiencia de la Policía Local del Municipio de Lanús en la Universidad Nacional de Lanús" (The scope of university training in police practice. The experience of the Local Police of the Municipality of Lanús at the National University of Lanús), and its continuation in the Project "La construcción del saber hacer en la función policial: de la formación inicial a la producción del 'criterio' para las prácticas cotidianas" (The construction of know-how in the police function: from initial training to the production of "criteria" for daily practices), both based at the Instituto de Problemas Nacionales, Universidad Nacional de Lanús.
2 Degree in Psychology, Specialist on Education, Ph,D. in Community Mental Health (UNLa). Reaserch Professor at the UNLa and the UBA. Director of the Citizen Security career (UNLa). Coordinator of university academic training of the Policía Buenos Aires 2 (2004–2008) and the Policía Local de Lanús (2014–2015), former National Director of Training of the SEDRONAR (2012–2013). Professor of the PFA Cadet School. Co-director of the research proyects of which this investigation is a part of.
3 Deegree in Sociology and P.h.D. in Social Sciences from the UBA Adjunt Professor in contest for the subject "Criminología", also dictating the subjects "Victimización, Inseguridad Subjetiva y Miedo al delito" and the seminar "Criterios criminológicos para el desarrollo de Observatorios de Seguridad" (Criminological criteria for the development of Security Observatories), Degree and Bachelor's degree in Citizen Safety, Universidad Nacional de Lanús. Director of the research projects of which this investigation is a part of.

4 Primarias Abiertas Simultáneas Obligatorias (Primary Open Simultaneous Compulsory): Voting system by which political parties and coalitions choose their candidates for the elections.
5 Fernández de Kirchner-Cobos (Frente para la Victoria): 45.28%; Carrió-Gustiniani (Confederación Coalición Cívica): 23.05% and Lavagna-Morales (Concertación para una Nación Avanzada): 16.91%.
6 The presidential formula Fernández de Kirchner–Cobos won in 21 out of the 24 provincial jurisdictions. The formula of Carrió–Gustiniani won in the Autonomous City of Buenos Aires, Rodríguiez Saa–Maya in the province of San Luis and the Lavagna–Morales binomial in Córdoba.
7 The Scioli–Balestrini formula won 48.17% of the votes. The opposition showed a greater dispersion of votes among the competing formulas. The Stolbizer–Linares formula (Frente Coalición Cívica) achieved 16.59%, while the De Narváez–Macri (Unión-Pro) got 14.97%.
8 Tensions between Fernández de Kirchner and Scioli weren't new. Up until his assumed governorship, Scioli had served as vice-president of the nation, accompanying CFK's husband, with whom he had maintained public conflicts.
9 This plan implicated a functional reorganization of the police force through a single step, the creation of the Policía Buenos Aires 2 and the integral reformulation of its training and formation policies.
10 On the day he took office as "General Operational Coordinator" of the police, the Superintendent Daniel Salcedo, who had served as head of the Scientific Police during Arslanian's administration, declared to the press that the aspiration to have a civilian leadership in the force had been a "mistake" of the policy makers in the matter, although he recognized that "the guilty ones for having suffered the intervention of the Police were the policemen". In this way Salcedo erased any possibility of being identified with Arslanian.
11 An accompanying commission, composed by the heads of the Academic Secretariat, the Department of Planning and Public, the Citizen Security Programme, and the Centre for Justice and Human Rights, was also considered for the organization scheme.
12 The Municipality of Lanús set up a team led by an actor with extensive experience in the field of provincial politics but no knowledge in the matter of education. Likewise, the people selected from the local staff to provide administrative support to the task showed enthusiasm and commitment to the task but no knowledge in matters of management.
13 Both in the initial reunion and all subsequent meetings, the improvisation of the provincial teams in charge of developing the proposal was evident. A few months before the start of classes the technical documentation of the course did not agree between the partial hourly loads of each subject and the total hours foreseen. In addition, two curricular spaces and their teaching hours were omitted.
14 https://www.facebook.com/pg/lacasitadelospibes/about/
15 By way of example, in the first administration of this evaluation, 20 applicants of UPPL La Plata were excluded.
16 "The scope of university training in police practice. The experience of the Local Police of the Municipality of Lanús at the National University of Lanús."
17 The Victimization Surveys that have been carried out – in a somewhat discontinuous way – in our country show that "police presence" tends to rank among the most highly valued measures among residents and at the same time constitutes a predictor that interacts directly with the levels of perceived insecurity.
18 Governor Daniel Scioli established through the Decreto 220/April 14th of 2014 the "Public Security Emergency". This entitled the provincial government to the

necessary human resources available, which subsequently enabled the reduction of the basic training time of the UPPL from a calendar year to six months.
19 From May of 2018, the Local Police Superintendence implemented a change of the UPPL uniforms, making them more like the rest of the PBA.

Bibliography

Ales, C., Fernández, G., Pereyra, S., Rosso, L. and Sokol, P. 2011. Propuestas para la regulación y el control del uso policial de la coerción y la fuerza en la Argentina [Proposals for the regulation and control of police use of coercion and force in Argentina] in *Regulación y control del uso policial de la coerción y la Fuerza en Argentina* [Regulation and control of police use of coercion and force in Argentina], ed. C. Ales, 209–283, Buenos Aires: Ministerio de Seguridad de la Nación.

Arslanian, C. L. 2008. *Un cambio posible. Delito, inseguridad y reforma policial en la Provincia de Buenos Aires* [A possible change. Crime, insecurity and police reform in the Province of Buenos Aires]. Buenos Aires: Edhasa.

Barreneche, O. 2007. La reforma policial del Peronismo en la Provincia de Buenos Aires, 1946–1951 [The Police Reform of Peronism in the Province of Buenos Aires, 1946–1951]. *Desarrollo Económico* 186: 225–248.

Barrera, N. 2013. Policía, territorio y discrecionalidad: Una etnografía sobre la espacialidad en las prácticas policiales en la ciudad de rosario [Police, territory and discretionality: An ethnography on spatiality in police practices in the city of Rosario] in *De armas llevar. Estudios socioantropológicos sobre los quehaceres de policías y de las fuerzas de seguridad* [Carrying weapons. Socioantropological studies on the work of police and security forces], ed. S. Frederic, M. Galvani, J. Garriga Zucal and B. Renoldi, 355–377, La Plata: Ediciones de Periodismo y Comunicación, Universidad Nacional de La Plata.

Bover, T. 2013. Una cuestión de criterio: Sobre los saberes policiales [A matter of judgment: On police knowledge] in *De armas llevar. Estudios socioantropológicos sobre los quehaceres de policías y de las fuerzas de seguridad* [Carrying weapons. Socioantropological studies on the work of police and security forces], ed. S. Frederic, M. Galvani, J. Garriga Zucal and B. Renoldi, 327–352, La Plata: Ediciones de Periodismo y Comunicación, Universidad Nacional de La Plata.

Carlés, R. 2010. El gobierno local del delito en la Ciudad Autónoma de Buenos Aires. Retóricas participativas y apelación a la comunidad [Local government of crime in the Autonomous City of Buenos Aires. Participatory rhetorics and appeal to community] in *La Policía Metropolitana de la Ciudad Autónoma de Buenos Aires* [Metropolitan Police of the Autonomous City of Buenos Aires] ed. G. Anitua, 63–86, Buenos Aires: Ad-Hoc.

Ciafardini, M. 2006. *Delito urbano en la Argentina. Las verdaderas causas y las acciones posibles* [Urban crime in Argentina. Real causes and possible actions], Buenos Aires: Ariel.

Cobler Martínez, E., Gallardo Campos, R. and Lázaro Guillamón, C. 2014. *Mediación Policial. Teoría para la gestión del conflicto* [Police Mediation. Theory for conflict management], Madrid: Dykinson.

Curbet, J. 2009. *El rey desnudo. La gobernabilidad de la seguridad ciudadana* [The Naked King. The governance of citizen security], Barcelona: Universitat Oberta de Catalunya.

Dammert, L. 2009. Políticas públicas de Seguridad Ciudadana: Innovaciones y desafíos [Public Policies on Citizen Security: Innovations and Challenges] in *Seguridad y ciudadanía: nuevos paradigmas, reforma policial y políticas innovadoras* [Security and citizenship: New paradigms, police reform and innovative policies] ed. G. Kessler, 119–142, Buenos Aires: Edhasa.

Dammert, L. 2000. *Violencia criminal y seguridad pública en América Latina: La situación en Argentina* [Criminal violence and public security in Latin America: The situation in Argentina], Santiago de Chile: CEPAL.

Eilbaum, L. 2004. La sospecha como fundamento de los procedimientos policiales [Suspicion as the basis for police procedures]. *Cuadernos de Antropología Social*20: 79–91.

Epele, M. 2007. La lógica de la sospecha. Sobre criminalización del uso de drogas, complots y barreras de acceso al sistema de salud [The logic of suspicion. On criminalisation of drug use, plots and barriers to access to the health system]. *Cuadernos de Antropología Social*25: 151–168.

Ferret, J. 2004. ¿Evaluar a la llamada policía de proximidad? Certezas e incertidumbres obtenidas de las experiencias francesas [Evaluating the so-called community policing? Certainties and uncertainties from the French experience]. *Revista Catalana de Seguretat Pública*14, 177–197.

Frühling, H. 2003. *Policía comunitaria y reforma policial en América Latina ¿Cuál es el impacto?* [Community policing and police reform in Latin America What is the impact?] Santiago de Chile: Centro de Estudios de Seguridad Ciudadana, Universidad de Chile.

Garriga Zucal, J. 2010. Se lo merecen. Definiciones morales del uso de la fuerza física entre los miembros de la policía bonaerense [They deserve it. Moral definitions of the use of physical force among members of the Buenos Aires police]. *Cuadernos de Antropología Social*32: 75–94.

Garriga Zucal, J. 2013a. Usos y representaciones del 'olfato policial' entre los miembros de la policía bonaerense [Uses and representations of 'police sense of smell' among members of the Buenos Aires police]. *Dilemas: Revista de Estudos de Conflito e Controle Social*3: 489–509.

Garriga Zucal, J. 2013b. Un correctivo. Violencia y respeto en el mundo policial [A corrective. Violence and respect in the police world] in *De armas llevar. Estudios socioantropológicos sobre los quehaceres de policías y de las fuerzas de seguridad* [Carrying weapons. Socioanthropological studies on the work of police and security forces], ed. S. Frederic, M. Galvani, J. Garriga Zucal and B. Renoldi, 147–168, La Plata: Ediciones de Periodismo y Comunicación, Universidad Nacional de La Plata.

Garriga Zucal, J. 2016. *El verdadero policía y sus sinsabores. Esbozos para una interpretación de la violencia policial* [The real policeman and his disappointments. Outlines for an interpretation of police violence] La Plata: Ediciones de Periodismo y Comunicación, Universidad Nacional de La Plata.

Garriga Zucal, J. and Melotto, M. 2013. La diversidad (in)visible. Identidad(es) entre policías bonaerenses [(In)visible diversity. Identity(ies) among Buenos Aires police officers]. *Avá, Revista de Antropología*21: 77–96.

González, G. 2011. Mapeando el trabajo policial. La in/experiencia en el "oficio" como variable de diferenciación [Mapping police work. In/experience in the "profession" as a differentiating variable]. *Delito y sociedad. Revista de Ciencias Sociales* 32, 55–85.

Jordán, J. 2017. Policía, mediación y gestión de conflictos [Police, mediation and conflict management]. *Working Papers*347: 1–40.

Kaminsky, G. 2005. Territorios inseguros, estigmas ciudadanos [Insecure territories, citizen stigmas] in *Tiempos inclementes. Culturas policiales y seguridad ciudadana* [Inclement times. Police cultures and citizen security], ed. G. Kaminsky, 16–62, Remedios de Escalda: Ediciones de la UNLa.

Kaminsky, G. 2011. Policía, política y filosofía. Apuntes para una crítica de la razón policial [Police, politics and philosophy. Notes for a critique of police reason] in *Mirada (de) uniforme. Historia y crítica de la razón policial* [Uniform gaze. History and critique of police reason], eds. D. Galeano, and G. Kaminsky, 411–448, Buenos Aires: Editorial Teseo.

Kaminsky, G.and Galeano, D. 2007. Descifrar el delito: Usos y desusos del saber estadístico[Deciphering crime: Uses and disuses of statistical knowledge] in *E l delito en la Argentina post-crisis: Aportes para la comprensión de las estadísticas públicas y el desarrollo institucional*[Crime in post-crisis Argentina: Contributions to the understanding of public statistics and institutional development], eds. G.Kaminsky, D.Kosovsky, and G.Kessler, 25–43, Buenos Aires: Universidad Nacional de Lanús.

Kessler, G. 2007. Miedo al delito y victimización en Argentina[Fear of crime and victimization in Argentina] in *El delito en la Argentina post-crisis: Aportes para la comprensión de las estadísticas públicas y el desarrollo institucional*[Crime in post-crisis Argentina: Contributions to the understanding of public statistics and institutional development], eds. G.Kaminsky, D.Kosovsky, and G.Kessler, 75–100, Buenos Aires:Universidad Nacional de Lanús.

Kessler, G. 2009. *El sentimiento de inseguridad. Sociología del temor al delito* [The feeling of insecurity. Sociology of the fear of crime], Buenos Aires: Siglo XXI.

Monjardet, D. 2010. *Lo que hace la policía. Sociología de la fuerza pública* [What the police do. Sociology of law enforcement], Buenos Aires: Prometeo Libros.

Muniz, J. 2012. *Discrecionalidad policial y aplicación selectiva de la ley en democracia* [Police discretion and selective application of the law in democracy], Caracas: Universidad Nacional Experimental de la Seguridad.

Nápoli, P. 2011. Policía y sociedad. La mediación simbólica del derecho [Police and society. The symbolic mediation of law] in *Mirada (de) uniforme. Historia y crítica de la razón policial* [Uniform gaze. History and critique of police reason], eds. D. Galeano, and G. Kaminsky, 255–281, Buenos Aires: Editorial Teseo.

Rangugni, V. and Russo D. 2010. El campo de la seguridad. Conceptos y definiciones [The field of security. Concepts and definitions], in *La seguridad ciudadana* [Citizen security], ed. C. Varela, 43–65. Buenos Aires: Cuadernos de Seguridad, Secretaría de Seguridad Interior.

Russo, D. 2017. *Intervención policial en sujetos intoxicados* [Police intervention on intoxicated subjects] in *Un libro sobre drogas* [A book about drugs], ed. P. González, 292–299, Buenos Aires: El gato y la caja.

Russo, D. 2020. *Cuidar a la fuerza. Sobre la intervención policial con personas intoxicadas por uso de drogas* [Caring by force. On police intervention with people intoxicated by drug use], Buenos Aires: La Docta Ignorancia.

Saín, M. 2008. *El Leviatán azul* [The Blue Leviathan], Buenos Aires: Siglo XXI Editores.
Saín, M. 2009. *La reforma policial en América Latina. Una mirada crítica desde el progresismo* [Police reform in Latin America. A critical look from progressivism], Buenos Aires: Nueva Sociedad.
Seri, G. 2011. Discrecionalidad policial y ley no escrita: gobernando en el estado de excepción [Police discretion and unwritten law: Governing under a state of emergency] in *Mirada (de) uniforme. Historia y crítica de la razón policial* [Uniform gaze. History and critique of police reason], eds. D. Galeano, and G. Kaminsky, 349–380, Buenos Aires: Editorial Teseo.
Sozzo, M. 2003. ¿Contando el delito? Análisis crítico y comparativo de las encuestas de victimización en la Argentina[Counting crime? Critical and comparative analysis of victimization surveys in Argentina]. *Cartapacio de Derecho: Revista Virtual de la Facultad de Derecho* 5:1–143.
Stortoni, C. 2014. Policías municipales en la Provincia de Buenos Aires: análisis de los proyectos de ley [Municipal police in the Province of Buenos Aires: Analysis of draft laws]. *VIII Jornadas de Sociología de la UNLP*. Universidad Nacional de La Plata.
Tiscornia, S. 2006. *Antropología de la violencia policial. El caso Walter Bulacio* [Anthropology of police violence. The Walter Bulacio case] (Tesis de Doctorado). Facultad de Filosofía y Letras, Universidad de Buenos Aires.
Tiscornia, S. 2004. Entre el imperio del «Estado de policía» y los límites del derecho. Seguridad ciudadana y policía en Argentina [Between the rule of the "police state" and the limits of law. Citizen security and the police in Argentina]. *Nueva Sociedad* 191: 78–89.
Varela, C. 2008. Contexto de surgimiento de los modelos policiales comunitarios [Context for the emergence of community policing models]. *1& Jornada de Investigación del Departamento de Planificación y Políticas Públicas*, Universidad Nacional de Lanús.

Legal references

Decreto 220/2014. Emergencia en materia de seguridad pública [Public security emergency]. 4 de Abril de 2014. Provincia de Buenos Aires, Argentina.
Decreto 373/2014. Creación de la Superintendencia de Seguridad Local [Creation of the Local Security Superintendence]. 30 de Junio de 2014. Provincia de Buenos Aires, Argentina.
Resolución 835/2014. Creación de la Policía Local [Creation of Local Police]. 2 de Julio de 2014. Ministerio de Seguridad de la Provincia de Buenos Aires. Argentina.

4

COMMUNITY JUSTICE AND CHINESE IMMIGRANTS

The perspective of law enforcement[1]

Jurg Gerber, Di Jia and Charles W. Russo

Community justice is a concept that has gradually developed with the rise of community policing. Inspired by community policing, some scholars further expanded the function of the community to the scope of providing support and integration for the entire judicial system, emphasizing that within the community, three core components of the criminal justice system, police, courts, and corrections, should be combined to jointly serve the safety of the community and improve the quality of life of the community by inviting/encouraging community members to cooperate and interact. Proponents of community justice argue that criminal justice agencies must tailor their interaction with the various "communities" and community groups to the latter's unique characteristics. What constitutes good police practices with one "community" or community group may not be appropriate with another one (Gerber & Jia, 2019; 2022; 2023). However, with the development of community justice research and practice, some theoretical research gaps and practical bottlenecks are gradually exposed. The main weaknesses are twofold: first, community justice is described as an integration model in general without considering the diverse characteristics of minority communities, Asian immigrants in particular. Second, there is a lack of research that looks into the community justice model from the practitioners' perspective.

Current project

The current project is part of a larger project that examines the relationships between Chinese migrants and police in China and the U.S. In the first stage,

DOI: 10.4324/9781003452379-5

we analyzed the beliefs and attitudes held by Chinese police officers of migrants within China (Gerber & Jia, 2019; 2022). We found that Chinese police officers hold nuanced opinions of Chinese migrants. Uneducated migrants who have migrated from rural to urban areas are seen as hardworking but are partly blamed for the crime problem in urban areas. Migrants who are young and tend to be well-educated are seen as an economic asset to the urban areas to which they migrate.

In the second stage of this research project, we analyzed attitudes and knowledge of Chinese immigrants in the U.S. about community justice initiatives of American police (Gerber & Jia, 2023). We found that recent Chinese immigrants to the U.S. tend to be well-educated, economically successful, and have limited contact with the police and the criminal justice system in general. However, they tend to be supportive of the police. If they live in cities with vibrant Chinese residential and business areas ("Chinatown"), they tend to perceive the police as being responsive to the Chinese immigrant community to a greater extent than if they live in a city that does not have a Chinatown. Conversely, immigrants in cities such as Denver, without a residentially isolated Chinese community, tend to become enculturated more quickly than residents in other cities.

This chapter reports on the third stage of our research project: attitudes and perceptions of U.S. police officers concerning Chinese immigrants. We implemented a pilot study in four U.S. cities: New York City, Houston, Daytona Beach, and Denver. The two first cities are cities with identifiable Chinatowns and sizeable Chinese immigrant communities, whereas the last two are not. It remains to be seen if these differences manifest themselves in differences among police officers.

Chinese immigrant communities and immigration

In some early studies, Chinese immigrants in the U.S. were introduced by researchers as being no different from those from Europe and South America but with more negative perceptions. Chinese immigrants were believed to "fear" and "misunderstand" the American social and legal systems (Alvarez et al., 2006). Both scholars and police were cautious and even questioned whether Chinese immigrants were able to integrate into the community and cooperate with law enforcement authorities (Albrecht, 1995; Yun et al., 2010). In fact, the integration of Chinese immigrants into the United States has gone through different historical stages and has distinctive characteristics.

The earliest time Chinese immigrants entered the United States by boat can be traced back to the 1850s and 1860s (Boyd, 1971). However, they cannot be called true immigrants. According to Boyd (1971), the early Chinese immigrants were cheap laborers recruited by the United States in China due to a shortage of domestic workers. Unlike today's immigrants, the purpose of these workers coming to the United States was not to start a new life in another country but to complete a work task. Most of these workers were men who came alone. They lived near the entry port in the West and looked forward to returning to China to reunite with their families after completing their work. Therefore, the initial Chinese immigrants lived in the United States as sojourners. Their labor status may have caused the government, even the workers themselves, not to consider the issue of labor community and integration. Eventually, half of the early workers who came to the United States returned to China, and the remaining 400,000 Chinese became citizens of the United States between 1850 and 1960.

Reviewing the literature, like immigrants from other Asian countries, the remaining Chinese immigrants' survival in American society has been widely influenced by World War II and the relationship between the West and the East. From the Chinese Exclusion Act in 1882 to the Repeal of the Chinese Exclusion Act in 1943, the history of Chinese–American communities throughout the early 20th century revolved around the development of U.S. Chinatowns (Zhou & Kim, 2001; Holland, 2007). After the Chinese immigrants who remained in the United States withstood the suppression of the massive Chinese Exclusion Act, they gained American citizenship and began to settle in the eastern region of the United States. Chinese immigrants abandoned thoughts of returning to their homeland and instead actively mobilized and arranged for other family members to come to the United States for reunions (Hong, 1976). The scope of this group membership in the United States gradually extends from the nuclear family to people connected by surname, dialect, and ancestral origins (Hong, 1976). Gradually, the vast majority of Chinese immigrants lived and worked in communities described as Chinatowns, which was a notable change that occurred in the immigration pattern of early Chinese immigrants. By living in Chinatowns, early immigrants could minimize interaction with most whites and avoid conflict, hostility, and humiliation, so this residential pattern became a form of defensive isolation to escape prejudice and discrimination (Yuan, 1963).

Hence, the efforts of Chinese immigrants to integrate into American society were limited during that time because most Chinese immigrants were isolated in Chinatown (Zhou & Kim, 2001). Chinese immigrants attempted to integrate into the community by establishing community social organizations, industry associations, churches, public welfare organizations, and other community institutions. However, the attempts of these organizations often took the form of striving for better business and trade opportunities, while cooperation and integration in political, legal, and judicial systems were minimal (Liou & Shenk, 2016; Zhou & Kim, 2001). Still, the primary need of most immigrants is how to survive in the United States by settling in Chinatown.

When the United States began to adjust its immigration policy in the late 1970s, especially the introduction of an equal immigration policy, the composition of Chinese immigrants changed dramatically (Chen, 1998). Scholars have identified this gradual transition as "new Chinese immigrants," the immigrants who migrated to the United States after China's reform and opening up policy who exhibited an unprecedented willingness to participate in criminal justice activities, safeguard their authority, and participate in public social welfare (Hooper & Batalova, 2015; Chen et al., 2021; Zhou & Liu, 2016).

According to 2019 U.S. statistics, there are approximately 14.1 million Asian immigrants in the United States, accounting for 31% of the total immigrants in the U.S. (Hanna & Batalova, 2021). One of the most populous groups among them is Chinese immigrants, who peaked in 2019 at 2.5 million and declined to under 2.4 million in 2021 due to the COVID-19 pandemic (Rosenbloom & Batalova, 2023). Many studies have demonstrated the distinct characteristics of new Chinese immigrant groups. For example, most recent immigrants have completed university education in the United States, obtained academic qualifications, and secured highly paid jobs (Leong & Tang, 2016). They are concerned about education and social resources and live in communities with diverse cultures (Tsai et al., 2021). Their residential choices in the United States have shifted from the original preference for cities with Chinatowns to more workplace or school district decisions. The Chinese immigrant groups include unskilled workers, small entrepreneurs, skilled workers, professionals, transnational capitalists, and political refugees (Zhou & Kim, 2001). Chinatown, which once symbolized a common origin, a transplanted village, and a common culture, has evolved into a national community with new international vitality, surpassing the original functions of Chinese residence and border protection (Zhou, 2011). In the eyes of the Chinese immigrants, the Chinese community is no longer a Chinatown or defined and understood through geographical ties. The living environment of different races makes Chinese immigrants pay attention to the importance of integration into local communities. Due to the widespread acceptance of higher education in the United States, they have developed a cross-cultural identity in their perception of the community, shifting their roles from residents to builders of the community. Some scholars have found that new immigrants have increased participation in the local communities, have a better image of the police, and have a higher enthusiasm for community policing (Gerber & Jia, 2023).

Nevertheless, research on how immigrants integrate into the country of immigration is far behind the rapid development of Chinese immigrant communities in the United States. Past scholars have explored the American Road and the American Dream of Chinese immigrants from different perspectives, but exploring the integration of Chinese immigrants into

American community life from the community justice perspective is almost absent. Community justice aims to strengthen neighborhoods and their moral order to prevent crime, seeking to manage cases and create a collective justice experience. Immigrants and their integration into community justice are critical components of community justice studies. In our research, we collected data from the experience and perspective of the police. We aim to further explore the criminal justice model in the context of immigration. Also, this social demographic change in Chinese immigrant communities has not been fully reflected in the research of the community justice model nor the dialogue between researchers and practitioners. We have been discussing where the breakthrough of community judicial construction is. The change in immigrant community structure can bring us significant inspiration and new entry points for a country of immigration. This phenomenon of social development is worthy of researchers' and practitioners' attention.

Police perceptions of community justice and the immigrant community

Community justice is a social governance model based on community policing, with the primary purpose of preventing crime, serving the community, and improving the quality of community life (Crawford & Clear, 2001; Sedgwick et al., 2021). Whether this model is successful or not is determined by the public who receives services and the police officers who participate. While a considerable amount of research exists on the public response to community justice, police officers have less often been the object of study (Lurigio & Skogan, 1994; Burke & Bush, 2013; Glaser & Denhardt, 2010; Nix et al., 2017). Such a difference in research focus is important because (1) the public and the police have different perceptions of community justice, and (2) the public believes that the degree of participation in community justice is much higher than the police's evaluation of the degree of public participation in community justice (Becerra et al., 2017; Carr & Maxwell, 2018)

How have the police been working in immigrant communities? Early in the 1990s, police practitioners started to think about the importance of reforming the police strategy in immigrant communities. According to a National Institute of Justice report in 1995, most police departments had formulated policing strategies for immigrant communities (Davis et al., 2001). Upon a national survey conducted for the National Institute of Police Administration, J. Thomas McEwan concluded that:

> the diverse cultural makeup of many communities requires new strategies, such as recruiting bilingual officers, training field personnel in cultural sensitivity, and offering foreign language training to officers. There are

reasons to believe that it is essential for criminal justice officials to make special efforts to encourage immigrants to report crimes and assist in their prosecution.

(Davis et al., 2001, p. 185)

Research on the police's perceptions of the participation of immigrant communities in community justice is still deficient. Research from the perspective of the police began with the difficulties of executing community justice work in immigrant communities (Wooden & Rogers, 2014). Among them, one of the most salient problems mentioned is that language is the primary obstacle in immigrant communities (Schneider, 1998; Liederbach et al., 2008; Lima-Nunes et al., 2013). But other studies presented paradoxical findings. In 2001, Herbst and Walker (2001) found that the language barrier was insignificant for police work in immigrant communities, and the misunderstanding caused by language barriers rarely occur, according to the empirical evidence from the 9-1-1 police dispatch and patrol data. However, based on data collected by police departments, community leaders, and residents in rural Missouri, Culver (2004) concluded that language barriers were the most significant challenge affecting police community work in Latino communities. Because of the language barrier, immigrants are afraid to contact the police, and it is difficult to cooperate with the police. Lewis and Ramakrishnan (2007) further pointed out that the police provided relevant language services to immigrant communities earlier than government departments, which shows that the police are concerned about their work in immigrant communities. Language is an essential factor that they believe affects the development of immigration work. These paradoxical findings implied that police perception of the immigrant community still needs to be fully examined.

In addition to the language issue, other factors significantly affect police views on immigrant community work. Greene (1989) found that police officers' career satisfaction will affect their views of the public. The more satisfied the police are with their work, the more they tend to think that the public is willing to cooperate with the police and the more willing they are to deal with the public. Recently, researchers (Todak et al., 2018) found that the police, whether white, black, Asian, male, or female, consistently understand the impact of race and culture. However, they believe there are differences in the enthusiasm and recognition of different immigrant communities regarding community policing. Bennett and Morabito (2006) suggested that the police's view of the degree of public cooperation depends on four main factors: personal factors, environment, institutional factors, and national factors. They further suggested that police officers with an immigration background can easily integrate into the community and obtain trust and assistance. Boateng et al. (2014) disclose a positive circle that the more the police emphasize a cooperative attitude toward serving community residents, the more they believe that residents are willing to cooperate with them. Meanwhile, the better their work in such a community is, the higher the efficiency reflected in crime control.

Interestingly, some researchers recently suggested a cognitive gap between the police and community residents regarding their perception of community collaborations. Ward (2013) found significant differences in the evaluation of police–civilian cooperation and the efficiency of community policing between police and residents. Through the interviews of residents and police officers in three communities, Stein and Griffith (2017) found support that the views of the police on residents in different regions are biased and also separate from the residents' self-reflection. Furthermore, they claimed that "police perceptions of the neighborhood are affected by the demographic characteristics of the residents" (p. 150). Nalla et al. (2018), using a sample of 581 uniformed police and 959 community members, found a significant variation between the police and the public regarding their perceptions on community work and the police–public relationship. Square-Smith (2017) suggested some consensus between the police and the public in community policing. For example, police and residents both agreed that community policing had improved the police interview rate and strengthened community unity and the relationship between the police and the people. However, this study did not include a detailed analysis and research on the community type, personal background, and other factors. Therefore, it is impossible to prove further whether the emergence of these consensuses will be different in different communities and their residents.

The above gaps are not reflected in the cognition between the immigrant community and the police. Beginning in 2018, the authors have studied community justice in immigrant communities. By interviewing Asian immigrants, we found that they are willing to participate in the work of community justice. At the same time, they also expressed their intense curiosity about their image in the eyes of the police, especially their cooperation in participating in community justice. They believe that understanding the evaluation of the police can help them better integrate into the work of community justice.

Based on the above gaps and research voids, we designed a study for this chapter. Through qualitative research, we hope to capture the overall impression of the current policy on community work in immigrant communities. We also aim to explore the reasons for these gaps further, seek the development path of community justice in immigrant communities, and provide a reference for the integrated development of immigrant communities. Unfortunately, it looks like those two terms are still ungeared to each other, especially for immigrant communities. Police officers implement the community justice model. However, until now, little research has been conducted at how community justice should be appropriately implemented in immigrant communities.

Methods

As part of a larger project (Gerber & Jia, 2019; 2022; 2023), we developed a list of discussion topics that guided our interview procedures and included four areas of questions: (1) Police perceptions of community justice; (2) Police perceptions of involving the Asian community in community justice; (3) Police's overall perceptions of the Chinese community and individuals, and (4) other issues not previously covered. Examples of questions included, among many others: (1) What do you know about any policing program related to community justice? (2) Do you have difficulty inviting Chinese residents to participate in community justice, and what are your main concerns? (3) Did you have any experience stopping a Chinese immigrant? Can you describe it? (4) Are there any issues that we did not address that are important in understanding the relationship between the police and Chinese immigrants?

The sample consists of 25 police officers who have experience collaborating with members of the Chinese Immigrant Community (CIC) in different cities around the nation. They are either currently employed or retired within five years. Some of them are (were) first-line officers, and some of them are (were) taking a leadership role (sergeant or above). The 45–60 minutes of online interviews were conducted from August 2022 to April 2023. The sample was a non-probability sample that was a *purposive* sample. Findings can, therefore, not be generalized to all police officers in the U.S. but are representative of cities that have either a large number of Chinese immigrants or are moderately representative of cities that do not. However, even police officers who work in areas with few Chinese immigrants tend to have experience interacting with ethnic minorities and immigrant communities, albeit not Chinese.

The Institutional Review Board of the Metropolitan State University of Denver approved the research.

Findings

Our respondents were law enforcement officers who served various agencies ranging from local police departments, sheriff's offices, state agencies, and specialized law enforcement agencies. Interviews, on average, lasted approximately 45 minutes in which participants were asked to respond to structured and follow-up questions from four (4) question areas and subsequent follow-up questions. The four (4) structured question areas were:

1. Police perceptions of the role of the Asian community and individuals in community justice
2. Police perceptions of involving the Asian community in community justice
3. Police overall perceptions of the Chinese community and individuals
4. Anything you want to add?

If/when the law enforcement officer indicated little interaction with the Asian immigrant community, the questions were applied to the wider immigrant community in general.

The community justice model in Chinese American communities is unclear

Most of our respondents were intimately familiar with the concept of community policing but seemed to have only a vague understanding of the broader concept of community justice. The police who hold leadership positions have a clearer understanding of the concept of community justice compared to other officers. Their understanding of community justice is in two aspects. For the implementation of community justice in the community, their statements are limited to the implementation of community policing, or they equate community justice with community policing.

All participants, except for one working for a state investigative agency, indicated their agencies participate in community engagement initiatives with all members/populations of the community. These initiatives include but are not limited to "walk and talks," broken windows practices, servant leadership models, citizen on patrol programs, minority outreach programs, citizen police academies, Police Athletic League (PAL), community meetings, and neighborhood watch programs. All viewed such engagement programs as a key component to the success of community justice.

A common theme from participants was that effective communication was key to relationship building. The importance of making those personal connections that seem to have been eroded over time was emphasized by participants. When language difficulties needed to be overcome, almost all participants indicated tools such as Language Line were available to remove language barriers when a local interpreter could not be located. To aid in making connections, participants called upon proper knowledge of the culture of the community, religion, food, practices, and family dynamics. To gain this understanding, participants indicated quality diversity training, not just "check the box training" was needed. It should be coupled with a push for higher education among officers to equip officers better to work with diverse populations.

Participants acknowledged the importance of community diversity in community justice. The participants indicated they are used to dealing with a diverse population due to their agencies being located in areas of international tourist destinations. In addition, the Central Florida area attracts those looking to relocate from around the world. Participants indicated that neighborhoods are often integrated, and there are not necessarily the ethnic pockets as may be found in other cities/areas of the United States.

Primarily, the minority communities contacted by the participants consisted of Hispanics and African Americans. Participants commonly addressed that Asians, including Chinese communities, are important components of the community justice model. However, those interviewed indicated there was no large Asian population within their area, and the community justice model with a specific focus on Chinese immigrants seems not clear.

Police perceptions of the Asian community in community justice are consistent with other minority communities

The police do not have the same understanding of the main difficulties of uniting residents to conduct community policing in Chinese immigrant communities. Some participants indicated there was no defined Chinese community in their respective areas. Some police officers believe that there is no significant difference between conducting community policing activities in Chinese immigrant communities and other ethnic minority communities. So, the question was applied to wider Asian immigrant communities in general. Some police officers believe that effective communication is the main obstacle to immigrants' participation in community policing. These barriers include language, culture, and trust in the police. At the same time, they also admit that the degree of these obstacles is different among Chinese immigrants of different ages. The degree of cooperation between the immigrant community and the police activities has no difference in race and ethnicity.

In terms of integrating immigrant communities into community justice activities, participants indicated that their agencies would frequently assign officers of similar demographics to reach out to specific communities. They will utilize local community resources like churches/religious organizations, community groups, and such to reach out to specific community demographics. When language barriers needed to be overcome, and an interpreter was not available, Language Line was once again mentioned as a resource to overcome this barrier. Languages frequently encountered by officers were reported to be Spanish, Portuguese, French, Creole, and German. A few instances of utilizing Language Line for Mandarin were noted by participants. Participants also reported using apps such as Google Translate on their mobile phones to overcome language barriers. Overall, the language barriers have not been a main concern for the police officers when talking about collaborating with the immigrant communities, especially for those police officers who are more familiar with accessing Apps and have international travel/working experience.

Police overall perceptions of the Chinese community and individuals are traditional

The police have a positive impression of the Chinese immigrant community and Chinese immigrants as a whole. Participants characterized Chinese immigrants as hard-working, welcoming, motivated, law-abiding, and friendly. The police believe that there is no language barrier in the communication between Chinese immigrants and police work. On the one hand, the language ability of Chinese immigrants has improved, and more importantly, a few police stations now have specialized multilingual translators or employ police officers who speak Chinese. Denver, for instance, supports this development by paying officers extra for foreign language skills. There is a perception among police officers that a generational difference exists among Asian immigrants in general: older immigrants are less likely to be bilingual and are, therefore, less communicative than younger immigrants. This may also be partially due to cultural norms and not just linguistic ability.

Interactions between the participants and the Chinese community were reported to be very infrequent. Few recalled specific interactions related to the call for service and remembered the individuals as being respectful and polite. Many participants responded to this question in a comparable manner after addressing the lack of Chinese/Asian interaction. "I portray the community people like everyone else....no different, everyone is the same. The only time I see someone different is when the person is a vegan, and I want to eat some meat." Another participant stated, "I wouldn't treat them any different than anyone else...no different than any other immigrant or anyone." As one participant stated, "I treat everyone the same and am respectful. Try to be kind to everyone....They are calling because they are having a bad day, and you must take this into consideration." The quotes from these three participants capture well the sentiments of all participants to this question.

Anything you want to add

When participants were asked this question, some senior participants added their introspection on community justice to the discussion based on their years of working experience. One felt that law enforcement needs to understand that fundamental differences exist between some cultures.

Another responded with, "The key is being able to evaluate, ask people where they are hurting, and then listen." From all participants, the overall sense was that outreach is extremely important and that there is always room for improvement. One participant summed up the dilemma facing the profession with, "I think it would be a benefit to provide more training; however, there is just so much money and just so many resources." Some of our respondents live in communities with very few Chinese immigrants. These respondents experienced difficulties in our research. However, they tended to respond to our interviews by stating repeatedly, "Everyone should be treated the same, regardless of ethnicity and race."

In addition to the need to improve training and education opportunities, recurring themes among participants, when asked about the main challenges to community justice, were recruiting future law enforcement officers and the negative media portrayal of law enforcement. With many agencies under-staffed, 20–30% being a common range, agencies are experiencing difficulties in meeting call-for-service demands. This shortage, according to participants, is attributed to the combination of good people leaving the profession coupled with the challenge of finding quality candidates to fill their vacancies. Increased staffing levels are often required to meet community justice and community engagement initiatives.

Negative media portrayal of law enforcement does not make it any easier for agencies to recruit new officers. Many participants called out the media for having "vilified the police," fueling negative perceptions, and engaging in sensationalism to sell/push ratings. As one participant stated, "Those outlets don't care no about what they are reporting. The humanity has been lost. Just pump it out." A series of public events and media reports on the police in the post-epidemic period have brought grave consequences to the image of the police. These have brought more unfavorable factors to the police's work in Asian communities, including Chinese immigrant communities. It is of foremost importance to recruit Asian police officers to serve the Asian community. However, with the increasing difficulty of police recruitment, the recruitment of Asian police officers is also difficult. This is a problem that needs to be solved.

Conclusion

The current project is part of a larger project that explores the relationships between police and Chinese migrants, the perceptions they have of each other, both in the United States and in China. On balance, while more work needs to be done, we are cautiously encouraged by the positive perceptions of each category of respondents. This holds true of the current respondents, U.S. police officers, as well as others we have interviewed (Chinese police officers and Chinese immigrants in the America). In general, our respondents have favorable attitudes about each other. Chinese police officers have favorable attitudes about at least some Chinese domestic migrants (Gerber & Jia 2019; 2022) and Chinese immigrants to the United States tend to view American police officers as professional and fair (Gerber & Jia 2023). The current research shows favorable attitudes of American police officers towards Chinese immigrants. It remains to be seen if the last category of respondents, Chinese domestic migrants in China, have an equally positive outlook on Chinese police.

Beyond the scope of the initial research questions, participant responses indicate areas worthy of additional exploration. The reoccurring themes of challenges facing police recruitment, the impact of negative media portrayal of law enforcement, and the issue of quality training versus "check the box training" were repeatedly raised by participants. These are all issues that require further exploration to determine the scope and severity of the impacts to not only community justice and immigrant populations but the greater law enforcement profession as a whole. These are all issues that can impact every aspect of the law enforcement profession, from law enforcement officers to the services provided to the community and the population served.

Note

1 An earlier version of this chapter was the focus of a poster presentation at the Annual Meeting of the American Society of Criminology in Atlanta, November 2022. Corresponding author: Jurg Gerber, Department of Criminal Justice and Criminology, Sam Houston State University, Huntsville, TX, 77341–2296. E-mail: gerber@shsu.edu

References

Albrecht, H. J. (1995). Ethnic minorities, culture conflicts and crime. *Crime, Law and Social Change*, 24, 19–36.

Alvarez, A. N., Juang, L., & Liang, C. T. (2006). Asian Americans and racism: When bad things happen to "model minorities." *Cultural Diversity and Ethnic Minority Psychology*, 12(3), 477.

Becerra, D., Wagaman, M. A., Androff, D., Messing, J., & Castillo, J. (2017). Policing immigrants: Fear of deportations and perceptions of law enforcement and criminal justice. *Journal of Social Work*, 17(6), 715–731.

Bennett, R. R., & Morabito, M. S. (2006). Determinants of constables' perceptions of community support in three developing nations. *Police Quarterly*, 9(2), 234–265.

Boyd, M. (1971). Oriental immigration: The experience of the Chinese, Japanese, and Filipino populations in the United States. *International Migration Review*, 5(1), 48–61.

Boateng, F. D., Makin, D. A., & Yoo, J. (2014). Let me speak: Officer perceptions of community members in Ghana. *International Criminal Justice Review*, 24(1), 22–38.

Burke, A. S., & Bush, M. D. (2013). Service learning and criminal justice: An exploratory study of student perceptions. *Educational Review*, 65(1), 56–69.

Carr, J. D., & Maxwell, S. R. (2018). Police officers' perceptions of organizational justice and their trust in the public. *Police Practice and Research*, 19(4), 365–379.

Chen, S. J. (1998). Characteristics and assimilation of Chinese immigrants in the US labour market. *International Migration*, 36(2), 187–210.

Chen, L., Tse, H. W., Wu, D., & Young, M. E. D. T. (2021). Cross-cultural researchers' positionality in immigrant health research: Reflections on conducting research on Chinese immigrants' experiences in the United States. *International Journal of Qualitative Methods*, 20, 16094069211052190.

Crawford, A., & Clear, T. (2001). Community justice: Transforming communities through restorative justice. *Restorative Community Justice: Repairing Harm and Transforming Communities*, 127–149.

Culver, L. (2004). The impact of new immigration patterns on the provision of police services in Midwestern communities. *Journal of Criminal Justice*, 32(4), 329–344.

Davis, R. C., Erez, E., & Avitabile, N. (2001). Access to justice for immigrants who are victimized: The perspectives of police and prosecutors. *Criminal Justice Policy Review*, 12(3), 183–196.

Gerber, J., & Jia, D. (2019). Community policing and community justice: Studying a marginalized population segment in the People's Republic of China. In E. W. Plywaczewski & E. M. Guzik-Makaruk (Eds.), *Current Problems of Penal Law and Criminology*, eighth edition (pp. 451–461). Beck.

Gerber, J., & Jia, D. (2022). Perceptions of police officers on the floating population: A pilot study of community justice initiatives in China. In J. Eterno, B. Stickle, D. Peterson, & D. Das (Eds.), *Police Behavior, Hiring, and Crime Fighting* (pp. 56–65). Routledge.

Gerber, J., & Jia, D. (2023). Chinese immigrants' perceptions of community justice in the U.S.: An exploratory study. *Białostockie Studia Prawnicze (Bialystok Legal Studies)*, 23(1), 173–196.

Glaser, M. A., & Denhardt, J. (2010). Community policing and community building: A case study of officer perceptions. *The American Review of Public Administration*, 40(3), 309–325.

Greene, J. R. (1989). Police officer job satisfaction and community perceptions: Implications for community-oriented policing. *Journal of Research in Crime and Delinquency*, 26(2), 168–183.

Hanna, M., & Batalova, J. (2021). *Immigrants from Asia in the United States*. Migration Policy Institute. https://www.migrationpolicy.org/article/immigrants-asia-united-states.

Herbst, L., & Walker, S. (2001). Language barriers in the delivery of police services: A study of police and Hispanic interactions in a midwestern city. *Journal of Criminal Justice*, 29(4), 329–340.

Holland, K. M. (2007). A history of Chinese immigration in the United States and Canada. *American Review of Canadian Studies*, 37(2), 150–160.

Hong, L. K. (1976). Recent immigrants in the Chinese American community: Issues of adaptations and impacts. *International Migration Review*, 10(4), 509–514.

Hooper, K., & Batalova, J. (2015). Chinese immigrants in the United States. *Migration Policy Institute*, 28.

Leong, F. T., & Tang, M. (2016). Career barriers for Chinese immigrants in the United States. *The Career Development Quarterly*, 64(3), 259–271.

Lewis, P. G., & Ramakrishnan, S. K. (2007). Police practices in immigrant-destination cities: Political control or bureaucratic professionalism? *Urban Affairs Review*, 42 (6), 874–900.

Liou, C. L., & Shenk, D. (2016). A case study of exploring older Chinese immigrants' social support within a Chinese church community in the United States. *Journal of Cross-cultural Gerontology*, 31, 293–309.

Lima-Nunes, A., Pereira, C. R., & Correia, I. (2013). Restricting the scope of justice to justify discrimination: The role played by justice perceptions in discrimination against immigrants. *European Journal of Social Psychology*, 43(7), 627–636.

Liederbach, J., Fritsch, E. J., Carter, D. L., & Bannister, A. (2008). Exploring the limits of collaboration in community policing: A direct comparison of police and citizen views. *Policing: An International Journal of Police Strategies & Management*, 31(2), 271–291.

Lurigio, A. J., & Skogan, W. G. (1994). Winning the hearts and minds of police officers: An assessment of staff perceptions of community policing in Chicago. *Crime & Delinquency*, 40(3), 315–330.

Nalla, M. K., Meško, G., & Modic, M. (2018). Assessing police–community relationships: Is there a gap in perceptions between police officers and residents? *Policing and Society*, 28(3), 271–290.

Nix, J., Pickett, J. T., Wolfe, S. E., & Campbell, B. A. (2017). Demeanor, race, and police perceptions of procedural justice: Evidence from two randomized experiments. *Justice Quarterly*, 34(7), 1154–1183.

Rosenbloom, R., & Batalova, J. (2023). Chinese Immigrants in the United States. *Migration Policy Institute.* https://www.migrationpolicy.org/article/chinese-immigrants-united-states.

Schneider, S. R. (1998). Overcoming barriers to communication between police and socially disadvantaged neighbourhoods: A critical theory of community policing. *Crime, Law and Social Change*, 30(4), 347–377.

Sedgwick, D., Callahan, J., & Hawdon, J. (2021). Institutionalizing partnerships: A mixed methods approach to identifying trends and perceptions of community policing and multi-agency task forces. *Police Practice and Research*, 22(1), 727–744.

Stein, R. E., & Griffith, C. (2017). Resident and police perceptions of the neighborhood: Implications for community policing. *Criminal Justice Policy Review*, 28(2), 139–154.

Square-Smith, D. R. (2017). *Police and Citizens' Perceptions of Community Policing in Richmond, Virginia* (Doctoral dissertation, Walden University).

Todak, N., Huff, J., & James, L. (2018). Investigating perceptions of race and ethnic diversity among prospective police officers. *Police Practice and Research*, 19(5), 490–504.

Tsai, W., Zhang, L., Park, J. S., Tan, Y. L., & Kwon, S. C. (2021). The importance of community and culture for the recruitment, engagement, and retention of Chinese American immigrants in health interventions. *Translational Behavioral Medicine*, 11(9), 1682–1690.

Ward, K. L. (2013). *Assessing Police-Citizen Communication by Identifying Perceptions of Community Policing Styles and Effectiveness* (Doctoral dissertation, University of Phoenix).

Wooden, K., & Rogers, C. (2014). Restoring public confidence: Perceptions of community police officers. *The Police Journal*, 87(3), 186–194.

Yuan, D. Y. (1963). Voluntary segregation: A study of new Chinatown. *Phylon (1960-)*, 24(3), 255–265.

Yun, I., Kercher, G., & Swindell, S. (2010). Fear of crime among Chinese immigrants. *Journal of Ethnicity in Criminal Justice*, 8(2), 71–90.

Zhou, M. (2011). Traversing Ancestral and New Homelands: Chinese Immigrant Transnational Organizations in the United States: A Report. Working Papers 1352, Princeton University, Woodrow Wilson School of Public and International Affairs, Center for Migration and Development.

Zhou, M., & Liu, H. (2016). Homeland engagement and host-society integration: A comparative study of new Chinese immigrants in the United States and Singapore. *International Journal of Comparative Sociology*, 57(1–2), 30–52.

Zhou, M., & Kim, R. Y. (2001). Formation, consolidation, and diversification of the ethnic elite: The case of the Chinese immigrant community in the United States. *Journal of International Migration and Integration*, 2(2), 227.

Zhou, M., & Lee, R. (2013). Transnationalism and community building: Chinese immigrant organizations in the United States. *The Annals of the American Academy of Political and Social Science*, 647(1), 22–49.

5

UNDERSTANDING OFFICER'S BEHAVIOR IN A NON-TRAFFIC SITUATION

Why will police officers use force and verbally attack citizens during a street stop?

Francis D. Boateng and Michael K. Dzordzormenyoh

Introduction

Numerous studies have examined the nexus between police stops, decision-making, behavior, and the use of force from different theoretical and methodological perspectives, with the primary goal of explaining the origins, processes, consequences, and predictive factors (Becker, 1963; Black, 1970, 1980; Black & Reiss, 1970; Kramer & Remster, 2018; Lundman, 1974; Lundman et al., 1978). These studies have contributed to both theory-building and practice in diverse ways. First, the studies have provided immense knowledge about the factors that influence police decision-making during stop encounters. Second, these studies have assisted policymakers in making the necessary policy changes to improve police–citizen relations (Kramer & Remster, 2018).

Currently, three major perspectives can be identified within the literature on the factors that affect police decision-making, behaviors, and the use of lethal force during stop encounters. The first posits that citizens' misdemeanor and hostility towards police officers during an encounter influence officers' decision-making, behaviors, and the use of force. While this perspective focuses mainly on the behavior of citizens, it has been widely criticized for overlooking situational, extralegal, and other factors that relate directly to officers (Smith & Klein, 1983, 1984; Worden & Pollitz, 1984; Smith et al., 1984; Smith, 1987; Worden, 1989). Second, some police scholars have suggested that the criminal background of a citizen influences officers' decision-making and not the misdemeanor or hostility of citizens (Klinger, 1994; Morrow et al., 2018; Fryer Jr., 2019).

DOI: 10.4324/9781003452379-6

The third perspective on determinants of officers' behavior attempts to address the weaknesses of the first two perspectives by arguing that situational, extralegal factors, factors related directly to police officers, and citizens' behavior—misdemeanor, hostility, and criminal background—together account for officers' decision-making, behaviors, and use of force during stop encounters (Bates et al., 2020; Kramer & Remster, 2018). These studies conclude that officers' decision-making, behavior, and use of force can have negative impacts on the citizens they are sworn to serve. Recent examples of cases that had significant adverse effects on citizens or suspects include the killings of Breonna Taylor (KY), George Flyod (MN), Eric Garner (NY), Jamar Clark (MN), Freddie Gray (MD), and Michael Brown (MO) (Eith & Durose, 2011; Morrow et al., 2018).

Although these studies have provided a tremendous understanding of factors influencing police decision-making and the use of force, there is a significant gap in the current literature. Specifically, existing research on police decision-making has largely focused on traffic stop encounters, with far less attention paid to non-traffic decision-making. This exclusive focus on traffic encounters has created an urgent need for studies specifically addressing issues and questions related to officers' behavior during non-traffic street stop situations. Thus, critical questions such as what prompts officers to use force against citizens that are stopped while walking and what factors influence officers to verbally assault citizens are left unanswered due to the gap in research.

To address this empirical gap, the current study explored factors that influence officers' decisions to use force and verbally assault citizens during non-traffic street stops. To achieve this purpose, we analyzed data from the Police–Public Contact Survey (PPCS) conducted by the United States Department of Justice and Bureau of Justice Statistics. By answering the above questions, we contribute to existing literature by theoretically and practically advancing existing knowledge and understanding of the variables that influence police decision-making in all encounters.

Literature review

Police use of force: A brief overview

Police use of force is not a new phenomenon in the United States; however, in recent years, the frequency of police use of force and the deaths of unarmed citizens have brought the issue to national attention (Hickman et al., 2008; Reppetto, 2012; Hyland et al., 2015; Motley Jr. & Joe, 2018). The nationally publicized deaths of Breonna Taylor (KY), George Flyod (MN), Eric Garner in New York City (NY), Jamar Clark in Minneapolis (MN),

Freddie Gray in Baltimore (MD), Michael Brown in Ferguson (MO), Tamir Rice in Cleveland (OH), and others through the use of lethal force by the police remain a national debate and have sparked various responses from citizens in the form of riots and calls to defund police departments (Wihbey & Kille, 2016).

Police use of lethal or excessive force can be defined as the application of force greater than that which a "reasonable" and "prudent" law enforcement officer would use under the circumstances (Bureau of Justice Statistics, 2016; Motley Jr. & Joe, 2018). Some examples of lethal force include (a) physical force against a person who is a free citizen; (b) physical force against a person who is already in police custody and is not resisting being in custody; and (c) physical force against a person who does not have a weapon or who a police officer should reasonably assume does not have a weapon (LawInfo, 2015).

Police scholars noted that the use of lethal force can be attributed to the involvement of the police force in fighting wars on crimes and drugs (Skolnick & Fyfe, 1993). The war on crime and drugs has led to most police departments in the U.S. transferring the use of lethal force to other areas of policing, such as traffic stops and patrols. Also, most of the police departments in the U.S. have policies and procedures that encompass a use-of-force continuum. Police officers are also trained about when and how to use force appropriately to resolve various situations they encounter (National Institute of Justice, 2015; Wilt, 2015). The use-of-force continuum typically consists of the following types of force:

1. Mere presence—police uniforms and distinctly marked cars—may influence people's behavior, causing them to comply with the law (e.g., reduce their speed when driving, refrain from jaywalking)
2. Verbalization—a red light or siren for a person to pull over, or an officer's use of a persuasive tone or command voice to achieve the desired results
3. Firm grips—to get an individual to remain still or move in a certain direction, but without causing pain (e.g., grips on parts of the body)
4. Pain compliance—to inflict pain without causing lasting physical injury in order to get a subject to submit (e.g., finger grips, hammerlocks, wrist locks)
5. Impact techniques—used to overcome resistance that is forcible but less than imminently life-threatening (e.g., kicks, batons, chemical sprays, TASER)
6. Lethal force—force capable of killing or likely to kill an individual (e.g., discharge of firearms)

The above continuum illustrates that the use of lethal force is the last resort for officers, after they have exhausted the other five options on the continuum. Statistically, between 75% and 83% of U.S. residents reported experiencing excessive use of force during encounters with the police (Durose et al., 2007; Hyland et al., 2015; Motley Jr. & Joe, 2018). Moreover, scholars have reported disparities between Black and White residents in their exposure to police use of lethal force and their perceptions of the use of lethal force (Durose et al., 2007; Hickman et al., 2008; Eith & Durose, 2011; Hyland et al., 2015).

Factors predicting officer behavior

In the past several decades, many scholars have focused on examining how extralegal factors can influence decisions by criminal justice actors (Lizotte, 1978; Weitzer, 1996; Reiman & Leighton, 2015; Van Cleve & Mayes, 2015). The role of citizens' demeanor, race, and socio-economic status, among others, have been examined by these scholars. Prominent among these studies are those that focused on juvenile demeanor and police arrest (Black & Reiss, 1970; Lundman et al., 1978), adults and police arrest (Lundman, 1974; Sykes et al., 1976), and studies that combined both young and older populations as well as different demographic characteristics (Black, 1980; Black & Reiss, 1970; Brown & Frank, 2005; Dunham & Alpert, 2009; Engel et al., 2000; Huggins, 2012; Lundman, 1974; 1994; Lundman et al., 1978; Smith, 1987; Smith & Klein, 1984; Smith & Visher, 1981; Smith et al., 1984; Sykes et al., 1976; Terrill & Paoline, 2007; Visher, 1983; Worden, 1989; Worden & Shepard, 1996; Worden & Pollitz, 1984). The findings of all these studies were consistent: demeanor or hostility is a prime indicator of police officer behavior. Thus, the officer's decision-making is largely driven by the demeanor of the suspect.

More specifically, Worden and Shepard (1996) examined data from 24 police departments and found that citizen displays of hostility and disrespect during contact with the police affect police behavior, decision-making, and the use of lethal force. Additionally, by analyzing data on a sample of juvenile offenders regarding issues of demeanor and hostility, Lundman (1994) concluded that misdemeanor was a big contributing factor in police behavior. Conclusively, these studies posit that citizens who demonstrate higher levels of disrespect toward officers during encounters risk receiving the most severe sanctions on the police list, lending tremendous support for the hostility and demeanor hypothesis. However, Klinger (1994) argued that individuals who displayed a hostile or disrespectful demeanor towards the officer were more likely to be arrested because they were more likely to engage in observable criminal behavior in the presence of or against police officers. This argument contradicts the observation that demeanor or hostility is a key determinant of police decisions and the use of lethal force.

Apart from demeanor, research has also examined the effects of other variables on officers' behavior. For instance, Brown & Frank (2005), using data from Cincinnati Police Division street-level officers between 1997 and 1998, identified that as criminal wrongdoing increased, so did the likelihood of police issuing a citation. Another important finding from this study was the effect of officers' race on their decision-making. Black officers were less likely to offer a citation compared to their white counterparts. Also, Huff (2021) identified that verbal assault, officer, and suspect characteristics were important predictors of police decision-making behavior during traffic stop interactions.

In conclusion, despite the empirical evidence identified above, there is still room for further studies to examine factors that influence police behavior and decision-making, specifically in relation to non-traffic encounters. While much is known about how the officer behaves toward a motorist, less is known about officers' behavior towards a citizen walking on the street. The recent citizen–police clashes and demands for defunding police departments due to excessive use of force by police officers clearly illustrate the need for further probing by scholars to understand the factors that influence the decision to use force in all situations.

Method

Data source and sample description

The study used data from the 2015 PPCS conducted by the United States Department of Justice and Bureau of Justice Statistics. The survey, using a nationally representative sample of households, aimed to uncover citizens' experiences with police contact during the 12 months prior to the survey. The PPCS is supplemental to the National Crime Victimization Survey (NCVS), an annual survey inquiring about information regarding crimes against persons 12 years of age or older and is typically administered every 3 years. The PPCS was administered to NCVS participants who were 16 years of age or older through either telephone interviews or computer-assisted personal interviews. The current analysis focused on responses from the 650 individuals who encountered the police during street stops.

Measures

Dependent variables

There are two dependent variables in this study. The first was the *police use of force* during the encounter. This variable was measured using 3 items capturing instances where the police used force against the suspect: at any point during this contact, did the police do any of the following: (1) threaten to arrest you, (2) actually push or grab you, and (3) handcuff you. Each of these items was dichotomously measured as 0 = no and 1 = yes. A factor analysis (Factor loadings ranged from .74 to .80; and about 59% total variance explained) indicated that these items measure the same construct. Therefore, they were combined to form the use of force scale, with an alpha of 0.66. The second dependent variable was *Verbal attack against citizen*, measured using two items: during contact did police officer shout at you and during contact did police officer curse at you. Both items were dichotomously measured as 0 = no and 1 = yes. A factor analysis indicated that these items measure the same construct. Therefore, they were combined to form the verbal attack scale, with an alpha of 0.70.

Independent variables

The effects of several variables on the dependent variables were examined. The first was the reason for stopping a suspect on the street. Reasons for the stop was a categorical variable measured as 1 = suspected you of something, 2 = match you to the description of someone they were looking for, 3 = seeking information about another person, 4 = investigating a crime, and 5 = providing a service or assistance to you. Option 5 was used as the reference category. *Verbal attack* on officers was measured using three items to gauge whether respondents verbally assaulted the officer(s) during the contact. These items had the same lead in question_during the contact: 1) did you complain to the officer(s), 2) did you argue with the police officer(s) and 3) did you curse at, insult, or verbally threaten the police officer(s)? All the items were dichotomously measured as 0 = no and 1 = yes. A factor analysis (Factor loadings ranged from .70 to .85 and about 70% total variance explained) indicated that these items measure the same construct. Therefore, they were combined to form the verbal assault scale, with an alpha of 0.90.

Control variables

Prior research has found several variables to influence police behavior and decision-making. The effects of some of these variables were accounted for in the current analysis of police decision-making during street-level interactions. Specifically, three variable sets—the officer's characteristics, the suspect's characteristics, and situational characteristics—were included. The effects of two officer characteristics, gender, and race, were explored. Both were dichotomously measured: gender (0 = female and 1 = male) and race (0 = nonwhite and 1 = white). Also, five suspect characteristics were examined in the models. Gender, measured as 0 = female and 1 = male; age, assessed in terms of years at the time of the survey; race (0 = other races, 1 = White and 2 = Black); and income (1 = less than $25,000, 2 = between $25,000 and 49,999, 3 = between $50,000 and 74,999, and 4 = $75,000 or more). Responses from those who reported an income of $75,000 or more were used as the reference category. Finally, one situational characteristic of the stop was included in our analysis of officer decision-making during street stops. This variable, location, measures the size of the place (in terms of population) where the stop occurred (1 = less than 100,000 and 0 = 100,000 and above).

Plan of analysis

To achieve the purpose of the study, we conducted several analyses. First, we conducted descriptive analysis to gauge the distribution of responses among the respondents. We also conducted collinearity analysis to determine whether there is any multicollinearity issue with our data. The results of this analysis indicate no concern for multicollinearity because none of the variance inflation factors (VIF) values were higher than 10 and no tolerance value was closer to 0. Regression analyses were conducted to estimate the effects on police decisions to use force as well as threaten to sanction a suspect. Specifically, we used ordinary least-squared regression to examine the effects of the predicting variables on the outcomes.

A detailed description of the respondents is provided in Table 5.1. Of the 650 individuals that experienced non-traffic stops, about 62% were stopped as a result of the police either investigating a crime or suspecting the individual of something. About 29% reported being stopped as a result of officers providing assistance to them. A majority of the suspects were whites (77%), with an average age of about 38 years. The youngest suspect was 16 years old, while the oldest was 85 years old. Most of the suspects were male (62%) and earn an annual income that is either less than $25,000 or $75,000 and above. In terms of officers' characteristics, the majority were male (96%) and white (91%). Officers verbally assaulting suspects as well as using force against them at street stops were less frequent.

Results

Factors predicting police verbal assault against suspects during non-traffic street encounters

To understand factors that influence police officers' behavior, especially regarding verbally assaulting suspects in non-traffic encounters, we conducted a multivariate ordinary least-squared regression analysis. The results of this

TABLE 5.1 Descriptive statistics of study variables (N =650)

	M	%	SD	Min.	Max.
Reason for the street stop:					
Suspect you of something		30.5			
Match you to the description of someone they were looking for		2.5			
Seeking information about another person		7.4			
Investigating crime		31.0			
Providing service or assistance to you		28.6			
Verbal assault–against officer	0.23		0.59	.00	3.00
Gender–stopping officer (Male)		96			
Race–stopping officer (White)		91			
Gender (Male)		61.7			
Age	37.99		16.47	16.00	85.00
Race:					
Black		15.4			
Other races		7.8			
White		76.8			
Income:					
less than $25,000		29.8			
between $25,000 and $49,999		24.2			
between $50,000 and $74,999		16.6			
$75,000 or more		29.4			
Location (Less than 100,000 population)		66.3			
Use of force	0.13		0.48	0.00	3.00
Police verbal attack	0.12		0.41	0.00	2.00

analysis are presented in Table 5.2. The model was significant (F = 11.50, p <.001) and explained about 65% of the variance in police verbal assault. After controlling for the effects of other variables in the model, verbal assault against officers (t = 10.67, p <.001), suspect's gender (male) (t = -1.93, p <.05), other races (t = -3.76, p<.001), and White (t = -1.98, p <.05) were found to be significant predictors of officers' verbal assault. Specifically, suspects who verbally assaulted officers were more likely to be verbally assaulted by police officers.

TABLE 5.2 Factors influencing police verbal assault against suspects during street (non-traffic) stops (N =650)

	b (SE)	Beta	t/F	Tolerance	VIF
Constant	-.22 (.10)		-2.33*		
Reason for the street stop[1]:					
Suspect you of something	.02 (.03)	.05	.59	.66	1.52
Match you to the description of someone they were looking for	.01 (.09)	.01	.10	.90	1.11
Seeking information about another person	-.01 (.05)	-.02	-.28	.83	1.21
Investigating crime	.01 (.03)	.02	.02	.76	1.32
Verbal assault against officer	.39 (.04)	.75	10.67***	.76	1.32
Officer characteristics					
Gender stopping officer (Male)	-.01 (.07)	-.01	-.17	.87	1.14
Race stopping officer (White)	.04 (.05)	.06	.85	.85	1.18
Suspect and situational characteristics					
Gender (Male)	-.05 (.03)	-.12	-1.93*	.93	1.08
Age	.01 (.01)	.06	.83	.79	1.26
Race[2]:					
Other races	-.32 (.08)	-.27	-3.76***	.76	1.317
White	-.09 (.04)	-.16	-1.98*	.56	1.79
Income[3]:					
Earn less than $24,999	-.02 (.03)	-.05	-.66	.64	1.55
Earn between $25,000 and $49,999	.03 (.04)	.05	.69	.76	1.32
Earn between $50,000 and $74,999	.01 (.04)	.02	.30	.77	1.30
Location (Less than 100,000 population)	-.01 (.04)	-.02	-.31	.67	1.49
Model fit			11.50***		
R-squared			0.65		

Notes: 1 = providing a service or assistance to you (RC), 2 = Black (RC), and 3 = $75000 or more (RC). b = unstandardized coefficient, SE = standard errors, and VIF = variance inflation factor. *p < .05, **p < .01 and ***p < .001

Moreover, suspects who were male, white, or of other races (excluding Black) were less likely to be verbally assaulted by the police than those who were female and Black. This means that being female and being black make one vulnerable to police verbal attacks.

Factors predicting police use of force against suspects during non-traffic street encounters

A multivariate ordinary least-squared regression analysis was conducted to understand predictors of police use of force during non-traffic street encounters. The results of this analysis are presented in Table 5.3. The model was

TABLE 5.3 Factors influencing police use of force against suspects during street (non-traffic) stops (N =650)

	b (SE)	Beta	t/F	Tolerance	VIF
Constant	-.23 (.13)		-1.84*		
Reason for the street stop[1]:					
Suspect you of something	.07 (.04)	.08	1.65	.66	1.52
Match you to the description of someone they were looking for	.00 (.12)	.00	-.03	.90	1.11
Seeking information about another person	.05 (.06)	.03	.76	.83	1.21
Investigating crime	.05 (.04)	.05	1.04	.76	1.32
Verbal assault–against officer	.94 (.05)	.91	19.43***	.76	1.32
Officer characteristics					
Gender–stopping officer (Male)	-.03 (.09)	-.01	-.31	.87	1.14
Race–stopping officer (White)	-.18 (.06)	-.13	-2.87**	.85	1.18
Suspect and situational characteristics					
Gender (Male)	.06 (.03)	.08	1.92*	.93	1.08
Age	.01 (.01)	.04	.85	.79	1.26
Race[2]:					
Other races	.04 (.11)	.01	.03	.76	1.32
White	.04 (.06)	.04	.64	.56	1.79
Income[3]:					
Earn less than $24,999	.02 (.04)	.02	.37	.64	1.55
Earn between $25,000 and $49,999	-.10 (.05)	-.10	-2.01*	.76	1.32
Earn between $50,000 and $74,999	-.04 (.05)	-.04	-.84	.77	1.30
Location (Less than 100,000 population)	.04 (.05)	.04	.76	.67	1.49
Model fit			33.72***		
R-squared			0.85		

Notes: 1 = providing a service or assistance to you (RC), 2 = Black (RC), and 3 = $75,000 or more (RC).). b = unstandardized coefficient, SE = standard errors, and VIF = variance inflation factor. *p < .05, **p < .01 and ***p < .001.

significant (F= 33.72, p <.001) and explained a significant portion (about 85%) of the variance in the use of force. After controlling for the effects of other variables in the model, verbal assault against officers (t = 19.43, p <.01), officer's race (white) (t = -2.87, p<.01), suspect's gender (male) (t = 1.92, p <.05), and income (between $25,000 and $49,999) (t = -2.01, p<.01) were found to be significant predictors of officers' use of force. Specifically, suspects who verbally assaulted officers and those who were males were more likely to experience the use of force by police officers. Moreover, suspects who earned between $25,000 and $49,999 were less likely to experience the use of force compared to those who earned $75,000 or more. Finally, white officers were less likely to use force than their non-white officers.

Discussion and conclusion

Although not too common compared to traffic stops, a significant number of people encounter the police through non-traffic street stops. These stops have received limited research attention, and as a result, less is known about the nature and dynamics of such contacts. Due to the limited research, important questions related to officers' decision-making processes, attitudes, and behaviors are left unanswered. To answer some of these questions, we analyzed self-reported data from citizens to explain police–citizens' interactions during non-traffic encounters. Specifically, we examined the factors that influence police use of force during non-traffic street stops and assessed the effects of variables predicting police verbal attacks against citizens during such encounters.

Our analysis revealed several important indicators of police behavior in non-traffic situations. First, the current analysis observes that male and non-white citizens are more likely to be at the receiving end of officers' verbal assaults. These observations echo the critical role individual characteristics such as gender, race, and demeanor play in influencing police officers' behavior. According to most prior studies, citizens' demeanor and hostility play a pivotal role in determining the direction and outcome of an encounter (Huggins, 2012; James et al., 2018; Huff, 2021). In essence, these researchers believed that hostile citizens and those who demonstrated a negative demeanor were more likely to receive severe sanctions from the police. The findings from this study support observations made by prior arguments about demeanor and suggest that citizens who verbally attack police officers by cursing or insulting them place themselves in a position where the police would use force and verbally assault them. Furthermore, ethnicity and race were equally essential factors to consider when explaining the police use of force and verbal assault on citizens.

Another revelation was the effects of race and ethnicity on officers' behavior. In this study we did observe race and ethnicity of both citizens and officers influencing officers' behavior, specifically the decision to use force and verbally assault citizens. These findings are consistent with previous observations, non-white race like blacks and Hispanics are strong predictors of officers' use of force and verbal assault. These citizens, compared to others, are at a higher risk for searches and arrests, and as demonstrated in this study, are more likely to experience force than other races. In addition, white officers are also more inclined to use force and verbal assault on citizens compared to officers with other races. While police behavior of targeting minorities has been well documented in the literature (Warren et al., 2006; Gau & Brunson, 2010), there have been mixed findings about why officers target minority groups.

Although the study made important observations, it is not without limitations, and as a result, we would caution readers against further interpretation of the study's findings. We acknowledge the possibility of desirability bias influencing the results of this study because the data were self-reported by citizens. During the survey, respondents may provide responses to questions that will make them look good and credible while, at the same time, making the officers' look bad. Again, using citizens' self-reported data about their encounters and experiences with an officer will not help to accurately measure and understand police–citizen interactions during street stop encounters, pertaining especially to the use of force against citizens. To address this limitation, we recommend further study using systematic social observation or a dataset that combines the responses of both citizens and police officers to provide insight about the factors that influence police officers' behavior, specifically the use of lethal force and verbal attacks on citizens during street encounters. Furthermore, we acknowledge that the current study is restricted in scope because it focused on only two dimensions of police behavior: police use of force and police verbal assault. Although helpful in understanding aspects of an officer's behavior, these two dimensions do not tell the whole story about the attitudes and behaviors of the officer on the street. We would suggest that future studies should consider including other dimensions of police attitudes and behavior, such as corruption, criminal conduct, and the decision to arrest or not to arrest.

Despite the above limitations, this study reveals some interesting and compelling findings that have implications for both theory and practice. Theoretically, the findings provide further understanding of the factors that influence officers' use of force and verbal assault on citizens during non-traffic stop encounters. This broadens our understanding of how certain variables, such as race, gender, and citizens' attitudes towards officers, can determine how an officer will behave in some situations.

These findings, however, provide further support for existing theories that have been offered to explain police behavior. Practically, the findings of this study have serious implications for developing better police–citizen interactions as well as improving public attitudes toward the police at the local and national level. Police trust always suffers significantly when the police are perceived to use force against citizens. Street-level bureaucrats like police officers, who have much discretion, need continued education and training to enhance their decision-making ability to know when to use lethal force and the amount of force needed to control a given situation. Additionally, following the recommendations of prior research we recommend that police administrators implement strict administrative policies to reduce police use of lethal force and verbal abuse on citizens.

Specifically, we support departments that will hold officers personally accountable for the decisions they make on the street. To hold officers accountable, departments should make officers financially liable for unnecessary use of force that will result in a civil lawsuit. By ensuring that officers pay a percentage of civil settlements in cases involving the use of force, officers will quickly learn the price of abusing their authorities and powers and will begin to engage in prosocial behavior such as using force appropriately and necessarily. Furthermore, citizens must be educated about how to interact with officers during stop encounters. These measures, if properly implemented and administered, can go a long way toward creating professional police officers whose mission is to serve and protect citizens.

References

Bates, L., Anderson, L., Rodwell, D., & Blais, E. (2020). A qualitative study of young drivers and deterrence based road policing. *Transportation Research Part F: Traffic Psychology and Behaviour*, 71, 110–118.

Becker, H. (1963). *Outsiders*. New York: Free Press.

Black, D. J. (1970). The social organization of arrest. *Stanford Law Review*, 23, 1087.

Black, D. J. (1980). *The Manners and Customs of the Police* (pp. 180–186). New York: Academic Press.

Black, D. J., & Reiss, Jr., A. J. (1970). Police control of juveniles. *American Sociological Review*, 35, 63–77.

Boateng, F. D., & Hsieh, M. L. (2019). Misconduct within the "four walls": Does organizational justice matter in explaining prison officers' misconduct and job stress? *International Journal of Offender Therapy and Comparative Criminology*, 63 (2), 289–308.

Brown, R. A., & Frank, J. (2005). Police-citizen encounters and field citations: Do encounter characteristics influence ticketing? *Policing: An International Journal of Police Strategies & Management*, 28 (3), 435–454.

Bureau of Justice Statistics. (2016). Use of force. Retrieved from http://www.bjs.gov/index.cfmty5tp&tid584.

Dunham, R. G., & Alpert, G. P. (2009). Officer and suspect demeanor: A qualitative analysis of change. *Police Quarterly*, 12 (1), 6–21.

Durose, M. R., Smith, E. L., & Langan, P. A. (2007, April). *Contacts Between Police and the Public, 2005* (Special Report NJC 215243). Retrieved from the Bureau of Justice Statistics website: https://www.bjs.gov/content/pub/pdf/cpp05.pdf.

Eith, C., & Durose, M. R. (2011). *Contacts Between Police and the Public, 2008*. Washington, DC: U.S. Department of Justice. Retrieved from http://bjs.gov/content/pub/pdf/cpp08.pdf.

Engel, R. S., Sobol, J. J., & Worden, R. E. (2000). Further exploration of the demeanor hypothesis: The interaction effects of suspects' characteristics and demeanor on police behavior. *Justice Quarterly*, 17 (2), 235–258.

Fryer Jr, R. G. (2019). An empirical analysis of racial differences in police use of force. *Journal of Political Economy*, 127 (3), 1210–1261.

Gau, J. M., & Brunson, R. K. (2010). Procedural justice and order maintenance policing: A study of inner-city young men's perceptions of police legitimacy. *Justice Quarterly*, 27 (2), 255–279.

Hyland, S., Langton, L., & Davis, E. (2015, November). *Police Use of Nonfatal Force, 2002–2011* (Special Report NCJ249216). Retrieved from the Bureau of Justice Statistics website: http://www.bjs.gov/content/pub/pdf/punf0211.pdf.

Hickman, M. J., Piquero, A. R., & Garner, J. H. (2008). Toward a national estimate of police use of nonlethal force. *Criminology & Public Policy*, 7 (4), 563–604.

Huff, J. (2021). Understanding police decisions to arrest: The impact of situational, officer, and neighborhood characteristics on police discretion. *Journal of Criminal Justice*, 75, 101829.

Huggins, C. M. (2012). Traffic stop encounters: Officer and citizen race and perceptions of police propriety. *American Journal of Criminal Justice*, 37 (1), 92–110.

James, L., James, S., & Vila, B. (2018). Testing the impact of citizen characteristics and demeanor on police officer behavior in potentially violent encounters. *Policing: An International Journal*, 41 (1), 24–40.

Klinger, D. A. (1994). Demeanor or crime? Why "hostile" citizens are more likely to be arrested. *Criminology: An Interdisciplinary Journal*, 32 (3), 475–493.

Kramer, R., & Remster, B. (2018). Stop, frisk, and assault? Racial disparities in police use of force during investigatory stops. *Law & Society Review*, 52 (4), 960–993.

LawInfo. (2015). What to do if police use excessive force. Retrieved from https://resources.lawinfo.com/criminal-defense/what-to-do-if-police-use-excessive-force.html.

Lizotte, A. J. (1978). Extra-legal factors in Chicago's criminal courts: Testing the conflict model of criminal justice. *Social Problems*, 25 (5), 564–580.

Lundman, R. J. (1974). Routine police arrest practices: A commonweal perspective. *Social Problems*, 22 (1), 127–141.

Lundman, R. J. (1994). Demeanor or crime? The Midwest City police-citizen encounters study. *Criminology: An Interdisciplinary Journal*, 32 (4), 631–656.

Lundman, R. J., Sykes, R. E., & Clark, J. P. (1978). Police control of juveniles: A replication. *Journal of Research in Crime and Delinquency*, 15 (1), 74–91.

Morrow, W. J., Berthelot, E. R., & Vickovic, S. G. (2018). Police use of force: An examination of the minority threat perspective. *Criminal Justice Studies*, 31 (4), 368–387.

Motley Jr, R. O., & Joe, S. (2018). Police use of force by ethnicity, sex, and socio-economic class. *Journal of the Society for Social Work and Research*, 9 (1), 49–67.

National Institute of Justice. (2015). The use-of-force continuum. Retrieved from https://www.nij.gov/topics/law-enforcement/officer-safety/use-of-force/Pages/continuum.aspx.

Reiman, J., & Leighton, P. (2015). *Rich Get Richer and the Poor Get Prison: Ideology, Class, and Criminal Justice*. New York, NY: Routledge.

Reppetto, T. (2012). *American Police: A History 1945–2012*. New York, NY: Enigma Books.

Skolnick, J. H., & Fyfe, J. J. (1993). *Above the Law: Police and the Excessive Use of Force*. New York, NY: The Free Press.

Smith, D. A. (1987). Police response to interpersonal violence: Defining the parameters of legal control. *Social Forces*, 65 (3), 767–782.

Smith, D. A., & Klein, J. R. (1983). Police agency characteristics and arrest decisions. *Evaluating Performance of Criminal Justice Agencies*, 19, 63–98.

Smith, D. A., & Klein, J. R. (1984). Police control of interpersonal disputes. *Social Problems*, 31 (4), 468–481.

Smith, D. A., & Visher, C. A. (1981). Street-level justice: Situational determinants of police arrest decisions. *Social Problems*, 29 (2), 167–177.

Smith, D. A., Visher, C. A., & Davidson, L. A. (1984). Equity and discretionary justice: The influence of race on police arrest decisions. *Journal of Criminal Law & Criminology*, 75, 234.

Sykes, R. E., Fox, J. C., & Clark, J. P. (1976). A socio-legal theory of police discretion. *The Ambivalent Force: Perspectives on the Police*, 3, 171–183.

Terrill, W., & Paoline, III, E. A. (2007). Non-arrest decision making in police–citizen encounters. *Police Quarterly*, 10 (3), 308–331.

Van Cleve, N. G., & Mayes, L. (2015). Criminal justice through "colorblind" lenses: A call to examine the mutual constitution of race and criminal justice. *Law & Social Inquiry*, 40 (2), 406–432.

Visher, C. A. (1983). Gender, police arrest decisions, and notions of chivalry. *Criminology: An Interdisciplinary Journal*, 21 (1), 5–28.

Warren, P., Tomaskovic-Devey, D., Smith, W., Zingraff, M., & Mason, M. (2006). Driving while black: Bias processes and racial disparity in police stops. *Criminology*, 44 (3), 709–738.

Wihbey, J., & Kille, L. W. (2016). Excessive or reasonable force by police? Research on law enforcement and racial conflict. Retrieved from https://journalistsresource.org/studies/government/criminal-justice/police-reasonable-force-brutality-race-research-review-statistics.

Weitzer, R. (1996). Racial discrimination in the criminal justice system: Findings and problems in the literature. *Journal of Criminal Justice*, 24 (4), 309–322.

Wilt, B. (2015, September). Police use of force: Training, community relations help township police ensure proper use of force. *Pennsylvania Township News*. Retrieved from http://www.cohenseglias.com/library/files/police_use_of_force_pa_township_news_carusone_2015.pdf.

Worden, R. E. (1989). Situational and attitudinal explanations of police behavior: A theoretical reappraisal and empirical assessment. *Law and Society Review*, 23, 667–711.

Worden, R. E., & Pollitz, A. A. (1984). Police arrests in domestic disturbances: A further look. *Law and Society Review*, 18, 105.

Worden, R. E., & Shepard, R. L. (1996). Demeanor, crime, and police behavior: A reexamination of the police services study data. *Criminology: An Interdisciplinary Journal*, 34 (1), 83–105.

6

THE DETERMINANT FACTORS OF RELIGIOUS RADICALIZATION

The case of Kyrgyzstan

Erlan Bakiev and Zairbek Kozhomberdiev

Introduction

Kyrgyzstan is a post-Soviet Central Asian Country bordered by China, Kazakhstan, Uzbekistan and Tajikistan. Being in the center of the Silk Road, which is the main trade artery of the region, makes Kyrgyzstan a key partner for many global players. After the collapse of the Soviet Union, we witnessed the end of 70 years of anti-religious policies that strictly censored religious expression and controlled religious institutions with the aim of affecting the demise of religion. The wave of religious freedom brought to the Central Asian region many radical and extremist groups from all religions and faiths all over the world. The helplessness of states in countering the destructive organizations was obvious. For instance, Kyrgyzstan ratified its Law on monitoring religious organizations (Law of the Kyrgyz Republic on Freedom of Religion) in 2008 after 17 years of its independence. Therefore, Kyrgyzstan still cannot identify the exact number of religious organizations functioning on its territory. Extremist organizations see Kyrgyzstan, the Island of democracy, as a springboard for their activities.

Religious extremism, with its destructive manifestations, poses a serious threat to the national security of any state. Under the light of the ongoing growth of tensions in the Middle East, as well as potential threats from the Afghani-Pakistani zone, sustainable counter-extremism and counter-terrorism measures for the Central Asian region are vital. However, despite enormous collaborative efforts by state, international organizations and non-profits, unfortunately, extremism remains a major concern for certain marginalized groups in the society. Especially the youth is actively involved in the religious radicalization process both as recruiters and as victims. For instance, in Kyrgyzstan most of the active members of the radical groups and the terrorist convicts are in the age range of 25 and 35 years.[1] It is safe to claim that extremists focus on youth and try to get fresh blood into their lines among them.

The extremist organizations such as, Hizb-ut Tahrir and Akromia (prohibited in Kyrgyzstan) actively recruit the youth in the South of Kyrgyzstan.[2] Moreover, we can observe the increase in the number of religious extremist groups and their joint interaction and efforts in building the so-called caliphate and the branch of the ISIS in Kyrgyzstan. Currently, 19 extremist and terrorist organizations are banned by courts of various instances in Kyrgyzstan.[3] Consequently, investigating and researching these organizations and their members would give new impetus in developing counter-extremism and counter-terrorism policies. Moreover, this research identifies factors that push people to radicalize and join extremist and terrorist organizations.

Literature

Religious extremism and radicalization are new terms for newly independent Kyrgyzstan. From the early 19th century in the Soviet Union the socialist system combated religious expression directly.[4] After the pursuit of religious leaders, their influence and the impact of religion has diminished, which followed with the closure of religious schools and madrasas, religious educational institutions. There is a debate among scholars on the success of the Soviets in their promotion of atheist society.[56] However, religious practice and identification among Muslims in Central Asia remained at least at the cultural level. Hann and Pelkmans state that previous points of reference did not disappear. The promotion of ethnonational categories and their endowment with standardized literary languages as well as a long list of cultural attributes, such as cuisine, costume, dance, burial process and marriage were an overwhelming success.[7] Moreover, in the Fall of 1943, the Soviet government agreed to develop the Spiritual Administration of Muslims of Central Asia and Kazakhstan in Tashkent. This opened a new page in the history of Islam in the USSR, which determined the development of the Ummah in the post-Soviet space until the present day.

After the collapse of the Soviets, a process of liberalization started not only in economics but also in religion. This liberalization process allowed various religious groups to enter Kyrgyzstan. Hann and Pelkmans state "While the Kyrgyz government had reckoned with the revival of locally rooted faiths – primarily Sunni Islam but also Orthodox Christianity – the liberal policies led within a few years to a proliferation of groups not previously active in the country."[8]

Accordingly, the Muslim population of the Central Asian countries began the process of reviving national values, as well as restoring the spiritual heritage. However, the very process of reviving the Islamic value system and the cultural-civilizational integration of this region into the Islamic world is fraught with a number of difficulties. One of them is cultural; for 70 years the Muslims of Central Asia were intellectually separated from the Islamic civilization, the modern political and legal thought of the East. The religious elite was educated with the materials and literature which passed through thorough sight of the secret services of the Soviets. Consequently, this situation caused a state of cultural Islam in Central Asia where the role of culture is predominant of the dogmas of Islam. Therefore, Muslims of Central Asia were socially and politically passive amongst the Soviets.[9]

The reason for the social and political passivity of the Muslim communities of the Central Asian countries is also that Islamic political thought in those countries has been stagnant for a long time due to objective reasons. One of them is that Islamic thought in the former USSR Muslim republics was separated by the "Iron Curtain" from the revolutionary influence of liberation movements of the Middle East against colonialism.[10] Furthermore, the ideology of scientific atheism of the USSR was directed against religion in general, which led to the fact that most of the Muslim clergy were repressed. The other part of the Muslim clergy did not work for the development of Islamic thought, but for preserving Islam in general, through folk traditions, religious rites, and rituals.[11] All this, as well as other factors, influenced the emergence of a fragmented and stereotyped understanding of Islam, which limited Islam only to questions of worship. This led to an even greater conservatism of Islamic thinking that already existed in the era of purely authoritarian formations in the form of khanates or emirates.[12]

An internal obstacle to the Islamic intellectual awakening of Kyrgyzstan is either a deficit or the absence of its own modern ideological base, that would have its own specific goals, objectives, and political system. Additionally, there has been an absence of Islamic ideology which is focused on solving specific issues and problems at the community level with its subsequent presentation to the general population through the Islamic prism. Another critical issue in this chain is the deficit of the Islamic political elite, lack scholars who would unify the Kyrgyzstani Muslims. This came about because of conceptual contradictions between aalyms (Islamic scholars) of Kyrgyzstan, which led to a breaking down into small fractions of jamaats with different views and beliefs. Intellectuals with state-oriented thinking directed themselves to external projects rather than national interests. The existing jamaats, movements, and groups in Kyrgyzstan are focused on the narrow interests of defending the rights of their jamaat without taking into account the protection of the rights of all segments of the population. With existing ideological and mazhabic contradictions between groups, different jamaats may lead to impatience and confrontation among believers.[13]

According to Abdyrahmanov, Krygyzstan's religious intelligentsia illustrated incompetence, religious illiteracy, a low level of scientific theosophical characteristics, and moral values.[14] This intelligentsia fails to lead its Ummah in the right direction. Moreover, they very often are convicted in corruption cases, and started the "commercialization" and the "arbitrariness" of such matters as the organization of hajj, funerals, collection of donations. The imams turned Islam into one of the sources of enrichment.[15] Therefore, contemporary Kyrgyz Islam's leadership pays more attention to ritual-commercial affairs than to its primary functions related to the service of Islam, such as releasing fatwas on present-day issues that Muslims in Kyrgyzstan face. The luxury lifestyle of the mufti of Kyrgyzstan who owns several villas and luxury automobiles is evidence for the above.[16] They left out of their field of vision such issues as bringing other, values – basic beliefs, religious practices, the Qur'an, the teachings of the Prophet Muhammad and Sharia – of Islam to the religious community, engaging the religious community based on these values, solving acute problems, and negative attitudes taking place in Kyrgyz Islam. Consequently, among the Kyrgyz Muslim elite, the quality of religious literacy, stability, constructiveness, and creativity have diminished.[17]

The weakness of the Muslim elite led the population to seek religious knowledge in venues outside an official non-government organization representing Muslims of Kyrgyzstan, the Spiritual Administration of Kyrgyzstan, such as the Internet or social media. In particular, Russian speaking Muslims cannot find sources in the Russian language because there is not a single imam or aalym (Islamic scholar) who preaches in Russian. Therefore, these young people find sources from websites of radical Salafi takfirist-jihadi organizations or institutions. Kyrgyzstan is a secular state; therefore, religion should be out of politics and outside of any state institution and public education. The Spiritual Administration of Kyrgyzstan (Muftiate) is a non-government organization formed by the Aalyms Council, which consists of 12 Islamic scholars. The Spiritual Administration of Kyrgyzstan reports to the State Commission for Religious Affairs of the Kyrgyz Republic. This Commission monitors the activity of all religious organizations and foundation across the country.

Religious extremism and terrorism in Kyrgyzstan

Kyrgyz officials claim that more than 800 Kyrgyz citizens have left the country to join jihad and side with terrorist organizations in Syria.[18] The Islamic State of Iraq and Syria (ISIS), formerly known as the Islamic State of Iraq and Levant (ISIL), although defeated, is still a threat not only to the region but also to the global community. In 2016, the Kyrgyz Police revealed 167 cases related to the recruitment, mercenaryism (activities of individuals, groups and organizations in planning, organizing, preparing and committing acts aimed at recruiting, using, training, financing and other material support for mercenaries) and travel of citizens of the Kyrgyz Republic to foreign countries where armed conflicts had been continuing, such as Syria, Iraq, Afghanistan, and Pakistan (North Waziristan).[19][20]

Despite the measures taken by the national police and security service, the number of Kyrgyz citizens who have joined terrorist groups in Syria, Iraq, Afghanistan, and Pakistan (specifically North Waziristan) remains high. As of May 2019, according to the Kyrgyz National Police and other national security authorities, a total of 803 Kyrgyz nationals (186 of whom were females) had left Kyrgyzstan to travel to these conflict zones.[21] A total of 63 foreign fighters originating from Kyrgyzstan were killed in various conflict zones.[22] The distribution of these people based on their hometowns and provinces in Kyrgyzstan is as follows: the city of Osh 100, Osh province 357, Jalal-Abad province 95, Batken province 104, Chui province 54, Talas province 4, Issyk-Kul province 34, and Naryn province 1.[23][24] According to the Kyrgyzstan Ministry of Interior and the State Service of Financial Intelligence, a total of 143 Kyrgyz citizens received financial aid from terrorist organizations to travel to conflict zones.

It is also important to note the role of the Internet in the recruitment activities of terrorist and extremist organizations. The majority of Kyrgyz citizens (60%) were recruited through social networks such as Odnoklassniki, Facebook, Instagram, and the mobile apps Telegram and WhatsApp. This was the result of weak preventive work on the Internet by state agencies, which failed to create counter narratives. The weakness of this preventive work is emphasized by the lack of legal and technological measures such as the ability to identify recruiters' IP addresses and the deficiency of counter narratives on social media. Moreover, 25% of citizens who left for war zones, such as Syria, are women, indicating the need for preventive measures specifically targeting women.

Additionally, the organized crime in Kyrgyzstan has changed in recent years. Earlier, organized crime and gang groups were guided by criminal traditions that came out of the criminal subculture.[25] However, today there has appeared a new trend of merging organized crime with religious extremists and radicals. Now, we see more gang leaders, convicts imprisoned for serious crimes and sentenced to life imprisonment, using religious ideology to attract youth. Non-traditional religious movements of a radical fundamentalist persuasion (i.e., Salafi or Wahhabi, in general) have infiltrated organized criminal groups. Adherents of the Salafi takfiri jihadist ideology actively began to spread their influence in the criminal environment.

In 2016, nine jihadists, members of the prohibited homegrown terrorist organization Jaysh al-mahdi in Kyrgyzstan, carried out a prison break from one of the most highly secured prisons near the capital, Bishkek. Jaysh al-mahdi first committed a terrorist attack using explosives in 2008 in Bishkek, and since then, the number of attacks has risen to dozens. In the late 1990s, the leaders of Jaysh al-mahdi (Islamov, Itibaev, and Abdrahmanov) were members of local gangs that operated under the protection of criminal organizations. According to Dubanaev, there is currently an active process of merging organized crime groups with terrorist organizations.[26] His research suggests that organized crime and terrorists/violent extremists share a common denial of statehood and constitutional order. Members of organized crime or other convicts serving sentences in correctional institutions can be susceptible to ideological radicalization under the influence of terrorists and extremists who are also serving sentences in the same institutions.[27]

Over the past few years, the Wahhabization of organized criminal groups has become a reality. As mentioned earlier, criminal activity was previously carried out using criminal traditions and governed by the criminal brotherhood. However, recently, certain criminals are attempting to portray their criminal activities as religious by using extremist ideas, terms, and slogans to justify and absolve themselves of their actions. For instance, there have been several robbery and extortion cases in which suspects have admitted to collecting money for the jamaat, for incarcerated individuals, or for "brothers" engaged in a jihad against "infidels". Consequently, organized criminal groups can now more easily legitimize their illicit activities in the eyes of society and are becoming more efficient in conducting their unlawful business.

The coalescence of criminal gangs and religious extremist groups, to a certain extent, occurs in prisons through the dissemination of religious and extremist ideas among convicts. Those who are convicted for religious extremism and terrorist acts, in general, do not entirely abandon their views while they serve their sentence in correctional institutions. On the contrary, they begin to engage in "davat-propaganda" among other convicts who were not believers or practitioners of traditional religious teachings before ending up in prison.

Table 6.1 illustrates the increasing trend in the number of convicts. Currently, there are more than 400 inmates convicted of religious extremism and

TABLE 6.1 Convicts on religious extremism and terrorism

Type of facility	2010	2011	2012	2013	2014	2015	2016	2017
Correctional inspections	0	0	0	4	29	87	158	123
Open prisons	17	17	21	22	24	33	31	108
Correctional facility	62	84	79	81	111	133	161	191
Total	79	101	100	107	164	253	350	422

terrorism. Among them, almost 22% were convicted of serious crimes, such as terrorism and activities involving the financing of terrorism, going to war zones in third countries, and engaging in recruiting new members for terrorist organizations. They were sentenced to over five years in special correctional institutions. The convicts in these special correctional institutions are held in locked cells and each person has an area of two square meters. The convicts are not allowed to move freely outside the cells and are even restricted from entering the dining room – they eat in their cells, along with using the restroom and bathrooms. Twice a year, they are allowed to meet with their family members, and once a day for an hour, they are permitted to go for a walk under the control of prison guards. Moreover, 14 people were sentenced to life imprisonment.[28]

The role of law enforcement in counter-terrorism strategies

In modern conditions, international terrorism and religious extremism have transformed into a complex socio-political phenomenon and represent a multifaceted threat on a global scale. Based on problems of a political, economic, territorial, spiritual, moral and religious nature, today terrorism and religious extremism are undergoing changes towards transnationalization. The scale and cruelty of the actions are increasing. The formation of terrorist threats to Kyrgyzstan is largely due to the continuing unfavourable situation in certain countries of the world.[29] Moreover, the importance of anti-terrorism activities is especially noted in the context of the continued growth of tension in the Middle East – Syria, Iraq – as well as potential threats from Afghanistan. As the analysis shows, soon, it will be jihadist organizations based on radical extremism that will pose a serious threat to the security of the state.[30]

There have been no cases reported of citizens from the Kyrgyz Republic being transferred to foreign countries where hostilities are ongoing. This suggests that the authorities in Kyrgyzstan may have effective measures in place to prevent citizens from being involved in conflicts abroad or being taken to such areas against their will. However, the analysis also states that the issue of returning terrorists from foreign conflict zones is a significant concern. This suggests that although citizens have not been transferred to conflict areas, some individuals from Kyrgyzstan have managed to travel abroad to engage in terrorist activities. It may indicate a need for increased efforts in preventing radicalization within the country and enhancing border control measures to prevent individuals involved in terrorism from returning.[31] The analysis mentions that international terrorist organization leaders are currently active and preparing for an active phase. This suggests that there may be an imminent threat posed by these leaders or the organizations they represent. It could imply a need for proactive measures by security forces to counter their activities and prevent potential acts of terrorism.

The Kyrgyz National Police (KNP) are actively cooperating with their counterparts in Central Asian countries to combat religious extremism and terrorism. KNP are specifically concerned about the arrival of highly trained militants who may use fake documents of citizens from Uzbekistan, Tajikistan, Kazakhstan, Russia, Ukraine, etc., who have not previously been flagged by law enforcement. It is anticipated that these militants may travel through a transit channel via the Russian Federation, passing through Turkey, Ukraine, Georgia, and Azerbaijan. The leaders and members of these international terrorist organizations also plan to collaborate with internal underground networks and criminal groups in an effort to destabilize the situation in the Central Asian region.[32]

The efforts of the KNP in countering threats from religious extremism and terrorism in the region is very significant. The police are actively collaborating with police forces in other Central Asian countries to exchange experiences and pool resources. This cooperation aims to enhance their effectiveness in fighting against these threats. In order to prevent individuals from returning to radical groups, the Department of Counter Terrorism identifies citizens who have joined or are currently participating in illegal armed groups abroad. This allows them to uncover and suppress potential terrorist and extremist actions in a timely manner. However, the task faced by law enforcement officers is becoming increasingly challenging due to the rising number of women and young people joining radical movements. Young individuals are often recruited through various messaging platforms and social networks, and there are even "Internet imams" who conduct online sermons. Tracking these activities is problematic, but efforts are made to warn young people about the dangers associated with radicalization. Preventive lectures are conducted in educational institutions to raise awareness among schoolchildren and students. Yearly, over 10,000 young individuals are covered through these lectures.[33]

Overall, the analysis highlights the proactive measures taken by the KNP to address the threats of religious extremism and terrorism. However, the emergence of new recruitment methods and the involvement of young individuals pose significant challenges to their efforts. The next important stage, as noted by the experts, is the prevention of radicalization in the country's prisons. According to some experts, prisons can become recruiting centers for militants.[34,35,36] A significant amount of work is also anticipated in this area, including training sessions for employees of the State Penitentiary Service. It is imperative to address the potential influence of extremists, as there have been cases in foreign countries where colony employees themselves fell under their influence. Although prisoners of this category are typically segregated, corruption provides some inmates the opportunity to control units using mobile phones.

The issue is the lack of a clear system to track individuals who have been released from prison. According to statistics, 50 percent of these released individuals continue to be loyal to recruiters even after their due date. The research implies that the event in question prompted experts to come up with recommendations. However, it also suggests that while the recommendations may have addressed various aspects related to the event, the problem of tracking released individuals was not fully resolved. The lack of a clear system to monitor individuals after their release from prison raises concerns about public safety. The fact that half of them remain loyal to recruiters is alarming and indicates a potential failure in rehabilitation and reintegration efforts.

To address this problem, it would be crucial to establish an effective tracking system that monitors individuals after their release from prison. This system should involve close collaboration among relevant authorities, including law enforcement, correctional facilities, and social services. It would also be important to focus on improving rehabilitation programs within prisons to reduce the likelihood of individuals being recruited or returning to criminal activities after release. These programs should address the underlying factors that contribute to re-offending, such as lack of education, job skills, mental health support, and social networks.[37]

Furthermore, a comprehensive approach involving community support and integration could help released individuals successfully reintegrate into society. This might involve providing access to housing, employment opportunities, educational support, and mentoring programs. Additionally, international collaboration and knowledge-sharing can play a significant role in addressing this issue. International experts, who have experience in dealing with such challenges, could continue to offer insights and support in developing and implementing effective strategies.

Overall, addressing the problem of released individuals remaining loyal to recruiters requires a multifaceted approach that focuses on improving tracking systems, enhancing rehabilitation programs, fostering community support, and leveraging international expertise. By implementing these recommendations, it may be possible to mitigate the risks associated with released individuals returning to criminal activities.

Methodology

This study utilizes open-source information and on-field professional experience to classify jihadists from Kyrgyzstan and reconstruct their life stories after being recruited by terrorist organizations. The study analyzes information from open sources and professional observations of apprehended/arrested extremists, jihadists, and terrorists. The information obtained from these sources was classified and used to organize subjects into three groups: (1) jihadists who have travelled to Syria to fight with ISIS, Jabhat al Nusra, or Al Qaida, (2) jihadists who joined IMT (Islamic Movement of Turkestan) in North Waziristan, Pakistan, and (3) jihadists who have returned to Kyrgyzstan from conflict zones and are currently under investigation or have been convicted. Additionally, one of the authors conducted on-field work at the Department of Anti-Extremism and Terrorism of the Ministry of Interior of the Kyrgyz Republic, which provided crucial insights for this study.

The life stories of the observees are reconstructed into several groups of variables. The first group of variables includes demographic characteristics such as age, gender, education, residence, family, parents, economic status, satisfaction with one's own economic situation, and the level of religiosity. The second group of variables is related to the circumstances of departure, including logistics, organization and financing, and the attitudes of relatives or intimate ones towards this decision. The third group of variables consists of the psychological characteristics of the fighters, including factors such as propensity to violence, aggression, and the determination to leave the country to participate in the war activities of terrorist organizations. Lastly, the fourth group of variables comprises the personal motivations of the fighters.

Information for this study was gathered between 2015 and 2017 from open sources and field operations activities such as the detention process, preventive work, and searches. Individuals who were suspected of extremism or terrorism were observed. Additionally, the evidence in this study includes information from operational visits to correctional institutions.

Since the Criminal Code of the Kyrgyz Republic does not contain a definition of the term "extremism," the classification of this category of crimes is included in the Law of the Kyrgyz Republic "On countering extremist activity." This classification covers the list of articles of the Criminal Code of the Kyrgyz Republic which are posed in the Review of Judicial Practice on the consideration of criminal cases on terrorism and extremism. However, the Criminal Code of the Kyrgyz Republic does contain statutes defining and sanctioning the act of terrorism' for instance, Article 226 "Act of terrorism," Article 227 "Hostage-taking," Article 228 "Knowingly false report on an act of terrorism," Article 232 "Hijacking of air or water transport or railway rolling stock," Article 298 "Diversion," Article 375 "Mercenary," and Article 376 "Attack on persons or institutions which are under international protection" of the Criminal Code of the Kyrgyz Republic.

However, it is important to note that open-sourcing information is a common practice in terrorism research and law enforcement. Open-source intelligence involves collecting, analyzing, and interpreting publicly available information, such as news reports, social media posts, academic research, and government documents. While open-source information certainly has its limitations, it is also a valuable source of data for researchers studying terrorism. It helps in understanding terrorist tactics, recruitment strategies, funding sources, and ideological motivations. Open-source information plays a significant role in identifying potential threats, analyzing trends, and informing counterterrorism strategies. Furthermore, it helps in debunking misinformation, propaganda, and conspiracy theories related to terrorism.

It is essential, however, to complement open-source information with other sources, such as classified data, human intelligence, and expert analysis, to have a comprehensive understanding of the issue. Open-source research alone may not always provide accurate or complete information, and it is crucial to verify and cross-reference multiple sources. This research has the limitation of utilizing complementary sources of information. Therefore, while there may be challenges and limitations in using open-source information for terrorism research, labeling it as a fallacy is an oversimplification. Open-source intelligence remains a valuable tool in better understanding and countering terrorism.

Findings and discussion

According to government data, the majority of foreign terrorist fighters (FTFs) from Kyrgyzstan are young males between 25–35 years old, accounting for about 65% of the total FTFs. Women, on the other hand, represent a growing number, making up as much as 25% of the citizens who have left the country to join foreign terrorist groups.[38] Currently, individuals convicted of terrorism-related offenses make up 4% of the overall prison population in Kyrgyzstan.[39] The number of violent extremist offenders has seen a tremendous increase from 79 in 2010 to 422 in 2017. Out of these 422 offenders (92% men, 8% women), 45 are in pretrial detention centers, 191 are in closed-type facilities, 108 are in open-type prisons, and 123 are serving non-custodial sentences.[40] Based on information from the State Penitentiary Service of the Kyrgyz Republic, it is safe to claim that extremist and terrorist organizations target relatively younger individuals. On-field observation revealed the following findings: most jihadists were between 22 and 30 years old when they left Kyrgyzstan to join the conflicts in Syria and Northern Waziristan. The majority of these militants were from Osh, Jalal-Abad, and Batken provinces in the south of Kyrgyzstan. However, there were seven individuals from Chui province, which is located in the northern part of the country.

The police data on arrests and the cases initiated on terrorism and violent extremism crimes indicate that the residents of the southern part of Kyrgyzstan are relatively more religious, and this factor plays a more significant role in the number of individuals joining the war in Syria and Northern Waziristan.[4142] In terms of their level of education, 32% of jihadists were high school dropouts, 52% had high school diplomas, and 26% had university diplomas.

The research on ISIL terrorist fighters indicates that most of the participants were from middle-class families. Only three of them were from the upper class, and only one of them was in debt.[43] Both male and female jihadists were making decent money doing their daily business by Kyrgyzstan standards. For instance, a young man who went to Syria from the Chui province used to make $1,000 USD a month. Among those who left for conflict zones was a businessman from Kara-Balta city, who owned several stores in the central market. Another young female from Kara-Balta city worked as a barber and used to make around $600 USD per month before leaving Kyrgyzstan.

Moreover, research on social media channels promoting radicalization in Kyrgyzstan indicates that the majority of violent extremists and radical jihadists were migrants in Russia, where they worked and supported their families.[44] The observations have revealed that most of the respondents' living standards were at mid and upper levels in comparison to other inmates who committed other types of crimes.

The evidence retrieved from open-source information and filed observations claims that social services in suburban stations, where individuals used to live, have completely failed. There were no opportunities for leisure activities, such as sports and other social engagements. Additionally, opportunities for education and social communication for women outside of the family are minimal. Consequently, based on experiences in other countries, this research suggests that the poor quality or absence of social services could be motivating factors for individuals to leave their permanent residence and join so-called jihad in conflict zones.

Sikorskaya states in her research report that the Internet, social networks, and new information technologies played a significant role in the radicalization process.[45] On-field observations indicated that arrested jihadists were recruited by watching videos of spiritual leaders of ISIS and other extremist religious organizations. Terrorist organizations professionally prepare their propaganda materials and broadcast them on the Internet, which can have a significant impact on specific segments of the population. Additionally, many online extremist propaganda platforms, using social networks, direct youth towards the radicalization process. However, youth are only radicalized after becoming permanent residents of the aforementioned platforms and changing their worldview through long and lively dialogues with radicalized online recruiters.

Moreover, based on observations, it is safe to claim that there are several layers of personal motivations that induce people to join terrorist organizations. These motivations include ideological factors related to religion, as well as other non-religious motivations such as financial gain, self-esteem, or the need for a sense of identity.

The ideological motivation related to religion includes the fight against "kafirs" (infidels) and enemies of Islam, the fight against sinners and political leaders, and the desire to participate in the establishment of the Islamic caliphate. It is important to note that the desire for martyrdom, to become a "shahid," and the desire to participate in "jihad" as per their understanding, are also significant motivating factors.

On the other hand, the non-religious aspect of ideological motivation was the quest for social justice. This manifested as a desire to be involved in the creation of a just state, the drive to actively shape one's own life and society, the determination to fight against regimes seen as authoritarian, and the fight for freedom and justice. Another layer of motivation is connected to what is commonly referred to as the "squalor of local life." Due to their living conditions and other indicators of disadvantage, people are more likely to experience social and financial insecurity.[46] The majority of militants and their spouses have limited exposure to well-established social services, adequate leisure time, and recreational activities. From a young age and after high school graduation, they anticipate entering the workforce and eventually immigrating to Russia as migrant workers, despite the challenges and difficulties involved.

It is evident that, at some point, they have a desire to break the "vicious circle" of everyday life, to see the outside world and go somewhere, and to participate in an adventure that will make their lives enjoyable and meaningful. Many of them were likely led by romance and the opportunity to self-actualize. For women, there is a desire to find a husband or groom in the "new world" and have a family according to Islamic Sharia law, as they define it, and the desire to realize their female identity the way they see fit. Many fighters from Kyrgyzstan were hesitant to return home because, according to Kyrgyz laws, they would be arrested, prosecuted, and convicted for participating in armed conflicts or military operations in a foreign state or undergoing terrorist and extremist training. However, it should be noted that it is not just one motivating factor, but various factors that could play a role in an individual's decision to travel abroad and engage in activities with terrorist organizations.

The story of a young man who joined the Islamic Movement of Turkestan (IMT) serves as an example. This man joined the group due to his unrequited love for a girl. The girl's parents denied his request to marry her. His family described him as shy, unstable, and unemployed, lacking status in society. After leaving for North Waziristan, he not only tried to cope with his personal trauma but also discovered his identity. It turns out that he is a talented "journalist," capable of creating and posting a series of advertisements promoting the IMT on the internet. Analysis of his verbal and non-verbal behaviors indicates that he is content with his fate, has found professional significance and identity, and feels happy and satisfied with his status.

Based on the demographic characteristics and analysis, this research reveals the following individual characteristics that are more likely to lead to participation in the activities of terrorist organizations in Central Asia. First, the decision to join a foreign terrorist organization is influenced by both external and internal factors. Individual decisions to engage in jihad can stem from social or educational immaturity or a narrow outlook. The socioeconomic status of the family does not significantly impact an individual's decision to join jihad, nor is it a significant obstacle. The individuals who leave the country to join terrorist organizations cannot be considered destitute or illiterate.

It is difficult to consider the level of religiosity as a decisive factor in an individual's decision to join a terrorist organization. However, religious illiteracy does affect the decision to embark on a "jihadist" path, as terrorist organizations create environments to target vulnerable individuals by deliberately misleading them. There are over 2,000 mosques in Kyrgyzstan where 12,000 Imams (individuals who lead prayers in a mosque) conduct services, with about 70% of them being self-taught and not having completed specialized Islamic educational institutions.[47]

The Internet and social networking have a significant impact on personal attitudes toward radicalization. A recruitment network, which operates in both Kyrgyzstan and abroad, carry out recruitment activities both face to face and through the Internet. Also, this network facilitates logistics and travel arrangements for the recruits so that they could travel to the conflict zones.

Policy implications and conclusion

Religious extremism poses a significant threat to the sovereignty of the Kyrgyz Republic. The war in Syria, escalating tensions in the Middle East, and potential dangers from the Afghani-Pakistani zone all highlight the crucial need for sustainable counter-extremism and counter-terrorism measures in the Central Asian region. This research employed open-source information and on-field observations provided by an active anti-extremism and terrorism officer of the Ministry of Interior of the Kyrgyz Republic.

This research identifies the factors that drive citizens to radicalize and join terrorist and extremist organizations in Kyrgyzstan. The data was collected through open-source information and on-field observations during the arrests of jihadist returnees from conflict zones and those already in correctional institutions nationwide in Kyrgyzstan. The analysis of this research clearly indicates that religious ideology, lack of social justice, and lack of self-esteem/actualization are the main determinants and motivators for religious radicalization in Kyrgyzstan. The nature of these motivational factors is complex, consisting of several layers. Ideological motivations related to religion are among the leading push and pull factors. Consequently, the official Spiritual Administration of Muslims of Kyrgyzstan, together with the State Committee on Religious Affairs, should focus on providing imams with deep religious education directed towards traditional Islam in order to develop counter-narratives to radical Salafi-jihadi ideology. It is important to fill the gaps where radical groups could interact with potential recruits.

Moreover, non-ideological motives, such as economic incentives, social justice, a desire for an enjoyable and exciting life, self-esteem/actualization, and fear of criminal charges upon returning home, are also significant factors in the radicalization of individuals. Therefore, it is important for the state to develop strategies that address these underlying causes in order for policies and programs aimed at countering violent extremism and terrorism to be more effective.

The government bears the primary responsibility in countering violent extremism and religious radicalization, especially among the youth. As a result, it should take the lead in implementing necessary measures and means to protect society, considering the extent of the radicalization process. Research indicates that the government should create a strategic plan that includes state measures relating to religion and offers opportunities for the self-realization of young people. To hinder the efforts of radical organizations, it is crucial to counteract the conditions that contribute to the radicalization of the population. This can be achieved through the establishment of a stable economic foundation for the population's livelihood, promoting apolitical attitudes, and immunizing individuals against radical ideologies.

Communicating the necessary information and counter-narratives on the topic of religious radicalization to society is effectively done through social media, television, and radio broadcasting. These tools have the greatest impact on the general population and can foster a tolerant attitude among young people towards representatives of various faiths. Combating religious extremism and terrorism requires collaborative efforts. Therefore, it is crucial to involve international and non-profit organizations, as well as civil society, in preventive activities and the process of reintegration/rehabilitation for convicts.

Notes

1. Bakiev, E. (2018). Which extremist organizations are banned in Kyrgyzstan: list. Retrieved from https://knews.kg/2018/02/07/kakie-ekstremistskie-organizatsii-zap reshheny-v-kyrgyzstane-spisok/ on 29.04.2020.
2. Mirsaitov, I. (2013). Islamic organizations in the south of Kyrgyzstan. *Central Asia and the Caucasus*, 14(4).
3. Bakiev, E. (2018). Which extremist organizations are banned in Kyrgyzstan: list. Retrieved from https://knews.kg/2018/02/07/kakie-ekstremistskie-organizatsii-zap reshheny-v-kyrgyzstane-spisok/ on 29.04.2020.
4. Hann, C., and Pelkmans, M. (2009). Realigning religion and power in Central Asia: Islam, nation-state and (post) socialism. *Europe-Asia Studies*, 61(9), 1517–1541.
5. Pipes, R. (1955). Muslims of Soviet Central Asia: Trends and prospects (Part I). *Middle East Journal*, 9(2), 147–162.
6. Hann, C., and Pelkmans, M. (2009). Realigning religion and power in Central Asia: Islam, nation-state and (post) socialism. *Europe-Asia Studies*, 61(9), 1517–1541.
    Human Rights Watch Report (2018). "We live in constant fear." Storage of extremist materials in Kyrgyzstan. Retrieved from https://www.hrw.org/ru/rep ort/2018/09/17/322302.
7. Ibid.
8. Ibid., p. 1528.
9. Tazmini, G. (2001). The Islamic revival in Central Asia: A potent force or a misconception? *Central Asian Survey*, 20(1), 63–68.
10. Naumkin, V.V. and Naumkin V.V. (2005). *Radical Islam in Central Asia: Between Pen and Rifle*. Rowman and Littlefield.
11. Tazmini, G. (2001). The Islamic revival in Central Asia: a potent force or a misconception? *Central Asian Survey*, 20(1), 63–68.
12. Malikov, K. (2012). Religious situation in Central Asia. *Centrasianews*, http://www.centrasia.ru/newsA.php?st=1355928060 Retrieved on 15.12.2019.
13. Ibid.
14. Abdyrahmanov, T. (2014). Religious situation in Kyrgyzstan and the weakness of the Islamic elite. *Kyrgyz flag*, 8(2), 5–6.
15. Ibid.
16. Usenaliev, R. (2018). Imam's luxury home and car is not haram. Interview with the Mufti of the Kyrgyz Republic. *Sputnik*. Retrieved from https://ru.sputnik.kg/society/20180814/1040617239/intervyu-muftij-maksat-toktomushev.html on 22.04.2020.
17. Abdyrahmanov, T. (2014). Religious situation in Kyrgyzstan and the weakness of the Islamic elite. *Kyrgyz flag*, 8(2), 5–6.
18. Speckhard, A., Shajkovci, A., & Esengul, C. (2017). *Analysis of the Drivers of Radicalization and Violent Extremism in Kyrgyzstan, Including the Roles of Kyrgyz Women in Supporting, Joining, Intervening in, and Preventing Violent Extremism in Kyrgyzstan*. Washington, D.C., ICSVE.
19. Bakiev, E. (2016). Extremists and their mentors. *Slovo Kyrgyzstana*. Retrieved from http://slovo.kg/?p=78655 on 12.12.2019.
20. Human Rights Watch Report (2018). "We live in constant fear" Storage of extremist materials in Kyrgyzstan. Retrieved from https://www.hrw.org/ru/rep ort/2018/09/17/322302 on 12.12.2019.
21. Bakiev, E. (2016). Extremists and their mentors. *Slovo Kyrgyzstana*. Retrieved from http://slovo.kg/?p=78655 on 12.12.2019.
22. Ibid.
23. Ibid.

24 Esenamanova, N.S. (2017). Public opinion on the factors and causes of radicalization in the religious sphere. *Bulletin of the Kyrgyz-Russian Slavic University*, 17 (4), 91–94.
25 Bakiev, E. and Donmez, M. (2015). Organized crime groups in Kyrgyzstan: The weakness of the government and law enforcement and solution proposals. *Bartın Üniversitesi I.I.B.F. Dergisi*, 6(12).
26 Dubanaev, B.S. (2015). What to do with terrorism? *Information Portal of the Ministry of Internal Affairs of the Kyrgyz Republic*. Retrieved from https://mvd.gov.kg/index.php/rus/mass-media/all-news/item/420-dubanaev-b-s-chto-nam-delat-s-terrorizmom on 10.07.2020.
27 Ibid.
28 GSIN (State Penitentiary Service of the Kyrgyz Republic) Report, 2017. Retrieved from http://www.gsin.gov.kg/presssluzhba/novosti/cystuplenie-predsedatelja-gsin-t.-zhaparova-v-minske.html on 20.12.2019.
29 Zenn, J. and Kuehnast, K. (2014). *Preventing Violent Extremism in Kyrgyzstan*. Washington, DC: US Institute of Peace.
30 Bakiev, E. (2016). Extremists and their mentors. *Slovo Kyrgyzstana*. Retrieved from http://slovo.kg/?p=78655 on 12.12.2019.
31 Babanoski, K. (2020). The threats of returning foreign terrorist fighters for the European security. *Journal of Applied Security Research*, 15(1), 10–27.
32 Panteleeva, E. (2016). Religious extremism has transformed into a socio-political phenomenon. *News Asia*. Retrieved from https://www.news-asia.ru/view/11519 on 22.12.2023.
33 Bakiev, E. (2018). Which extremist organizations are banned in Kyrgyzstan: list. Retrieved from https://knews.kg/2018/02/07/kakie-ekstremistskie-organizatsii-zapreshheny-v-kyrgyzstane-spisok/on 29.04.2020.
34 Esenamanova, N.S. (2017). Public opinion on the factors and causes of radicalization in the religious sphere. *Bulletin of the Kyrgyz-Russian Slavic University*, 17 (4), 91–94.
 Greeley, A. (1994). Marital infidelity. *Society, 31*(4), 9–13.
35 Malikov, K. (2012). Religious situation in Central Asia. *Centrasianews*, http://www.centrasia.ru/newsA.php?st=1355928060 Retrieved on 15.12.2019.
 McDermott, S., Gleeson, R., & Healthcare, C. (2009). *Evaluation of the Severe Domestic Squalor Project*. Social Policy Research Centre.
36 Mirsaitov, I. (2013). Islamic organizations in the south of Kyrgyzstan. *Central Asia and the Caucasus*, 14(4).
37 Panteleeva, E. (2016). Religious extremism has transformed into a socio-political phenomenon. *News Asia*. Retrieved from https://www.news-asia.ru/view/11519 on 22.12.2023.
38 United Nations Peacebuilding Priority Plan Kyrgyzstan (UNPPP) (2017). Peacebuilding Priority Plan on supporting efforts by the Government of the Kyrgyz Republis to prevent radicalization potentially leading to violent extremism. Bishkek, Kyrgyzstan. Retrieved from https://kyrgyzstan.un.org/en/31253-peacebuilding-priority-plan-ppp on 10.09.2020.
39 GSIN (State Penitentiary Service of the Kyrgyz Republic) Report, 2017. Retrieved from http://www.gsin.gov.kg/presssluzhba/novosti/cystuplenie-predsedatelja-gsin-t.-zhaparova-v-minske.html on 20.12.2019.
40 Ibid.
41 Alisheva A. & Alisheva A. (1999). Religious situation in Kyrgyzstan. *Central Asia and Caucasus* (4), 56–59.
42 Bakiev, E. (2016). Extremists and their mentors. *Slovo Kyrgyzstana*. Retrieved from http://slovo.kg/?p=78655 on 12.12.2019.

43 Sikorskaya, I., (2017). *Action Research within the Framework of the Project "Social Media for Deradicalization in Kyrgyzstan": A Model for Central Asia.* Search for Common Ground. 74 Erkindik Boulevard, Bishkek, Kyrgyzstan 720045.
44 Ibid.
45 Ibid.
46 McDermott, S., Gleeson, R., & Healthcare, C. (2009). *Evaluation of the Severe Domestic Squalor Project.* Social Policy Research Centre.
47 Kurbanova, N. (2014). Islamic education in Kyrgyzstan. *Central Asia and the Caucasus: Journal of Social and Political Studies*, 15(1), 102–117.

7
CAMERAS, COMMUNITY, AND POLICE

Possible correlations in the evaluation of the body-worn cameras for the Brazilian Federal Highway Police

Otávio Lacerda, Eduardo Magrone, Vicente Riccio and Wagner Silveira Rezende

The police are the most visible institution in diverse societies. Given their importance for maintaining order and social peace, the police are also the target of criticism. In this way, the mistakes made by the police impact society much more than their successes. Furthermore, this reveals tensions and social conflicts rooted in these contexts. Due to technological advancements, the use of cameras appears to be a way of controlling police activity. The aim is to reduce abuses and increase the transparency of their actions.

The adoption of cameras gained momentum in the United States and spread to several countries. An event of great public commotion that reinforced the theme of the cameras was the murder of Michael Brown in 2014. The murder of this young black man, unarmed, by a white policeman (Darren Wilson), triggered a great crisis because the event was recorded on video. The problem stemmed from the acquittal of the police officer responsible for generating a series of protests (*New York Times* 2020). The impacts of protests generated the so-called "Ferguson effect." For the agents, there was a lot of criticism of the police, with impacts on interactions, community relations, and the entire way of acting of the police institution. Agents became more inert, fearful, and disincentivized to fight crimes (Deuchar et al. 2018, p. 13).

The US Federal Government has developed a package of measures determining new lines of action for US police (USA 2015). The Task Force on Policing in the 21st Century, convened by President Barack Obama, brought, among other innovations, the institution of the use of cameras by police officers (Body-worn cameras, BWC). The BWC adoption was recommended

DOI: 10.4324/9781003452379-8

with the aim of regaining public trust in the police. Thus, there was an expectation of improvement in police proactivity, greater acceptance by civilians, and a reduction in the impacts of the "Ferguson effect." The cameras were intended to affect the legitimacy of the officers. According to Tyler (2004), legitimacy is related to the acceptance of police authority and explains people's obedience to the law and agents' commands.

The use of cameras by police officers is a reality. The popularization of smartphones allowed the population to film the approaches and confront the agents' statements. In this way, the adoption of technology by the police is growing in several countries.

Brazilian police forces are in the process of adopting the tool. Some states already have legislation mandating the use in police forces. However, there is resistance from certain sectors, including the police, to the use of this technology.

Unlike the US, Brazil disposes of its police forces between the Federal Units and the Union, discharging this task to the municipalities. In the States and in the Federal District, the police forces with the largest contingents and attributions are the Civil and Military, responsible for investigation and street patrolling,[1] respectively. The Union has the Federal Police and the Federal Highway Police (PRF). The Federal Police are responsible for investigations, operations, and surveillance, while the Federal Highway Police have focused on street patrolling. The Federal Highway Police are responsible for "ostensive patrolling of federal highways" (Brasil 1988), with surveillance and repression of criminality on Brazilian federal highways. The institution has the second largest budget in the Public Security portfolio of the Brazilian Federal Government, with 3.411 billion reais, and is made up of 12,000 police officers (Brasil 2023a).

Given the different attributions, profiles, and institutional behaviors of the Brazilian police, it is natural that the use of BWC in each police organization has different objectives, requirements, and criteria. Thus, this chapter will carry out a quantitative analysis to identify factors related to the positioning of PRF agents regarding the use of cameras. The tool needs to be properly implemented so that its main positive impacts are achieved. It is expected to demonstrate a relationship between the recognition of the importance of the community for policing and the support of police officers in the use of technology. To carry out the analysis, data obtained from the research project "Social Complexity and Police Action: An analysis from the Federal Highway Police", produced by researchers from the Federal University of Juiz de Fora (Brazil) and the National Academy of the Federal Highway Police, will be used.

This chapter will be divided into five sections: the first deals with aspects related to the use of cameras; the second, reflections on the concept of legitimacy and the factors that influence it; the third analyzes the relationship between the police and the community with a focus on Brazil, the fourth presents the methodology; the fifth presents the simple linear regression with the results obtained in testing the hypothesis, and the discussion of the results.

1 The use of cameras by police – a solution for the crisis

As discussed before, in the years 2013 and 2014 episodes of police violence against young black people reduced trust in the police in the US (Gaub et al. 2016, p. 277). The murder of Michael Brown, in Ferguson, resulted in a lot of criticism of the police. Civilian protests led to a series of changes in the relationship between police and citizens (Deuchar et al. 2018, p. 2).

In response to the effects caused by the Ferguson episode, the Obama administration created a task force to address the problems between the population and the police (St. Louis et al. 2019, p. 307). The high number of incidents involving the use of force, especially with black and Hispanic people, motivated the development of the Task Force on Policing in the 21st Century. Its aim is generating solutions and recommendations to face this problem (Lum et al. 2019, p. 95). By the year 2020, more than half of the police agencies in the country already used BWC, encouraged by the Task Force (Nix et al. 2020, p. 398).

The implementation of BWC is an innovation by the State to demonstrate greater institutional control over its agents, deter bad behavior, and recover the prestige and legitimacy of the police before citizens (St. Louis et al. 2019). An empirical study by Hedberg, Katz, and Choate (2017), carried out with the police department in the city of Phoenix, Arizona, demonstrated the change in behavior of agents and civilians just with the implementation of the cameras. Police officers were required to activate their camera only in serious incidents. This led to a 62% reduction in complaints (Hedberg et al. 2017, p. 644). There is an even greater decrease in the use of force by the police when the activation of the recording by the cameras is automatic, not determined by the evaluation of the agent (Ariel et al. 2016).

In the Florida city of Orlando, body cams were observed to decrease the tendency for officers to use force, and complaints against officers (Jennings et al. 2015). Rankin (2013) identified the general downward trend in the use of force in the US after the implementation of BWC. However, the definition of "use of force" can change the analysis of this trend (Henstock and Ariel 2017, p. 739).

The reduction in arrests following the implementation of BWC is unproven. There is divergence in the identified results: certain studies indicate an increase in arrests, while others point to a decrease in arrests when police officers use BWC (Lum et al. 2019, p. 101). On the other hand, reports of domestic violence increase with the use of BWC. This is mainly due to the ease of obtaining evidence and the reduction in the number of victims who give up on pursuing complaints (Morrow et al. 2016; Katz et al. 2014). Mortality and crime rates, in turn, are impacted by facts unrelated to the behavior of the police or civilian. The impact of BWC on these rates is not known for sure (Lum et al. 2019, p. 109).

The adoption of technology has led to a general decline in civilian complaints against police, even from agents who did not use cameras – although lower from those who were using the tools (Lum et al. 2019, p. 95; Rankin 2013; Miller et al. 2014). The camera affects the officer's friendliness towards the civilian and vice versa. In addition, the police follow the technical protocols of action more rigorously, as they know that non-compliance with these rules will be recorded (Ariel 2016).

Despite the great expectations around BWC, there are experiences and arguments against their use. Incidents possibly resolved through dialogue, or with a simple warning by the police officer, are necessarily seen with greater severity (Hamilton-Smith et al. 2019). Decreased police discretion can be seen in opposition to the use of technology (Nowacki and Willits 2018, p. 849). Implementation costs, image storage, and threats to the privacy of civilians and police are challenges to the uptake of body cams (Guzik et al. 2021, p. 102). The possible discomfort and difficulty in using the camera is also a problem cited by police officers (Gaub et al. 2016, p. 286).

Despite negative scores about the cameras, there is strong support for their adherence. Prior to the implementation of the BWC, most agents advocated the use of technology across the US (Sousa et al. 2015). In Orlando, Florida, there was also support for the technology even before its use began (Jennings et al. 2014). After a year of BWC implementation, there was increased advocacy for the technology (Jennings et al. 2015). Police officers encouraged the adoption of the tool for officers who were not yet using it and understood that body cams improve their productivity, both in making reports and gathering evidence (Jennings et al. 2015).

In certain regions of the US, technology adoption is impacted both by police organizational factors (administration, interpersonal relationships, etc.) and by the community's violent crime rate (Nix et al. 2020, p. 401). The police officer's position on law enforcement efforts, administrative pressure for results, the police view on civilian cooperation in public security policy, and trust in citizens are also relevant to the agents' position in relation to the use of the body cam (Phillips et al. 2020).

In Brazil, the use of cameras is under discussion. By the year 2021, the states of Rondônia, São Paulo, and Santa Catarina were the most advanced in adopting the technology, carrying out the institutional implementation of the equipment in their Military Police (G1 2021). Prior to that, in 2012, the

Federal District carried out an experiment to adopt the technology with military police officers from ROTAM – *Rondas Ostensivas Táticas Motorizadas*, a special battalion of the district Military Police – (Agência Brasília 2012), but did not implement the technology. The state of Bahia also experimented with the technology at large events, from 2018 to 2020.

In the state of Rondônia, the use of the technology aims to "record evidentiary material regarding the criminal action of those involved and support the Justice in the evaluation of the use of force by law enforcement officers" (FRBL 2018). In São Paulo, until August 2021, there were 18 Military Police battalions using the technology. According to the State Legislative Assembly, the so-called COP – Portable Operational Cameras – "serve to protect security agents and the population, by preserving the transparency of operations" (São Paulo 2021). The state of Santa Catarina acquired 2,425 cameras and 130 were put into circulation in 2019.

According to the state government's advisory board, with the advent of technology, "the Military Police's actions and interactions with citizens during incidents will be filmed, helping to collect evidence in the act and preventing false accusations." (Santa Catarina 2019).

The Federal Highway Police still does not use body cam technology. Currently, the institution conducts studies on the feasibility of using technology (Brasil 2023b). The use of cameras emerged with the aim of restoring the relationship between police and civilians. The camera affects both the way an approach is conducted and the reaction of civilians to police commands, as well as the population's view of the institution and of the agent himself – which can be associated with the recognition of police legitimacy. Thus, with technology, it is expected to increase police legitimacy.

2 Legitimacy and procedural justice – ways to recover the relationship between civilians and police

The recognition of legitimacy is crucial for police action. As shown by Tyler (2006), people tend to obey the law when they recognize legitimacy in the authority that orders them. Acceptance of the police as an authority is more influenced by the behavior of agents than by the results of security policy. During an approach, the police officer needs to issue commands to the citizen. It is necessary to determine that the civilian stops the car, identifies himself, or delivers some document, for example. When the police officer approaches with cordial treatment, using transparent criteria in his decisions, and demonstrating respect for the citizen, the officer tends to obtain a better response from the person approached (Natal et al. 2016, p. 161).

The police officers' behaviors are related to the concept of procedural justice – the perception of the protocols adopted by the police officer during the interaction. It is through the recognition of legitimacy that obedience to the law occurs. Procedural justice, agent effectiveness, and moral similarity between civilians and police officers are important for the legitimacy of authority (Tyler 2006). Skogan and Riccio (2018, pp. 19–20) understand that legitimacy is related, first, to proper treatment by the police, the so-called procedural justice; second, with practices that reinforce equal treatment by the police to civil groups, reinforcing the belief that everyone responds to the same rules and is equal, the so-called "distributive justice"; and third, with police effectiveness in maintaining order and fighting crime (Skogan and Riccio 2018, pp. 19–20).

Tyler and Jackson (2014) highlight two factors as determinants for the recognition of police legitimacy: trust and normative alignment. The authors demonstrate that there is a correlation between people's adherence to the law and their view of the legitimacy of the police. The acceptance of police authority occurs due to the behavior of the public agent, his effectiveness in the role, and the existence of a moral alignment between the applied rule and the worldview of civilians (Tyler and Jackson 2014, p. 85).

In England and Wales, moral alignment between citizens and police has also been shown to be relevant to obedience to the law, as well as agent behavior and effectiveness (Jackson et al. 2012). It is important to highlight, on the other hand, that civilians with morality different from that of police officers do not tend to disobey the law more. Therefore, moral similarity can increase the legitimacy of the police, but the absence of these values, by itself, will not prevent the law from being followed (Jackson et al. 2012, p. 9). Although it does not constitute an obstacle to obeying the law, police, and civilians will have greater difficulty in relating when their values regarding a certain behavior are not common (Zanetic 2016). Moral alignment stands out and becomes perceptible to the citizen when the police offer respectful and correct treatment, concepts of procedural justice (Van Damme et al. 2013).

Bottoms and Tankebe (2012) demonstrate the impact of police effectiveness on building trust and civilian cooperation during an arrest. Civilians have greater difficulty conferring legitimacy on police whose effectiveness is not recognized (Bottoms and Tankebe 2012, p. 168). Police effectiveness is about the ability to keep communities safe. In places where there is a greater perception of crime, the need to fight crime, with recognition of greater police effectiveness, is seen as the most necessary factor for a good evaluation of the police (Skogan and Riccio 2018, p. 21). In São Paulo, it was found that among the reasons for trusting the police is the "ability to maintain tranquility in the streets" – a factor related to effectiveness. In this study, "education" – a factor related to procedural justice – was an even more important factor for trust in the police (Zanetic 2016, p. 11).

In order to have procedural justice, the authority's posture towards the civilian must follow four key factors: 1) civil participation, 2) dignity and respect, 3) neutrality, and 4) motivation (Mezerolle et al. 2013, p. 35). Procedural justice approaches tend to generate positive civilian perceptions of the police. Confidence that there will be procedural justice leads to greater civilian cooperation with the police (Van Damme et al. 2013, p. 15)

The recognition of legitimacy is impacted by the social context of individuals (Antrobus et al. 2015). When members of a community perceive procedural justice in an approach, that community is more likely to obey the law. The greater variety of community ties increases the tendency to recognize police legitimacy, while people with more restricted community ties tend to confer less police legitimacy (Antrobus et al. 2015, p. 13).

Victimization experiences also affect the perception and impact of procedural justice. People who have experienced criminal victimization prior to a police approach gain relatively greater trust in police officers compared to people who have not suffered crimes (Wolfe et al. 2016). The increase in confidence in police behavior with greater neutrality and equal treatment – what is conventionally called the "distributive effect" of procedural justice – is greater in people with a great fear of crime, or who live in disorderly communities (Wolfe et al. 2016, p. 24).

The impact caused by procedural justice is greater on people with previously positive perceptions of police treatment (Tyler and Jackson 2014, pp. 87–88). A positive experience with the police, with a procedure seen as fair, has lasting effects on the perception of those approached by the state agent (Mezerolle et al. 2013, p. 48). The use of procedural justice in the approach creates long-term effects on individual and community evaluation of the police (Tyler 2004, p. 92). By recognizing the procedural justice practiced by the agent, the citizen creates a future expectation of good treatment of the whole institution and starts to deposit confidence that the next action will also be correct, giving greater legitimacy to the police officers (Zanetic 2016, p. 5).

Confidence that there will be procedural justice leads to greater civilian cooperation with the police (Van Damme et al. 2013, p. 15). The police officer's decision-making process and the correctness of treatment are relevant to the recognition of authority legitimacy (Tyler and Jackson 2014). There is, therefore, a correlation between procedural justice and feelings of obedience and trust in the police (Wolfe et al. 2016, p. 18). Trust is more affected by the perception of procedural justice than the need for obedience (Wolfe et al. 2016, p. 27). Tom Tyler (2006) understands that legitimacy is impacted by the behavior of state agents. People obey voluntarily only when they confer legitimacy on the agent or the rule. When citizens do not grant legitimacy to police officers, violent enforcement becomes necessary for policing.

The absence of procedural justice results in difficulties in police work. When the stops do not have transparent criteria and the police are not controlled by the State, the population tends not to cooperate during the stops. This occurs due to distrust of agents (Hedberg et al. 2017, p. 628). Legitimacy, therefore, is capable of impacting law-abiding citizens. Authority behavior affects perceptions of moral alignment and police effectiveness. These factors, in turn, are also capable of making authority more legitimate.

Policing is directly affected by the way agents relate to citizens, as a greater perception of procedural justice is associated with increased trust, cooperation, and cordiality. When the relationship between police and civilians is positive, public safety tends to improve. In addition to the use of cameras, there are other state initiatives to reinforce this relationship, such as community policing methods. When the police approach the community, there is a tendency to improve the relationship between the groups.

3 The importance of the relationship with the community and the experiences of community policing in Brazil

The police have a strong institutional culture and tend to resist change (Campeau 2015, p. 3). Changing the relationship between police and civilians requires an institutional culture in tune with social advancement. Technological innovation is only effective when the police institution is in tune with technological progress. In the context of BWC adoption in Brazil, the evolution of policing methodologies is of particular importance. Community police experiences can be facilitated with the implementation of BWC technology, or even indicate ways to encourage adoption of the technology by police officers.

In the 1930s, the US police underwent several reforms. The changes were intended to eliminate political influences, professionalize agents and introduce principles of professional administration to police corporations (Batitucci 2011, p. 66). The use of technology was one of the flagships of this process, which resulted in the use of patrol cars, radios for internal communication, and telephones for public access. (Batitucci 2011, pp. 68–70). The professional model of policing began to be questioned in the 1970s, as there was no development in crime prevention (Skogan 2004, p. 17). In this context, community policing began to take shape. Crime prevention and problem-solving determine police priorities in this model.

Community policing aims at solutions to community issues not directly related to crime. With the confrontation of social ills, even if the reduction of crime did not occur, the fear of the population would decrease. Thus, the proximity of the police to the citizens is encouraged, as well as the implementation of technology to improve data analysis and also the integration of the police with other public sectors (Skogan 2004, p. 18).

Community policing is "a strategic organizational adaptation to a changing environment. [...] a blend of three new and interrelated organizational postures" (Skogan 2004, p. 23): decentralization, community engagement, and problem-solving. Decentralization would aim to reduce the existing bureaucracy, through the distribution of commands to localities, in order to improve community communication with the local police institution. Community engagement would occur by encouraging the formation of partnerships between the police and community groups, demonstrating a posture of collective construction and listening by the police to collectivities. Finally, and as a result of the distribution of corporations and the partnerships created, the police would be closer to local realities and would have a deeper understanding of existing social problems. Thus, the innovations of this policing method are crime prevention with community organizations; the encouragement of non-emergency State services; the deployment of policing; and public participation in policing (Mesquita Neto 2004).

There are six objectives to this method of policing: 1) to increase the importance of the community, aiming at greater police legitimacy by establishing a political base in the locality; 2) enhance the purposes of the police, including, in addition to maintaining order and combating crime, conflict resolution; 3) the decentralization of decisions, emphasizing the importance of the line police; 4) promotion of community relations; 5) focus on citizens' demands; and 6) new evaluation measures, with the objectives of reducing fear and popular satisfaction (Batitucci 2011, p. 88).

In Brazil, community policing focuses on problem-solving. In order to increase police legitimacy, it was necessary to deal with diverse social topics, from the institution of respect for human rights in militarized police forces to issues of health, cleanliness, and public lighting (Riccio et al. 2013). The first practices began in the 1980s. In 1983, the Military Police of Rio de Janeiro introduced community policing practices, producing literary content on the subject, aimed at military police officers, and inaugurating practical initiatives in the Copacabana neighborhood. In the 1990s, the state of São Paulo developed community policing projects and even carried out experiments in the cities of Bauru and Ribeirão Preto (Mesquita Neto 2004).

In the early 2000s, the Policing Group for Special Areas – GPAE (Grupamento de Policiamento de Áreas Especiais), a program carried out in the communities of Pavão Pavãozinho, in the city of Rio de Janeiro, was another experience inspired by the model of community policing. Police integration was GPAE's main objective. In addition, it sought to reduce access to firearms, keep young people away from crime and contain violence. Police officers began, right at the beginning of the program, to receive social demands other than those involving criminality, such as medical and educational assistance, as well as access to public institutions. GPAE was initially successful, managing to reduce the number of homicides in the community. However, with the expansion of the program, there was an increase in resistance from residents and the emergence of other problems, such as disorganization, political pressures, and excessive demands (Riccio et al. 2013).

Following the GPAE, there was the creation of the Pacifying Police Units (UPPs – Unidades de Polícia Pacificadora). The program operated in four stages: "intervention, stabilization, community policing and the consolidation of state authority" (Riccio and Skogan 2018). Another Brazilian program, also developed with the aim of strengthening the relationship between the police and the local population, including the presence of police in schools, is the State Drug Resistance Program – PROERD (Programa Estadual de Resistência as Drogas). According to the Ministry of Education, the program aims to keep young people away from involvement in drug trafficking and consists of a course "given by volunteer military police officers, pedagogically trained, in partnership with parents, teachers, students and communities" (Brasil 2010).

The aforementioned programs are examples of the presence of community policing principles in the Brazilian scenario. Among the objectives of community policing, there is the decentralization of policing, with an increase in the role of the base police, which generated antagonism from sectors at the top of the police hierarchy. In addition, the initiatives required large financial investments, a large police contingent and joint action with other agencies, which made it difficult for them to continue in times of cost contingency.

The main objective of community policing is to strengthen the communities themselves to face crime. In this scenario, the police organization needs to establish the proper structure and training for police officers. In addition, citizens need to be encouraged to interact with the police, report crimes and collaborate with agents. Trust and cooperation are fundamental for this method to be effective (Skogan and Riccio 2018, pp. 17–18).

Fostering public safety projects, demonstrating control over police agents, and providing social assistance are ways for the police to approach communities. These initiatives allow for the establishment of community ties. The use of cameras by police officers acts precisely in demonstrating that there is control over the agents, leading to increased cordiality and a positive relationship between the groups. It is through these practices that the police tend to obtain greater collaboration and approval from the civilian population. The use of cameras and community policing are directly related topics, as both aim to increase police legitimacy.

4 Research methodology

The hypothesis defended in this work is the existence of a positive correlation between the tendency of the PRFs to use the camera and the position regarding the relationship with the community. For this, a simple linear regression was performed on the variables "relationship with the community" and "support for the use of cameras". Data provided by the research project "Social Complexity and Police Action: An Analysis from the Federal Highway Police", carried out in partnership with UFJF (Universidade Federal de Juiz de Fora) professors and the National Academy of the Federal Highway Police will be used.

The researchers of the project "Social Complexity and Police Action" sent, via the Internet, between 2019 and 2020, a questionnaire to all police officers linked to the Brazilian PRF during the period. The themes of the questionnaire were the following: 1) Profile; 2) Violence, justice and criminality; 3) Relationship with the community; 4) Use of force; 5) The structure of the PRF; 6) The PRF and other public security institutions; 7) Appreciation of the Federal Highway Police; 8) Relationship with the media; and 9) Education and training at the PRF. These questions were based on the questionnaire developed by Skogan and colleagues (2015) for the Chicago Police. For the purposes of this research, they were translated into Portuguese.

The theme "Relationship with the community" is composed of nine questions. For the questions asked, the respondents indicated their degree of agreement with the proposed assertion, with the answers "I totally agree"; "I agree"; "I slightly agree"; "I disagree a little"; "I disagree"; or, "strongly disagree". The assertions presented in this theme were the following:

1. Citizens can be trusted most of the time.
2. It is naive to trust citizens.
3. Officers should not take time to listen the citizens' complaints about their problems.
4. Officers need to show interest in what people have to say, even if it is not going to change everything.
5. In certain areas of the city, it is more useful for an officer to be aggressive than courteous.
6. People who break the law do not deserve to be treated with respect.
7. In this job making judgments based on appearances is inevitable.
8. Explaining your decisions to the public is a waste of time.
9. How do you rate the cooperation of the police with citizens to solve problems?

The topic on supporting the use of cameras by police officers is in block n& 08, "The relationship between the media and the PRF". The questions that are of interest in this article are numbers 62 to 69. Question number 62 asks for the level of usefulness and brings the answer options "Very useful"; "useful"; "relatively useful"; "possibly useful"; "not very useful"; or, "completely useless"; the other questions of interest bring the degree of agreement of the respondent, with answers "totally agree"; "I agree"; "I slightly agree"; "I disagree a little"; "I disagree"; or, "strongly disagree". These are the assertions:

1. 62) The use of cameras attached to the police uniform
2. Does it have any kind of utility?
3. 63) The use of cameras attached to police uniforms reduces your authority.
4. 64) A fleeing suspect has less respect for a police officer with a camera attached to the uniform.
5. 65) The existence of cameras in vehicles reduces misconduct by the police.
6. 66) The use of cameras attached to the uniform reduces the violence of police officers.
7. 67) The popularization of surveillance cameras and smartphones facilitates proof of misconduct by the police.
8. 68) From the popularization of smartphones, the population began to frequently question the action of the police.
9. 69) The use of video serves to justify situations involving the use of force by the police.

For testing the hypothesis through linear regression, the questions of interest were selected and the answers were transformed into discrete numeric variables. By transforming the variables into numerical ones, they were organized in somatic scales and reconfigured to vary equally from 01 to 10. Testing the confidence in the correlation between the answers obtained in the questionnaires, using Cronbach's Alpha (1951), was a reality. Next, the value of Pearson's correlation, measured by r, will be identified. Also, the null hypothesis was tested through the analysis of the variance between the variables, the ANOVA (p). Finally, after carrying out all the previous tests, Hypothesis H1 was tested using the Determination Coefficient, represented by R^2. All these data will be verified by the statistical software IBM SPSS Statistics.

The questions of interest were selected to carry out the statistical analysis and were transformed into variables. In the theme of the relationship with the community, questions numbered 11, 12, 14, 15, 16 and 17 were selected. Questions numbered 10, 13 and 18 were discarded for bringing repeated themes. As for support for the use of cameras, questions 62 to 69 were selected, only question 68, whose topic is not pertinent, was excluded.

The frequencies of responses to the selected questions are shown in the tables below. Respondents' blank answers are indicated in the "NOA" option, an acronym in English for none of the answers. The indicated percentage excludes the disregarded responses from the total.

The distribution of responses in Table 7.1 deals with the relationship with the community. Among the respondents, 90.7% show considerable disagreement (indicating the responses of disagreement or total disagreement with the statement) that it is more useful for the police to be aggressive than courteous (question number 14). Only 3.6% agree to some extent with this idea. Of this same group, 79.4% strongly disagreed that the police should not "waste time" listening to complaints from civilians (question number 12). Still, 66.2% of the responding police strongly disagree that explaining their decisions is a "waste of time" (question number 17), a number that rises to 83% if we also consider the police officers who disagree a little with this assertion.

Table 7.2 also brings relevant data on the positioning of the respondents. For example, 75.4% consider the use of cameras to be very useful or useful. Furthermore, 77.1% of officers disagree or strongly disagree that the camera reduces their authority, while 73.4% disagree or strongly disagree that the camera negatively impacts a fleeing suspect. Still, 79.3% of respondents agree or strongly agree that the camera serves to facilitate proof of police misconduct and 78.3% agree or strongly agree that the video can justify situations involving the use of force. The answers indicate the high support of the respondents for the use of technology, as well as the recognition of its benefits in the production of evidence and in the relationship with civilians.

TABLE 7.1 Distribution of the 532 answers to the questions that make up the relationship with the community variable

Question/ Frequency	Strongly Agree	Somewhat Agree	Slightly Agree	Slightly Disagree	Somewhat Disagree	Strongly Disagree	NOA
11	13 (2.5%)	124 (23.4%)	141 (26.6%)	107 (20.2%)	127 (24%)	18 (3.4%)	02
12	03 (0.6%)	11 (2.1%)	35 (6.6%)	60 (11.3%)	284 (53.6%)	137 (25.8%)	02
14	01 (0.2%)	0 (0%)	18 (3.4%)	30 (5.7%)	244 (46%)	237 (44.7%)	02
15	01 (0.2%)	09 (1.7%)	24 (4.5%)	52 (9.8%)	276 (52.1%)	168 (31.7%)	02
16	34 (6.4%)	147 (27.8%)	159 (30.2%)	49 (9.2%)	113 (21.3%)	27 (5.1%)	02
17	03 (0.6%)	27 (5.1%)	60 (11.3%)	89 (16.8%)	271 (51.1%)	80 (15.1%)	02

Source: "Social Complexity and Police Action: An Analysis based on the Federal Highway Police"

After the construction of the tables, the sums of the answers about the relationship with the community can take the values from 06 to 36, while the sums of the answers about the support for the use of the cameras from 07 to 42. These values will be reprogrammed on a scale of 01 to 10, with higher values attributed to greater recognition of the relationship with the community and greater support for the use of cameras.

Then, the confidence test in the correlation between the answers obtained in the questionnaire is carried out. Cronbach's Alpha for the relationship with the community guarantees a confidence index of 0.6337048913. The confidence index, with Cronbach's Alpha, for supporting the use of cameras was 0.724683335. Calculations were provided by IBM SPSS Statistics and demonstrated considerable data reliability. Pearson's Correlation Coefficient, also identified through IBM SPSS Statistics, demonstrates that the value of r is 0.321. It is indicated that there is an average correlation between the variables, that is, they are directed in the same direction.

The null hypothesis (H0) serves to exclude the negative hypothesis, tested before the central hypothesis of the work. Contrary to what is sustained in H1, H0 argues that there is no correlation between the described variables. For testing H0, then, the analysis of variance between the variables (ANOVA) was performed. ANOVA is also provided through the equations performed by the IBM SPSS Statistics program. After analyzing this significance (ANOVA), with $p \leq 0.001$, H0 was rejected. The indication that the variables are unrelated is less than 0.001. With this, it is possible to proceed with the testing of H1.

The H1 test will be through the Determination Coefficient, represented by the R^2. The identification of R^2 is done by performing simple linear regression. Calculations were performed using the IBM SPSS Statistics program. On the Model Summary is the data provided by the program:

TABLE 7.2 Distribution of the 532 responses to the component questions of the support variable for using cameras

Categories/ Question	Very useful	Somewhat useful	Slightly useful	Eventually useful	Little useful	Completely useless	NOA
62	235 (44.5%)	163 (30.9%)	64 (12.1%)	41 (7.8%)	16 (3%)	9 (1.7%)	04
Question/ Frequency	Strongly agree	Somewhat agree	Slightly agree	Slightly disagree	Somewhat disagree	Strongly agree	NOA
63	04 (0.8%)	14 (2.6%)	48 (9%)	55 (10.4%)	253 (47.8%)	155 (29.3%)	03

Categories/Question	Very useful	Somewhat useful	Slightly useful	Eventually useful	Little useful	Completely useless	NOA
64	09 (1.7%)	33 (6.3%)	42 (8%)	56 (10.6%)	241 (45.6%)	147 (27.6%)	04
65	94 (17.8%)	245 (46.5%)	101 (19.2%)	36 (6.8%)	40 (7.6%)	11 (2.1%)	05
66	56 (10.6%)	226 (42.9%)	141 (26.8%)	42 (7.9%)	50 (9.5%)	12 (2.3%)	05
67	112 (21.2%)	307 (58.1%)	81 (15.3%)	13 (2.5%)	13 (2.5%)	02 (0.4%)	04
69	108 (20.5%)	305 (57.8%)	80 (15.2%)	20 (3.8%)	15 (2.7%)	0 (0%)	04

Source: "Social Complexity and Police Action: An Analysis based on the Federal Highway Police"

TABLE 7.3 Model summary

Model	R	R^2	R^2 adjust	Estimation error pattern	Altered stats					Durbin-Watson
					R^2 alter.	F alter.	df1	df2	Sig. F alter	
1	.321☐	.103	.101	1.35821	.103	52.443	1	457	.000	1.949

Predictor: (Constant), Indicator of perception about the community relationship – general. B. Dependent variable: Support indicator on camera use – general

TABLE 7.4 ANOVA b

Model		Sum of squares	df	Mean square	F	Sig
1	Reg.	96.742	1	96.742	52.443	.000☐
	Res.	843.041	457	1.845		
	Total	939.784	458			

Predictor: (Constant), Indicator of perception about the importance of the relationship with the community – general. B. Dependent Variable: Indicator of perception about the use of cameras – general

In the analysis carried out, the result of simple linear regression, as shown in the models above, the correlation between the dependent variable (support for the use of cameras) and the independent variable, the predictor (relationship with the community), identifies $R^2 = 0.103$. This is a considerable correlation index. It is possible to state that 10.3% of the trend towards camera use is correlated with community policing.

TABLE 7.5 Coefficients

Model		Non-standard coefficients		Standardized coefficients	t	Sig	95.0% confidence interval for B	
		B	standard error	Beta			Inferior limit	Superior
1	Constant	4.877	.397		12.291	.000	4.097	5.657
	perception indicator about the importance of relationship with the community – general	.395	.054	.321	7.242	.000	.287	.502

Dependent variable: Indicator of perception about the use of cameras – general

5 Discussion

Simple linear regression indicates, by the coefficient of determination (R^2), that 10.3% of the PRFs' support for the use of body cams is related to the agents' favorable attitude towards the community. This data is important for the correct implementation of the technology, the formation and training of agents, and the elaboration of public security policies.

The implementation of technology aims to achieve institutional control and reduce the negative behavior of agents. However, greater state control over agents may indicate that the police organization does not trust its members. The behavior of police officers towards citizens is affected by their relationship with the administration. Hedberg et al. (2017), demonstrates that the concept of procedural justice exists both externally to the corporation (aimed at civilians) and internally (designed for police officers). The police organization achieves greater internal procedural justice when its processes are conducted more transparently, which makes the results more understandable and acceptable by the police officers involved (Hedberg et al. 2017, p. 630). In the event of adherence to technology without considering the positions of the police, the organization will be adopting a posture of opposition to procedural justice.

A change in police prerogatives and discretion, decided without the participation of agents, does not seem to be a transparent decision. The component factors of procedural justice, therefore, will be shaken. This could impact the police officer's assessment of the use of cameras. If police agents' behavior towards civilians is undermined, the goals of the technology will be compromised. The police's internal culture can be an obstacle, not only to the adoption of BWC but to the development of the expected benefits of the technology (Hedberg et al. 2017, p. 629).

In the community policing model, the police need to develop ties with the community and be willing to deal with problems of a non-criminal nature. In Brazil, this policing model is little implemented. The tendency towards militarization of the Brazilian police and the wide domain of territories by criminal factions imposes the need to exercise ostensive, combative and violent policing, which creates a challenge of legitimation to the police. As a rule, before exercising a healthy relationship with the population, policing in Brazil is focused on combating violent crime. In certain cases, it is up to the police to reverse, by force, the domination of territories by groups that challenge the state. This reality, naturally, tends to undermine police legitimacy, as it asserts the antagonism between civilians and the police and emphasizes police action through force.

All Brazilian police suffer from difficulty in relationships with the community. Community policing programs face civil and police resistance. Information on the correlation between support for body cam use and community relations is relevant. The PRF, an institution with a billionaire budget and more than 12,000 police officers is also impacted by the lack of police legitimacy. Also, because it is a large organization, with high complexity and organizational control, the institution tends to face difficulties in technological innovation (Nowacki and Willits 2018). Thus, for the technology to be well received in the institution and reach its potential, the organization needs to act appropriately on the agents. Fostering behaviors associated with supporting technology adoption can generate greater acceptance of BWC and facilitate the positive results of the tool. With this, the police will be able to use the body cam and get closer to the desired results, increasing their legitimacy before the population.

Note

1 Article 144 Brazilian Federal Constitution

References

Agência Brasília. 2012. Polícia Militar do DF adota tecnologia inédita no Brasil: Há uma semana, homens da Rotam testam o uso de microcâmeras nos uniformes para registrar as apreensões. Estratégia do Distrito Federal é pioneira [The Military Police of the DF adopts unprecedented technology in Brazil: A week ago, men from Rotam tested the use of micro-cameras on their uniforms to register apprehensions. Federal District Strategy is a Pioneer]. December 3. Retrieved from: https://www.agenciabrasilia.df.gov.br/2012/12/03/uso-de-cameras-em-operacoes-rotam-fotos/.

Antrobus, E.; Bradford, B.; Murphy, K. and Sargeant, E. 2015. Community norms, procedural justice, and the public's perceptions of police legitimacy. *Journal of Contemporary Criminal Justice*, 1–20. doi:10.1177/1043986214568840.

Ariel, B. 2016. Increasing cooperation with the police using body worn cameras. *Police Quarterly*, 19, 326–362.

Ariel, B.; Sutherland, A.; Henstock, D.; Young, J.; Drover, P.; Syker, J. and Henderson, R. 2016. Increases in police use of force in the presence of body-worn cameras are driven by officer discretion: A protocol-based subgroup analysis of ten randomized experiments. *Journal of Experimental Criminology*, 12, 453–463. doi:10.1007/s11292-016-9261-3.

Batitucci, E. 2011. A polícia em transição: O modelo profissional burocrático de policiamento e hipóteses sobre os limites da profissionalização das polícias brasileiras. [The police in transition: The professional bureaucratic model of policing and hypotheses about the limits of the professionalization of the Brazilian police]. *DILEMAS: Revista de Estudos de Conflito e Controle Social*, 4 (1), 65–96.

Bottoms, A. and Tankebe, J. 2012. Beyond procedural justice: A dialogic approach to legitimacy in criminal justice. *The Journal of Criminal Law and Criminology*, 102 (1), 119–170.

Brasil. 1988. *Constituição da República Federativa do Brasil de 1988* [Constitution of the Federative Republic of Brazil of 1988]. Congresso Nacional. October 05. Brasília, DF.

Brasil. 2010. Programa mostra a estudantes como ficar longe das drogas [Program shows students how to stay away from drugs]. Ministério da Educação. September 28. Retrieved from: http://portal.mec.gov.br/ultimas-noticias/211-218175739/15910-programa-mostra-a-estudantes-como-ficar-longe-das-drogas.

Brasil. 2023a. Órgãos que mais aplicam recursos na área de segurança pública e Maiores Favorecidos [Agencies that most apply resources in the area of public security and greater beneficiaries]. Portal da Transparência. March 26. Retrieved from: https://portaldatransparencia.gov.br/funcoes/06-seguranca-publica?ano=2022.

Brasil. 2023b. PRF desenvolverá estudo científico sobre o uso de câmeras corporais por seus agentes [PRF will develop a scientific study on the use of body cameras by its agents]. May 10. Retrieved from: https://www.gov.br/prf/pt-br/noticias/uniprf/2023/marco/prf-desenvolvera-estudo-cientifico-sobre-o-uso-de-cameras-corporais-por-seus-agentes.

Campeau, H. 2015. Police cultures at work: Making sense of police oversight. *British Journal of Criminology*. January, 55 (4). doi:10.1093/bjc/azu093.

Cronbach, L. 1951. Coefficient alpha and the internal structure of tests. *Psychometrika*, 16.

Deuchar, R.; Fallik, S. and Crichlow, V. 2018. Despondent officer narratives and the 'post-Ferguson' effect: Exploring law enforcement perspectives and strategies in a southern American state, *Policing and Society*. doi:10.1080/10439463.2018.1480020.

FRBL – Fundo de Reconstrução de Bens Lesados. 2018. Parecer 001/2018/FRBL [Advice 001/2018/FRBL] November 11. Retrieved from: https://arquivos.mpro.mp.br/docs/frbl/convenios/PARECER%20SPI%20-%20final%20Dr%20Shalimar.pdf.

G1. 2021. Veja como é a adoção de câmeras corporais da PM em cada estado: O Fantástico mostrou que a implementação de câmeras acopladas ao uniforme da polícia fez com que a letalidade nas ações caísse [See how the adoption of body cameras by the PM is in each state: Fantástico showed that the implementation of cameras attached to the police uniform caused the lethality in the actions to drop]. October 17. Retrieved from: https://g1.globo.com/fantastico/noticia/2021/10/17/veja-como-e-a-adocao-de-cameras-corporais-da-pm-em-cada-estado.ghtml.

Gaub, J.; Choate, D.; Todak, N.; Katz, C. and White, M. 2016. officer perceptions of body-worn cameras before and after deployment: A study of three departments. *Police Quarterly*, 19 (3), 275–302.

Guzik, K.; Sesay, A.; Oh, O.; Ramirez, R. and Tong, T. 2021. Making the material routine: A sociomaterial study of the relationship between police body worn cameras (BWCs) and organisational routines, *Policing and Society*, 31 (1), 100–115, doi:10.1080/10439463.2019.1705823.

Hamilton-Smith, N.; McBride, M. and Atkinson, C. 2019. Lights, camera, provocation? Exploring experiences of surveillance in the policing of Scottish football, *Policing and Society*. doi:10.1080/10439463.2019.1696800.

Hedberg, E.; Katz, C. and Choate, D. 2016. Body-worn cameras and citizen interactions with police officers: Estimating plausible effects given varying compliance levels. *Justice Quarterly*. Advance online publication. doi:10.1080/07418825.2016.1198825.

Henstock, D. and Ariel, B. 2017. Testing the effects of police body-worn cameras on use of force during arrests: A randomised controlled trial in a large British police force. *European Journal of Criminology*, 14 (6), 720–750.

Jackson, J.; Bradford, B.; Hough, M.; Myhill, A.; Quinton, P. and Tyler, T. 2012. Why do people comply with the law? Legitimacy and influence of legal institutions. *British Journal of Criminology*, 1–21. doi:10.1093/bjc/azs032.

Jennings, W.; Fridell, L. and Lynch, M. 2014. Cops and cameras: Officer perceptions of the use of body-worn cameras in law enforcement. *Journal of Criminal Justice*, 42, 549–556.

Jennings, W.; Lynch, M. and Fridell, L. 2015. Evaluating the impact of police officer body-worn cameras (BWCs) on response-to-resistance and serious external complaints: Evidence from the Orlando police department (OPD) experience utilizing a randomized controlled experiment. *Journal of Criminal Justice*, 43, 480–486.

Katz, C.; Choate, D.; Ready, J. and Nuño, L. 2014. *Evaluating the impact of officer worn body cameras in the Phoenix Police Department*. Phoenix, AZ: Center for Violence Prevention & Community Safety, Arizona State University.

Lum, C.; Stoltz, M.; Koper, C. and Scherer, J. 2019. Research on body-worn cameras: what we know, what we need to know. *Criminology and Public Policy*, 18 (1), 93–118. doi:10.1111/1745-9133.12412.

Mesquita Neto, P. 2004. Policiamento comunitário e prevenção do crime: a visão dos coronéis da Polícia Militar [Community policing and crime prevention: the view of military police colonels]. *São Paulo em Perspectiva*, 18 (1), 103–110.

Mezerolle, L.; Antrobus, E.; Bennet, S. and Tyler, T. 2013. The Queensland Community Engagement Trial, (QCET): An overview of key findings. American Society of Criminology. *Criminology*, 51 (1). doi:10.1111/j.1745-9125.2012.00289.

Miller, L.; Toliver, J. and Forum, P. 2014. *Implementing a body-worn camera program: Recommendations and lessons learned*. Washington, DC: Office of Community Oriented Policing Services.

Morrow, W.; Katz, C., and Choate, D. 2016. Assessing the impact of police body-worn cameras on arresting, prosecuting, and convicting suspects of intimate partner violence. *Police Quarterly*, 19, 303–325.

Natal, A.; Oliveira, T.; Paes Manso, B. and Zanetic, A. 2016. Legitimidade da polícia: segurança pública para além da dissuasão [Police legitimacy: public security beyond deterrence]. *Civitas – Revista de Ciências Sociais*, 16 (4), 148–173.

New York Times. 2020. No charges for Ferguson officer who killed Michael Brown, new prosecutor says. July 30. Retrieved from: https://www.nytimes.com/2020/07/30/us/michael-brown-darren-wilson-ferguson.html.

Nix, J.; Todak, N. and Tregle, B. 2020. Understanding body-worn camera diffusion in U.S. policing. *Police Quarterly*, 23 (3).

Nowacki, J. and Willits, D. 2018. Adoption of body cameras by United States police agencies: An organisational analysis, *Policing and Society*, 28 (7), 841–853, doi:10.1080/10439463.2016.1267175.

Phillips, S; Kim, D. and Gramaglia, J. 2020. The impact of general police officer outlooks on their attitudes toward body-worn cameras. *Policing: An International Journal*, 3, 451–467. doi:10.1108/PIJPSM-10-2019-0163.

Rankin, H. 2013. *End of program evaluation and recommendations: On-officer body camera system*. Mesa, AZ: Mesa Police Department.

Riccio, V. and Skogan, W. 2018. Gangs, drugs and urban pacification squads in Rio, 135–150. In: Riccio, V. and Skogan, W. *Police and Society in Brazil*. New York: Taylor & Francis, Routledge. ISBN: [978-971-4987-6903-7].

Riccio, V.; Ruediger, M.; Ross, S. and Skogan, W. 2013. Community policing in the Favelas of Rio de Janeiro. *Police Practice and Research: An International Journal*, 14 (4), 308–318. http://dx.doi.org/10.1080/15614263.2013.816494.

Riccio, V.; Souza, A.; Magrone, E.; Vieira, M. and Rezende, W. 2023. Uso de câmeras e justiça procedimental: uma análise a partir da polícia rodoviária federal brasileira [Use of cameras and procedural justice: an analysis based on the federal brazilian highway police]. *Revista de Estudos Empíricos em Direito*, 10. doi:10.19092/reed.v10.785.

Santa Catarina. 2019. Câmeras individuais passam a integrar serviço da Polícia Militar de Santa Catarina [Individual cameras become part of the service of the Military Police of Santa Catarina]. July 22. Retrieved from: https://www.sc.gov.br/index.php/noticias/temas/seguranca-publica/cameras-individuais-passam-a-integrar-servico-da-policia-militar-de-santa-catarina.

São Paulo. 2021. Parlamentares da Assembleia Legislativa de São Paulo debatem uso de câmeras portáteis por policiais militares: Durante sessão extraordinária, deputados propuseram convite ao coronel responsável pelos estudos das câmeras [Parliamentarians of the Legislative Assembly of São Paulo debate the use of portable cameras by military police: During an extraordinary session, deputies proposed an invitation to the colonel responsible for studying the cameras]. By Daniele Oliveira and Matheus Batista. August 04. Retrieved from: https://www.al.sp.gov.br/noticia/?id=425726.

Skogan, W. 2004. *Community Policing – Can it work?*Thomson Wadsworth.

Skogan, W. and Riccio, V. 2018. Police and Society in Brazil, 1–25. In: Riccio, V. and Skogan, W. *Police and Society in Brazil*. New York: Taylor & Francis, Routledge. ISBN: [978-971-4987-6903-7].

Skogan, W.G.; Van Craen, M. and Cari, L.H., 2015. Training police for Procedural Justice. *Journal of Experimental Criminology*, 11 (3), 319–334.

Sousa, W.; Miethe, T. and Sakiyama, M. 2015. *Body worn cameras on police: Results from a national survey of public attitudes* (Research in brief). University of Nevada, Las Vegas: Center for Crime and Justice Policy.

St. Louis, E.; Saulnier, A and Walby, K. 2019. Police use of body-worn cameras: Challenges of visibility, procedural justice, and legitimacy. *Surveillance & Society*,

17 (3/4), 305–321. https://ojs.library.queensu.ca/index.php/surveillance-and-society/index | ISSN: 1477-7487.

Tyler, T. 2004. Enhacing police legitimacy. *The Annals of the American Academy of Political and Social Science*, 593, 84–99.

Tyler, T. 2006. *Why do people obey the law*. 2nd ed. Princeton, NJ: Princeton University Press.

Tyler, T. and Jackson, J. 2014Popular legitimacy and the exercise of legal authority: Motivating compliance, cooperation, and engagement. *Psychology, Public Policy, and Law*, 20 (1), 78–95. doi:10.1037/a0034514.

USA – United States of America. 2015. *President's Task Force on 21st Century Policing: Final report of the President's task force on 21st century policing*. Washington, DC: Office of Community Oriented Policing Services.

Van Damme, A.; Pauwels, L. and Svensson, R. 2013. Why do Swedes cooperate with the police? A SEM analysis of Tyler's Procedural Justice Model. *European Journal on Criminal Policy and Research*. Springer Science and Business Media Dordrecht. doi:10.1007/s10610-013-9224-4.

Wolfe, S.; Nix, J.; Kaminski, R. and Rojek, J. 2016. Is the effect of procedural justice on police legitimacy invariant? Testing the generality of procedural justice and competing antecedents of legitimacy. *Journal of Quantitative Criminology*, 32 (2), 253–282.

Zanetic, A. 2016. Ação institucional, confiança na polícia e legitimidade em São Paulo [Institutional action, trust in the police and legitimacy in São Paulo]. *Revista Brasileira de Ciências Sociais*, 32 (95), 1–19.

8

OFFICER SUICIDE

Agency protocol and prevention strategies

Charles W. Russo, Jarrod Sadulski and Matthew Loux

Family safety

Support networks and families are vital in preventing suicide amongst law enforcement officers (U.S. Department of Justice COPS, 2021). Officers are exposed to many potential dangers on the job. Still, they may not recognize related risks such as exposure to environmental hazards, traumatic events, and critical incidents (U.S. Department of Justice COPS, 2021). A survey by Mills et al. (2020) found that law enforcement's repeated exposure to trauma and dangers created an environment where officers are more likely to experience suicidal thoughts. Mills et al. also found that law enforcement survey participants who experienced traumatic reactions in three to five incidents were two times more likely to have suicidal thoughts. Because of the exposure to critical incidents and other dangers, officers must seek help, but they are often reluctant to do so.

Law enforcement officers who have suicidal thoughts are reluctant to seek help because of agency culture barriers, including changes in employment status and prospects for future promotion, as well as a fear of stigmatization and isolation (Barton, 2019; Donnelly et al., 2015; Collins & Genovese, 2020). In law enforcement, it is a frequent misconception that those who ask for assistance are weak. The typical belief is that law enforcement officers are conservative, masculine, cynical, isolated from the community and loyal to other officers (Burns & Buchanan, 2020). Burns and Buchanan also point to officer training that promotes courage, control, and strength which can conflict with officers seeking help and engender the belief that they are weak

DOI: 10.4324/9781003452379-9

if they seek assistance. Police officers usually fear their agency may find out if they seek assistance from a psychology service or employee assistance program (EAP). Officers fear being passed up for promotions or receiving other stigmatizations for reaching out for help. Unfortunately, this leads many officers not to get help, and as chronic stress builds through handling consistent traumatic events in the field, the stress can lead to suicidal ideation as indicated in the study by Mills et al.

Police family members may be hesitant to ask for help or guidance from the officer's agency because of the police culture in circumstances where they suspect the family member (officer) may show signs of depression, self-medication, or other indicators. It may be an unsafe environment. The family's reluctance to seek assistance or help can result in those in close contact with the officer being in a dangerous environment with the potential for lasting psychological distress. A family member perceiving the officer as not handling the stress and attempting to speak with the officer, is just one of those potentially dangerous situations that can lead to an adverse reaction from the officer. The culture of policing tends to promote an image in an officer's mind that weakness cannot be displayed. Burns & Buchanan (2020) add that the perception or stigma of being incompetent or weak may imply to others that they may not be fit for duty or career advancement can impact their willingness to seek help. An officer in psychological distress and approached by a family member may lead to the officer becoming angry and defensive towards that family member and even lead to family violence.

The American Psychological Association (n.d.) defines psychological distress as:

> A set of painful mental and physical symptoms that are associated with normal fluctuations of mood in most people. In some cases, however, psychological distress may indicate the beginning of major depressive disorder, anxiety disorder, schizophrenia, somatization disorder, or a variety of other clinical conditions. It is thought to be what is assessed by many putative self-report measures of depression and anxiety.

The emotional and mental safety of family members is also vital. According to Aiken (2010), someone with a mental illness (diagnosed or undiagnosed), causes stressors that impact the welfare and lives of family members negatively (pp. 132–151). Cohen et al., 2011 identify specific stressors such as lack of communication and career support, absenteeism, reduced family cohesion, need to sacrifice, and limited care options. According to Iseselo et al. (2016) family members have a burden of caring for those with mental illness. Iseselo identified that psychosocial problems of those with mental illness could cause a decrease in the quality of life (QOL) of the person and their family, such as an increase in social distance. Iseselo et al. identified themes such as disruptive family function, stigmas, lack of support, financial constraints, and disruptive behavior. Officers who do not manage cumulative law enforcement stress are at risk of bringing violence into their homes.

Cohen et al. (2011) interviewed family members who cite acute and chronic stress because of living with someone with a mental illness (diagnosed or undiagnosed). Those interviewed by Cohen's research team said that there was a lack of understanding of their situation and thus, there was reduced social support and interactions for what they were experiencing. Those interviewed also said they were not able to express experiences and concerns about their situation which caused stress and impacted their mental health negatively. Iseselo and colleagues point out that psychiatric professionals see family members as a support network and can act as "co-therapists" (para. 10). Iseselo notes that those with mental illness can create a burden on family members that may result in family members being critical of the family member with mental illness and may lead to a relapse in the mental illness.

Individuals living and supporting someone with a mental illness (diagnosed and undiagnosed) frequently mentioned sacrifice in their lived experiences. Individuals living and supporting someone with a mental illness often place their lives "on hold" to assist them, resulting in fewer activities and hobbies, careers, and other pursuits (Cohen et al., 2011). Siddiqui and Khalid (2019) found that the longer the span of the illness, the more burden put on caregivers and the higher the number of hours caregivers provide to those with mental illness.

Concerning emotional safety, research shows that family members including children of those with mental illness, are at risk of diminished mental well-being. Dharampal and Ani (2020) found that young caregivers have a higher risk of mortality and mental health issues when the person they are taking care of has a mental illness or abuses substances. Psychological distress of family members can lead to neurological difficulties if the mental health of the officer is left untreated (Mathew et al., 2016; Bunston et al., 2017). There need to be steps taken to help untreated officers in destress as well as their family members, especially for their physical and mental well-being.

Addressing firearms

A firearm is a tool and, in the trained hands of an officer, this tool can be very effective in accomplishing a task. Unfortunately, in discussing law enforcement suicide, this is definitely the case of a firearm being an effective tool. A firearm, whether loaded with a duty round or blanks, can bring about a fatality (Zdravkovic et al., 2009).

Among the general population, 85% of suicide attempts with a firearm end in death (Drexler, 2013). The Educational Fund to Stop Gun Violence (2021) notes that three in five gun deaths relate to suicides and in 2019, there were 23,941 deaths by firearm suicide in the U.S. Suicide by firearm has been increasing with a 12.5% increase between 2010–2019 (Educational Fund to Stop Gun Violence, 2021). Police officers training incudes firearms proficiency and efficiency in neutralizing a threat (Reaves, 2016; Orange County Sheriff's Office, 2020). Because of the extensive firearms training of police officers, it can be assumed that law enforcement suicide rates with a firearm result in more deaths.

The Israeli Defense Force was able to reduce its suicide rate among young soldiers by requiring soldiers to leave firearms secured on base when not on duty (Ramchand et al., 2019). There is often an expectation for officers to carry a firearm on-duty and it is cited in most police department policies, but also often extends to off-duty carrying of a firearm. There are potential limitations to carrying a firearm off-duty in situations such as consuming alcohol or participating in a sporting event (Orange County Sheriff's Office, 2020; Palo Alto Police Department, 2019). Based on policies allowing off-duty carrying of a firearm, it is not practical to require officers to secure firearms at the department at the end of a shift. Thus, whether on or off-duty, officers will always have access to a firearm. A firearm is a convenient tool for officers who may have impulsive suicidal thoughts.

Can effective steps be taken to keep that firearm out of the law enforcement officer's hand if and when impulsive thoughts of suicide form? Although various tools are available to safeguard a firearm for law enforcement at their residences, such as safes and lockboxes, this typically just adds one or two extra steps to the officer's attempt to retrieve the firearm. When the policeman is not on duty and not at their residence, there are typically no further barriers restricting an officer's access to a firearm when suicidal thoughts arise on the spur of the moment.

An officer's well-being is the most valuable means to try and prevent officers from using firearms to commit suicide. It must be stressed that ensuring a police officer's positive mental well-being and mental health is the best proactive method in preventing officer suicide. Some methods to focus on mental well-being include chaplain services, EAP, peer support, psychiatrist or psychologist support, and promoting self-awareness (Ramchand et al., 2019).

Domestic violence issues

Domestic violence is a serious problem in law enforcement families (Anderson & Lo, 2011; Ávila, 2015; Klinoff et al., 2015). There are links between law enforcement culture and domestic violence issues. In general, domestic violence rates amongst police officers are higher than in the general public (Ammons, 2005; Cheema, 2016). According to Klugman (2020) studies found that a minimum of 40% of law enforcement families experience domestic violence compared to 10% of the general population.

Aspects of the law enforcement culture, like authoritarianism and exhaustion, have fueled domestic violence. This association has been explained by the development of internalized elevated stress levels and the adoption of a crime-fighting mindset (being in charge at work, demanding compliance, and being able to employ force) (Blumenstein et al., 2011; Stinson & Liederbach, 2012). Domestic troubles were noted in 34 cases of the 2018 data set, which can be attributed to someone having suicidal tendencies or thoughts, a crime-fighting mentality, and heightened stress (Johnson, 2022).

In a study of officers responding to officer-involved domestic violence calls, Saunders et al. (2016) identified recommendations by responding officers including employee assistance programs and/or counseling. Officers are hesitant to seek EAP assistance for fear of adverse career implications (Barton, 2019; Donnelly et al., 2015; Collins & Genovese, 2020). The fear of adverse career implications reduces an officer's willingness to seek assistance to remediate the issue(s) that led to the incident. If not treated, additional strain on relationships and families can result.

Victims of officer domestic violence are also less likely to report incidents of abuse to law enforcement. There is an inherent fear that the offending officer would not be arrested, the incident be "covered up", the inability to escape the circumstances as there is nowhere to turn for help or potential retribution (Ammons, 2005). There is substantial strain in families and relationships involving officer-involved domestic violence cases because either the officer is hesitant to seek help or the victim reluctant to report the incident. In the 2018 officer suicide data set, Johnson (2022) found that in almost 11% of the instances, a homicide had occurred before the suicide. In three additional cases, a great bodily injury attempt had been made before the suicide (Johnson, 2022).

The relationship between drinking or substance abuse and domestic violence seen in the general public also applies to law enforcement (Cheema, 2016). In addition to substance and alcohol abuse, an officer's frequent experiences on the job of violence and the outcome of that violence can add to the effect of an increased likelihood of domestic violence at home in their own families or relationships (Cheema, 2016; Stinson & Liederbach, 2012). Of the officers arrested for domestic violence-related offenses, approximately one-third resigned or were terminated but almost 50% of officers arrested and convicted of domestic violence related offenses left their department (Stinson & Liederbach, 2012).

Mennicke and Ropes (2016) advocated for the creation of specific resources for use by law enforcement personnel as well as those who have experienced domestic abuse. These resources would allow everyone involved to seek help without immediately triggering a formal law enforcement investigation, such as an EAP. Cheema (2016) said that by using EAP rather than a formal investigation may "open the door" to addressing other issues such as suicidal tendencies or mental illness. Using EAP instead of a formal internal investigation would require a change in the law in many states as there is mandatory reporting to and by law enforcement agencies (Durborow et al., 2010). Another potentially negative image of using EAP rather than a formal investigation may give the perception of preferential treatment to law enforcement by the community.

Police officers experience traumatic and hazardous incidents at work that can cause stress resulting in physical aggression and the potential for violence at home (Anderson & Lo, 2011; Lambert et al., 2017). Increased emotions and deviant behavior that can lead to incidents of intimate partner violence because of officer stress (Anderson & Lo, 2011). Domestic violence in police families shows a need for support from prevention programs and a need for coping strategies (Anderson & Lo, 2011; Klinoff et al., 2015).

Induced stress off the job can be the result of police stress that can negatively impact an officer's relationships (Clark-Miller, & Brady, 2013; Gul & Delıce, 2011; Karaffa et al., 2015). Conflict can be the result of police officer stress that creates challenges in keeping positive emotions in police-family relationships (Karaffa et al., 2015; Roberts et al., 2013). Carrying stress from the job into their private lives and relationships can cause problems for the officer and their families which further solidifies the need for stress management to keep stress at work (Gul & Delıce, 2011; Karaffa et al., 2015). Queirós et al. (2020) note that policing is stressful and highlight the need for coping strategies as their study found that over 87% of officers have high occupational and organizational stress, with over 53% of officers showing low coping resiliency. Officers need to keep the characteristics and attributes of policing on the job to help manage or reduce officer stress.

Karaffa et al. (2015) looked at issues that exist in law enforcement marriages as a result of the stress that officers go through throughout their jobs. Although spouses frequently express pleasure in their relationship with a law enforcement official, several factors negatively affect police enforcement, including financial difficulties, trauma experienced by officers while on duty, and poor public perceptions (Karaffa et al., 2015). Emotional weariness is brought on by dealing with two main stresses in law enforcement marriages which include everyday trauma on the job and work–family conflict (Gul & Delıce, 2011; Karaffa et al., 2015). Support from someone else, such as assistance from family and friends, as well as open communication within the partnership, are crucial elements in addressing how law enforcement stress affects officer marriages (Gul & Delice, 2011; Karaffa et al., 2015).

Kunst et al. (2017) conducted a study concerning secondary traumatic stress (STS) and secondary posttraumatic growth (SPG) in Dutch liaison officers. Kunst et al. found a small correlation between risks such as personal trauma history, age, experience, and support from others and STS and SPG. Kunst et al. noted that some stressors of traumatic events can lead to negative life events. Exposure, whether direct or indirect, witnessing others' exposure or even learning of a close relative or friend's exposure to trauma can cause stress. This stress can therefore negatively impact the relationships between the officer and their family.

Stress from the job can increase the risk of divorce for police officers (Galatzer-Levy et al., 2013; Gul & Delice, 2011). Police officers also have a higher risk of divorce than other jobs that can be related to the high stress performing officer duties (Russell, 2014). Shift work, long hours, conflict between work and family roles, and perceived changes in the officer's personality between work and home are factors that have an adverse impact on officer marriages (Karaffa et al., 2015). Sleep patterns can have a negative impact on officers as shift work is often used to provide proper coverage. Working several shifts and long hours can cause stress at home because officers frequently struggle to acquire time off for family functions (Sadulski, 2017). Officers must constantly be ready to protect themselves and act promptly when on duty. When police are not on duty, it can be difficult for them to adjust their perspective, which can cause tension to build up and issues at home (Sadulski, 2017). To spend time with their family when their shifts are over, officers need to make a conscious decision to put work responsibility aside. Officers tend to be analytical and assertive while working to stay safe, which could lead to tension at home. High levels of aggressive behavior and reduced affection are linked to divorce rates in policing (Roberts et al., 2013).

A supervisor must deal with scenarios where an officer encounters a challenging situation that causes stress before the end of a shift. When a traumatic event occurs, such as a serious child accident, a violent crime scene, or mass killings, leadership must address cops who are under stress. An organization should consider setting up a peer-support structure where certain officers are assigned to assist other police who have gone through a traumatic occurrence (Sadulski, 2017). The International Association of Chiefs of Police (IACP) (2019) said that almost 90% of respondents to a 2018 police officer survey would recommend peer support as being helpful, and 80% said they would ask for support again from peers. The IACP also noted that over 50% of respondents who used peer-support services found their personal life was improved and they performed their job better.

Communication with peer officers privately about an incident should be available to all officers. There is less likely to be conflict in the officer's home life if the stress is managed before the shift ends. Spouses must also gain a deeper understanding of these issues through communication and literature. Spouses can provide further support for officers and can foster support by allowing the officer to talk as much or as little about the traumatic events they experience. A law enforcement support network can be valuable to their families. One idea that can be beneficial is to provide care for children so an officer and the officer's spouse can spend time together. Improving police–family relationships by having alone time with significant others or spouses is often overlooked, but this quality time could strengthen police families. The peer support network that can include those who faced similar experiences or challenges can relate to the challenges of coping as a police family.

There are more strategies to lessen the negative effects of law enforcement tension on a marriage. When they are not on duty, officers should strive to keep a separate identity. This can be achieved by taking up hobbies or engaging in extracurricular pursuits unrelated to law enforcement. Officers can lessen the stress of constantly feeling like they are working by having a different life and identity from the police. While getting to know other law enforcement families can be helpful, it is equally crucial to maintain relationships with couples who are not in law enforcement and have other occupations. This is useful because spouses and officers can both gain from learning conflict resolution techniques and outlooks on life that are unrelated to the attitude of a law enforcement officer. Additionally, agencies play a significant role in fostering officer marriages (Sadulski, 2017). While it can be helpful to provide literature and information to law enforcement spouses to help them better understand the stressors that are typical in their line of work, agencies can also provide counseling and support services to spouses who are going through secondary trauma because of what their spouse is going through in the field. Counseling options for individuals and couples might be beneficial for police enforcement families.

Within a law enforcement family, the likelihood of domestic violence might also be increased by spousal stress. Media criticism of the officer's actions, an apparent increase in violence against law enforcement officers that puts their spouse in danger, and the worry of the constant hazards their officer spouse encounters while on duty can all lead to spousal stress. One of the best ways for partners to relieve stress and family tension is through communication (Sadulski, 2018). When an officer's personal life has become tense on its own, one might assume this will carry over to increase the stress associated with police work. Instead, stress should be addressed in law enforcement marriages so that both partners may take action to cope with it (Sadulski, 2018).

Substance use and abuse

Johnson's (2022) study of 108 officer suicide cases analyzed from 2018 data showed that 13 indicated evidence of substance abuse. Many people have questioned the relationship between substance misuse and suicide. Since the middle of the 1960s, numerous investigations have shown linkages. However, these phenomena have various components that have been shown to contribute to both (Pompili et al., 2010).

The nature of the profession, events, and incidents encountered, combined with the closed law enforcement culture, influence law enforcement officers' need to self-medicate with alcohol and other substances to cope and relax. Substance abuse is estimated to involve 25% of the law enforcement population (Ballenger et al., 2010), compared to only an estimation of under 10% for the general population (Ballenger et al., 2010). If not addressed, pressures can lead to substance misuse and addiction, post-traumatic stress disorder (PTSD), other physical and mental health conditions, injuries, and diseases.

According to Brunault et al. (2019), PTSD is a significant predictor of substance abuse, particularly alcohol consumption. They contend that the drug's qualities help the user deal with PTSD symptoms because PTSD was discovered to exist prior to substance misuse. Due to the nature of their work, law enforcement personnel are frequently exposed to situations and occurrences that could result in PTSD (Russo & Hunziker, 2019). Post-traumatic stress disorder (PTS) affects 20–25% of all first responders (All Clear Foundation, 2020). An officer who has been through traumatic situations in the field may experience vivid flashbacks brought on by dreams. This could serve as a red flag to spouses that the cop is exhibiting PTSD symptoms. Other signs include self-destructive behaviors, extreme attentiveness, and various anxiety states, as well as when officers exhibit severe distress when confronted with real or imagined recollections of the trauma they had suffered on the job.

Alcohol misuse is the most prevalent substance abuse in the world (Pompili et al., 2010). When compared to social drinkers, heavy alcohol users are said to have a five times higher risk of suicide (Pompili et al., 2010). Connections are showing that roughly 40% of people seeking treatment for alcohol misuse or use had tried suicide at least once (Pompili et al., 2010). Alcohol was found in the blood of around 30% of American suicide victims (Pompili et al., 2010).

Substance abuse or use may play a role in someone's decision to terminate their life in various ways. The usage of drugs may help the person feel less anxious about performing the act. According to Pompili et al. (2010), alcohol may also be used to make a person less sensitive to the pain of the act and/or to give them the courage to carry it out.

Those close to someone who struggles with substance misuse may notice warning signs that point to suicide or a suicide attempt. One of these early warning signs might be someone breaking up important relationships. Unfortunately, folks close to a substance abuser frequently do not take suicide signals or threats seriously (Wolk-Wasserman, 1986). There may also be a sense of relief in the activities of the person who has decided to commit suicide since they have given up on the stressors burdening them. To family and friends, it may seem that the officer is handling stress better, but in truth, they may be preparing to commit suicide. Even the notion that circumstances have improved or that the officer is no longer in danger may be present. Despite being in a horrible situation, they suddenly seem like their former selves. This is a major red flag that must be handled right away. There are instances where a person has accepted their decision to terminate their life and now presents as calm or "normal." They are now content with their choice and feel more comfortable. Suicidal ideation warning signs need to be recognized and handled.

Injuries are another frequent aspect of policing that can cause an officer to take drugs. Injured officers may be prescribed a strong pain reliever, such as an opioid. The addictive potential of opioids like oxycodone, hydrocodone, and fentanyl is substantial. When the prescription runs out and a reliance has set in, the problem arises for the police. This might put cops at a higher risk of looking for illegal means to obtain the medication or it can lead to the officer abusing another drug, such as alcohol, to cope with stress and discomfort. Following an injury, officers should be regularly followed by their doctor and family members to ensure the medication is taken as directed and is not overused. Officers should be allowed to seek treatment without fear of retaliation from the department or supervisors if they become drug dependent or have a drug issue as a result of properly prescribed painkillers (Schlosser & McAleer, n.d.). McAleer and Schlosser (n.d.) identify opioid use as a national health crisis with 2015 statistics showing 52,000 deaths from drug overdoses and over 32,000 overdose deaths from prescription pain relievers and heroin. McAleer and Schlosser said that police officers are on the front lines of the crisis. However, little attention is given to the potential for officers to develop an opioid use disorder. Law enforcement is prone to developing a substance abuse disorder more than the average population because of the risk factors law enforcement face, such as physical demands and injuries (McAleer & Schlosser, n.d.). McAleer and Schlosser continue to identify the potential pain officers may encounter from driving a patrol car for extended periods and wearing heavy equipment and a gun belt.

This environment should be utilized as a vehicle for suicide prevention efforts if people are encouraged to seek help for substance use and misuse.

Prevention rates of suicide among law enforcement professionals can be improved by establishing any suicidal signs, fostering tools to manage life, and cultivating methods to combat depression, substance use, and abuse treatment (Pompili et al., 2010).

Murder/suicide

A person is homicidal if they are suicidal. When learning how to cope with suicidal people, law enforcement cadets in the academy have heard this for years. Officers were told that if a person plans to kill themselves, an officer's life will not mean much if it gets in the way of them doing it (K. Duffy, personal communication, September 9, 2020). The concepts of cop suicide and an individual threatening an officer compelling that officer to kill that individual, are also taught to officers. Patton and Fremouw (2016) identify law enforcement as secondary victims of suicide by cop. Patton and Fremouw also point out that in suicide-by-cop incidents, officers are often thought of as the subjects and the person wanting to be killed as the victim, which can cause stress on law enforcement. Trauma is not always the outcome of a "good" shooting, in which the police have every right to kill someone to protect their own life or the lives of others. Even in circumstances where using force is warranted, officers participating in "suicide-by-cop" incidents may suffer trauma and regret their actions during the killing.

Violanti (2007) investigated 29 incidents of law enforcement officer suicides that occurred after the commission of a homicide (or homicides) by that law enforcement officer in 2007. In three cases, the victim was an officer's child. He also discovered that the victim was often a current or previous romantic partner. These 29 incidents show a probable set of indicators for future events as various characteristics recur frequently. Law enforcement personnel frequently encounter harrowing and dangerous circumstances where their lives are in jeopardy. Officers are frequently exposed to the trauma of fatal auto accidents, suicides, and homicides. If the cumulative stress from these situations is not addressed, the officers' psychosocial functioning may suffer significantly (Marchand et al., 2015; Steinkopf et al., 2015).

Domestic violence in the officer's own home, in addition to the officer's exposure to violence and consequent desensitization to it, were found to be common causes of homicide-suicide incidents (Violanti, 2007). Unfortunately, given the officer's position and responsibilities, little can be done to reduce the officer's exposure to violence. However, there are other aspects that an organization may control that might lessen the officer's stress (Violanti, 2007). When an officer witnesses violence connected to their line of duty, they must not internalize what they see. Agencies can impact things like patrol and narcotics assignments, lengthy and unpredictable workweeks, and job unhappiness that includes burnout and excessive use of sick leave. Offering officers the chance to switch up their work duties through specialized units and possibilities for new tasks within the law enforcement organization might be beneficial. By taking proactive measures in these areas, an officer may experience less stress, which will benefit both their personal and professional lives.

Klinoff et al. (2015) examined the issue of cops having a higher probability of committing domestic homicide than the general population, followed by suicide. Data was gathered from 43 domestic homicides committed by law enforcement that were followed by suicides by the officers (Klinoff et al., 2015). According to Klinoff et al., domestic violence poses a serious threat to law enforcement and can potentially be fatal. They found that divorce and domestic violence are both risk factors for homicide, followed by occurrences involving suicide.

As mentioned earlier in this chapter, agency culture barriers frequently prevent law enforcement officers who are having suicidal thoughts from seeking help. Due to their familiarity with agency culture, spouses and partners are hesitant to request advice or support from the officer's agency. This hesitation puts other people in danger because a suicidal person might turn murderous. Twelve (12) of the 108 cases of officer suicide from 2018 data that were examined involved a homicide before the suicide, and three other cases featured an attempt at grave bodily harm to another person before the suicide (Johnson, 2022).

Early intervention into the elements that may cause a homicide-suicide event appears to be the key to lowering their incidence. Lowering the number of homicide-suicide incidents, treatment and/or settlement of interpersonal issues, domestic violence, and substance misuse could have a positive effect (Violanti et al., 2017).

Funeral protocol

For many years, the number of officers who committed suicide outnumbered those killed in the line of duty (Hyman et al., 2018). However, few organizations have written funeral protocols for suicide deaths. The suicide of a member of the law enforcement community has an impact on everyone in that community; however, there is no clear protocol for how that agency should respond. Unfortunately, agencies of all sizes have struggled with this issue, and the responses have been as diverse as the agencies themselves (R. Durkee, personal communications, August 13, 2020; Confidential, personal communications, August 14, 2020).

When they are a part of an agency's policy and procedure handbook, line-of-duty death protocols are frequently extremely specific and extensive.

Every detail of the funeral, including the who, what, where, when, why, and how of the event, is frequently described in specifics (Orange County Sheriff's Office, 2017). Very little is documented regarding the agency's protocol for handling suicide deaths. There is no reference to funeral procedures when the cause of death is suicide in agency policy and procedure guides from the US and Canada. Unfortunately, a lot of organizations seem unprepared for such occurrences.

The largest single law enforcement agency in the United States received phone calls due to the absence of documented protocols. It is generally known that police officers in New York City (NYPD) commit suicide; ten did so in 2019. (Katersky & Jacobo, 2020; Johnson, 2022). This led to a treatment response for individuals in need across the organization.

Unfortunately, there was no formal funeral protocol provided for cops who commit suicide in this response. There is no documented procedure for handling these incidents, according to a representative of the Ceremonial Unit of the New York City Police Department. When asked how the Ceremonial Unit handles these events, the response was, "We consult with the family and just go from there based on their wishes" (Confidential, personal communications, August 14, 2020).

Some organizations have published suggestions on this subject, including the Badge of Honor Memorial Foundation (2019, pp. 19–20), the International Association of Chiefs of Police (2017, pp. 22–24), and the Illinois Association of Chiefs of Police (n.d., p. 12). In the little that is written in agency procedure, the resounding themes center on respecting the officer's way of life and working with the family to decide how to proceed. Agencies might at first try to respect family wishes and line-of-duty death protocol. The agency and family may try to stray from traditional line-of-duty death protocols, though, as the officer's actions or activities leading up to the suicide were criminal and/or damaged the reputation of the officer or agency. Whatever the reason, the organization needs to be ready to explain its involvement—or lack thereof—in memorial and burial ceremonies.

Authorities seem ready to handle a death in the line of duty. Sadly, if a person commits suicide, this is not the case (Orange County Sheriff's Office, 2017; R. Durkee, personal communications, August 13, 2020; Confidential, personal communications, August 14, 2020). Agencies should be ready for both as officer suicides are more likely to have an impact than deaths in the course of duty. A straightforward change to current funeral policy and procedureis needed, for instance:

> If the death was a result of a suicide, consultation between the Agency and the deceased's family should be held. Although each instance should be treated individually (case-by-case), and the circumstances

investigated, generally, unless the Suicide was a result of an action by the deceased that brought discredit to themselves or the Agency, the appropriate funeral protocols should be afforded and allowed.

(Illinois Association of Chiefs of Police, n.d., p. 12)

This language offers the first instructions on how to proceed in the event of suicide. In addition to the wishes of the deceased's family, it bases its response on the agency's line-of-duty death protocol. Agencies are highly advised to provide a formal process for serving former officers who commit suicide. The best time to prepare for such an incident is in advance rather than in the tumultuous aftermath, when stress and emotion may impair judgment.

Media and social media regarding suicide death

It should not come as a surprise that media in all its forms impacts suicide deaths, given how much media seems to affect every other aspect of our lives. According to Mueller (2017), careless reporting about suicide is frequently linked to a rise in the suicide rate among people exposed to the media. Does the same hold true for individuals who work in law enforcement? Does it "suggest" suicide?

The "defund the cops" campaign and protests against law enforcement officials have been actively covered by the media. Making officers believe their work is pointless is the quickest way to sap their morale. Constant media portrayals of law enforcement being physically attacked, verbally abused, or the subject of demonstrations have a negative effect on officers' morale and may change how they perceive the significance of their work. Within the first few weeks after George Floyd died in Minneapolis, more than 2,000 law enforcement personnel were hurt (Sadulski, 2020). Between May 25 and July 31 of 2020, there were 8,700 protests across the country and 574 riots that were officially declared, both of which were characterized by violence and other criminal activity that disproportionately targeted law officers (Sadulski, 2020). The defund the police campaign, echoed by other politicians and in the media, emerged after the riots in the summer of 2020. Law enforcement stress and officer suicidal thoughts can be significantly impacted when the media and social media demoralize the field of law enforcement. The media must portray law enforcement with fairness and accuracy.

A rise in suicide deaths is associated with media coverage of a high-profile person's suicide (Fahey et al., 2018). Additionally, news of adolescent suicide appears to increase youth suicide in the neighborhood (Mueller, 2017). Similar trends seem to apply to social media, which seems to have the power to affect suicidal behavior (Luxton et al., 2012). For a variety of reasons, traditional media coverage of law enforcement suicide has been patchy; nonetheless, social media sites that are actively seeking to "fix the problem" routinely cover these instances. The effect of this reporting on a law enforcement officer who is thinking about suicide can only be conjectured. However, when examining Muller's prior reporting, it is possible that officers could imitate other examined subcultures, and that such reporting causes a rise in police officer suicides (2017).

There may be some benefits to social media and its possible impact on suicide inside the law enforcement community, even though this may cast social media in a negative image in relation to this subject. Social media platforms have shown that they can connect with those who are difficult to engage. It is not unreasonable to include law enforcement officials in this group. Social media platforms could be a useful tool for providing "an anonymous, accessible, and judgment-free place for exchanging experiences" (Robinson et al., 2016). People who use social media for suicide prevention-related goals cited the encouraging community fostered there and the freedom to express oneself without fear of judgment from others as advantages of this suicide prevention tool (Robinson et al., 2016). Consequently, using these platforms may be a good way to provide aid to those in need (Keasar et al., 2022).

Teo et al. (2020) investigated how military veterans used social media platforms to avoid suicide. Their investigation focused on how veterans handled distressed "friend" veterans. Teo et al. (2020) have attempted to pinpoint potential therapies that might be used. While some veterans were hesitant to discuss problems on social media, they found that these same soldiers were open to reaching out to other veterans who were acting in a disturbing way. They expressed a wish for more training to enable them to assist other veterans more effectively.

These results suggest that operators and moderators of law enforcement social media platforms may require training in suicide prevention. The community of law enforcement who run, moderate, and are otherwise active on law enforcement social media platforms is a potential resource in the identification of officers who are experiencing distress, much like the population of military veterans. Once the officer has been identified, these skilled professionals could then connect him or her with the resources needed to assist them.

Other factors may also impact officer suicide due to social media. Many people are aware of the wealth of data gleaned from social media, such as details on psychological pressures that may be used to anticipate suicidal tendencies. Deep learning-based approaches (algorithms) were used by Du et al. (2017) to identify tweets more effectively about suicide than other tried-and-true techniques. Coppersmith et al. (2018) also looked at social media data mining as a screening technique to identify suicide risk. Coppersmith et al. (2018) found that technology can identify signals and data identifying a suicide risk before involving that person with the healthcare system, similar to the findings by Du et al. (2017).

If a law enforcement organization were to keep tabs on its employees' social media activity, it might be able to spot warning signs of impending suicide and take steps to provide the person with the help they needed. In fact, Keasar et al. (2022) identified that outreach on social media by suicide prevention volunteers can provide a good strategy in an attempt to stop suicide. In Keasar's study, almost 70% of responses to suicidal posts were positive and the strategy of outreach on social media to suicidal posts may prompt those individuals to seek help. With so many social media sites available, it would be difficult to decide which ones to monitor or not monitor. Such agency conduct may also raise legal concerns (Luxton et al., 2012). However, that is a subject outside the purview of this work.

Pre-employment screening and testing

When a prospective law enforcement officer applies to an organization, a lengthy and intricate process begins. The past life of that person is examined in every detail. The person is assessed for both duty-fitness and goodness-of-fit for that agency. A thorough investigation should be made into the applicant's attention to detail in properly completing the application, as well as their driving, job, and military service histories (if applicable). The person will frequently go through an oral board and be asked a series of direct questions to give the board insight into the person's judgment, character, and capacity for quick thinking. This process frequently concludes with a medical examination, drug test, polygraph, and psychological examination (Russo, 2014).

This procedure's component for medical and drug testing is simple. As part of the medical examination, the person's overall physical health is verified. Flexibility, strength, electrocardiogram (EKG), heart and lung function, as well as vision are commonly tested to see if a person is physically capable of performing the required tasks. To check for any anomalies and to check for drugs in the person's system, blood is typically collected and submitted to a lab (Russo, 2014). You can find a sample drug policy at Woodbury, New Jersey, Police Department.

In order to verify information provided by the candidate, several organizations use polygraphs and/or vocal stress analysis (CVSA) as part of the pre-employment screening process. If used by the agency, this phase entails a thorough pre-interview conducted by a qualified person who asks the applicant a series of questions and gives them the opportunity to disclose any additional information that might have been purposefully or unintentionally left out of the application (Russo, 2014). This is followed by using a device, such as a polygraph, that is intended to identify autonomic arousal and microtremors rather than necessarily lying by monitoring changes in heart rate, blood pressure, breathing, skin conductivity, and stress in speech (Damphousse, 2008). These autonomic arousals and microtremors are difficult for individuals to manipulate and control; thus, under stress, changes in these are detected by the equipment and/or operator. A post-assessment interview is often conducted depending on the results of the polygraph test, particularly if deception is detected or some responses are inconclusive. Remington (2022) says some departments use the CVSA as an alternative to the polygraph but both tests have been criticized for their accuracy; however the tools are just that, one tool in the arsenal of evaluation measures for an applicant.

The purpose of the psychological examination is to ascertain whether the subject has any serious mental flaws or personality problems that would provide a challenge for someone working in law enforcement. Depending on agency preferences, agencies may utilize various techniques and/or professionals to arrive at this conclusion. A paper-and-pencil test with an interpretation session with a psychologist or other qualified therapist, who will then produce a report for the agency, is one example. The material in the report may range from a matrix classifying a person into one of three risk categories (low, medium, or high) to a paragraph stating whether or not they are deemed suitable for the obligations and responsibilities of the position (Russo, 2014).

In contrast to high-risk applications, agencies prefer low-risk individuals; however, they frequently give medium-risk candidates serious consideration. High-risk people risk making the front page of the newspaper—and probably not for positive reasons. Low-risk people have a chance of being on the main page, but only for good things, whereas medium-risk people might get there (Russo, 2014).

The interaction between the officer and the clinician ends here for most agencies. A consultation with a mental health professional is frequently reserved for officers who have experienced some kind of psychological trauma while performing their duties, such as witnessing a colleague die in the line of duty, coming close to passing out while performing their duties, being at the scene of a horrific accident, seeing the results of crimes against children, using deadly force, or handling a homicide (Courtney & Russo, 2012).

Theoretical conceptualization: information extracted and implemented

In police enforcement, discussions about mental health after first employment are uncommon. The agency can promote mental health wellness while simultaneously working to lessen or eliminate the stigma associated with officers seeking help and assistance by involving psychologists or other trained clinicians in frequent in-service training sessions and introducing them to new officers early in their careers, such as during initial agency indoctrination.

Including stress management in the discussion of an officer's yearly personnel review is one way in which law enforcement agencies and supervisors can have a beneficial impact on identifying issues related to stress in law enforcement officers. Supervisors have a great opportunity to ask officers about their stress levels during counseling sessions related to employee reviews for officers. During the annual personnel review, the boss needs to probe the cop to determine if they are dealing with PTSD symptoms. Supervisors should also inquire about how field stress affects the officers' personal and family relationships. The supervisor should take use of this time to talk to the officers about stress management techniques and the tools that are available to them, such as employee help programs. Stress in the police force is also significantly influenced by workplace culture (Biggs et al., 2014). In order to improve law enforcement culture and properly manage officer stress, front-line supervisors are crucial. Additionally, law enforcement supervisors supporting officers by accessing these resources when needed can help overcome some of the stigma associated with police seeking professional treatment when they are battling with their stress.

Officer burnout can be caused by the ongoing stress of law enforcement, which has prompted researchers to study the connection between stress and burnout (Don & Brett, 2011; Padyab et al., 2016; Schaible & Six, 2016; Yanan et al., 2014). Don and Brett (2011) conducted research on law enforcement stress and burnout in policing and the potential role of prior military service as a mediation factor affecting burnout for both prior and non-military service officers. To compare the effects of variables on stress amongst law enforcement officers with and without prior military experience, the researchers employed t-tests and multivariate regression analysis (Don & Brett, 2011). Don and Brett (2011) found that tough events had a negative burnout effect on all officers and that stressful situations impacted the stress levels of the study's non-military officers. Police burnout can have several serious repercussions. Officers who are burned out frequently develop cynicism, and their work may become less effective over time. Officers may experience health issues as a result of burnout. Personality traits and job satisfaction have an impact on law enforcement burnout. Agencies may not have any control over the personality traits of their employees, but by improving job satisfaction, they can mitigate the impact of burnout. Public acknowledgment of the officer's accomplishments, opportunities for advancement, and transparent and standardized agency policies and processes can all help with this.

Regular and frequent interactions with a clinician can lessen the stigma associated with requesting assistance and enhance officers' use of clinicians and other options to improve mental wellness. In the same way that physical strength is encouraged in training sessions, mental wellness is also highlighted Clinicians and agency management can support and encourage officers to seek therapy before a problem(s) badly impacts their personal and professional lives (Butterworth, 2001; Donnelly et al., 2015). COPS (n.d.) highlighted the 2017 Law Enforcement Mental Health and Wellness Act in January 2018, which recognizes the need and support for law enforcement's mental health. The Law Enforcement Mental Health and Wellness Act expands peer mentoring programs, ensures privacy, helps to develop crisis lines, and provides avenues for mental health checks for law enforcement through additional funding (COPS, n.d.).

The training and curriculum at the academy actively work to reduce the number of times that law enforcement personnel fail, make mistakes, and commit errors. But not every contact and event will result in what can be considered a success, given that there are more than 701,000 law enforcement officers servicing more than 320 million people every day in the United States (Bureau of Justice Statistics, 2011; Davis & Hyland, 2019). Officers may take responsibility for "less than successful outcomes" when occurrences have them. The way a particular officer responds to these "failures" can and will have a significant impact on both his or her wellbeing and the wellbeing of the agency as a whole.

Law enforcement academies and field training initiatives anticipate that fresh recruits will eventually mature into appropriately performing officers in a variety of variable and occasionally harsh conditions. Officers are expected to develop and make decisions for the future on their prior education and experiences. Officers are taught to recognize their skills and flaws and to make the most of them. Success and failure frequently reveal one's talents and limitations. Agencies should be accepting of failure and be prepared to learn from it if they want to foster a culture of wellbeing (Makin, 2016).

Wellness culture

A wellness culture values wellbeing and fosters development and resiliency. An organization that promotes wellness should develop in its officers the drive to do better in the face of difficulty, and adaptability when presented with negative outcomes. Promoting a culture of wellness starts at the top of the organization and leaders must create a culture of acceptance to remove the stigma associated with officers seeking help (Olson & Wasilewski, 2020). An officer can make the proper decision on the street and the appropriate decision in other areas of his or her professional and personal life by continually assessing the situation and the many factors. Every time something bad happens, an unanticipated consequence arises, or a situation changes, a course correction may be necessary. When it becomes apparent that taking a specific course would result in less-than-ideal results, an agency should train its personnel to feel comfortable "changing direction". The agency will have succeeded in developing a wellness culture once officers feel at ease with these ideas and procedures.

A peer support group is one element that can help in the establishment and creation of a culture of well-being. A unit like that might be useful in spotting and preventing potentially suicidal behavior (Courts & Mosiniak, 2015; Violanti et al., 2017; International Association of Chiefs of Police, 2019). These services enable people to share personal experiences, express their feelings, learn stress-reduction techniques, and, if necessary, make recommendations. Members of peer support units, which are made up of volunteer fellow law enforcement officers who have received specialized training, are seen as having greater levels of trust by their fellow officers than formally trained and licensed mental health specialists (Courts & Mosiniak, 2015; Violanti et al., 2017). Peer support programs effectively reduce the stigma of speaking with a psychologist or needing outside help. Peer support helps to share positive recovery messages while reducing barriers to seeking help (International Association of Chiefs of Police, 2019). Peer support can also make seeking help more normal and promote healthy coping skills (International Association of Chiefs of Police, 2019). An officer is more likely to talk to another officer with whom they have been friendly and have trusted over time, both before and after the horrific experience. When the peer officer has gone through similar traumatic experiences to what the officer is going through now and is able to share how they overcame the trauma from those events, peer support programs are highly beneficial. Evidence from these peer support groups has shown that they increase social contacts among the officers they assist while decreasing individual suffering (Violanti et al., 2017).

In medium and large-sized organizations, a peer support unit can frequently be developed within, although it must follow standards for confidentiality. A regional peer support organization that shares resources among its many member agencies might be established for the many smaller agencies that comprise the larger law enforcement community. In law enforcement, this shared services approach is popular. Multi-agency special weapons and tactics (SWAT) teams frequently use it (French, 2016). The multi-agency peer support unit can deploy a larger pool of skilled officers to help whenever necessary by expanding the talent pool of possible members. Peer support programs should start as soon as possible after a traumatic event while the officer is still on duty, and they should take place in a private meeting space away from the public eye and the gaze of the media (Sadulski, 2017). Following an incident, group peer support meetings should be held separately from agency debriefings. Trained peer officers should also keep in touch with the officer who had the traumatic experience and keep an eye out for any signs that the officer may be experiencing post-traumatic stress disorder or may be dealing with the trauma in a way that could result in self-destructive behaviors or suicidal ideation.

According to the IACP, peer support networks should be used for interventions in addition to suicide prevention, for instance in helping around challenges in an officer's life such as relationship problems or potential substance misuse. The IACP recommends that when agencies develop a peer support team, selecting support team members requires five main areas of consideration. They should set expectations for members to avoid selecting someone seeking "gain" such as promotion, financial, or to bolster their resume. They should also involve a minimum of one mental health professional, consider nominations by other officers in seeking someone who is genuine, sets boundaries, and practices self-care. Finally, the IACP recommends developing peer group members to build confidence and coaching skills.

There might not be a "one size fits all" answer to the problem of police officer suicide. The mix of agency, colleagues, family and other outside assistance for the specific officer facing suicidal thoughts and/or psychological stress is seen to be the key to finding solutions. This two-pronged strategy is deemed to have a better chance of helping the officer with suicidal thoughts and psychological distress.

References

Aiken, C. (2010). *Family experiences of bipolar disorder: The ups, the downs and the bits in between.* Jessica Kingsley Publishers.
All Clear Foundation. (2020). There is a human behind every first responder's badge. https://allclearfoundation.org/.
American Psychological Association. (n.d.) *APA dictionary of psychology*. Retrieved November 25, 2020, from https://dictionary.apa.org/psychological-distress.
Ammons, J. (2005). Batters with badges: Officer-involved domestic violence. *Women Lawyers Journal*, 90(5), 28–39.
Anderson, A.S., & Lo, C.C. (2011). Intimate partner violence within law enforcement families. *Journal of Interpersonal Violence*, 26(6), 1176. doi:10.1177/0886260510368156.
Ávila, A. (2015). When the batterer wears a badge: Regulating officer-involved domestic violence as a line-of-duty crime. *American Journal of Criminal Law*, 42(3), 213–239. http://ajclonline.org/.
Badge of Honor Memorial Foundation. (2019). *2019 agency casualty assistance guide.* http://www.bohmf.org/media/2019-agency-casualty-assist-guide.pdf.

Ballenger, J.F., Best, S.R., Metzler, T.J., Wasserman, D.A., Mohr, D.C., Liberman, A., Delucchi, K., Weiss, D.S., Fagan, J.A., Waldrop, A.E., & Marmar, C.R. (2010). Patterns and predictors of alcohol use in male and female urban police officers. *The American Journal on Addictions*, 20, 21–29.

Barton, L. (2019). Silent no more: Officers need a lifeline, too. *Police1*. https://www.police1.com/health-fitness/articles/silent-no-more-officers-need-a-lifeline-too-5K2bGshSBw9XCDiE/.

Biggs, A., Brough, P., & Barbour, J.P. (2014). Exposure to extra organizational stressors: Impact on mental health and organizational perceptions for police officers. *International Journal of Stress Management*, 21(3), 255–282. doi:10.1037/a0037297.

Blumenstein, L., Fridell, L., & Jones, S. (2011). The link between traditional police sub-culture and police intimate partner violence. *Policing: An International Journal of Police Strategies & Management*, 35(1), 147–164.

Brunault, P., Lebrigre, K., Idbrik, F., Mauge, D., Adam, P., El Ayoubi, H., Hingray, C., Barrault, S., Grall-Bronnec, M., Ballon, N., & El-Hage, W. (2019). Posttraumatic stress disorder is a risk factor for multiple addictions in police officers hospitalized for alcohol. *European Addiction Research*, 25, 198–206.

Bunston, W., Franich-Ray, C., & Tatlow, S. (2017). A diagnosis of denial: How mental health classification systems have struggled to recognize family violence as a serious risk factor in the development of mental health issues for infants, children, adolescents and adults. *Brain Sciences*, 7(10), 133. https://www.ncbi.nlm.nih.gov/pmc/articles/PMC5664060/.

Bureau of Justice Statistics. (2011). *Census of state and local law enforcement agencies, 2008* (NCJ 233982). https://www.bjs.gov/content/pub/pdf/csllea08.pdf.

Burns, C., & Buchanan, M. (2020). Factors that influence the decision to seek help in a police population. *International Journal of Environmental Research and Public Health*, 17(18), 6891–. https://doi.org/10.3390/ijerph17186891.

Butterworth, I. (2001). The components and impact of stigma associated with EAP counseling. *Employee Assistance Quarterly*, 3, 1–8.

Cheema, R. (2016). Black and blue blood. Protecting police officer families from domestic violence. *Family Court Review*, 54(3), 487-500. https://scholarlycommons.law.hofstra.edu/hofstra_law_student_works/10/.

Clark-Miller, J., & Brady, H. (2013). Critical stress: Police officer religiosity and coping with critical stress incidents. *Journal of Police & Criminal Psychology*, 28(1), 26. doi:10.1007/s11896-012-9112-8.

Cohen, L., Ferguson, C., Harms, C., Pooley, J.A., & Tomlinson, S. (2011). Family systems and mental health issues: A resilience approach. *Journal of Social Work Practice*, 25(1), 109–125.

Collins, J., & Genovese, M. (2020). How police leadership can respond to officer mental health crises. *Police1*. https://www.police1.com/chiefs-sheriffs/articles/how-police-leadership-can-respond-to-officer-mental-health-crises-3zrmdFnjtpoYLOyR/.

Coppersmith, G., Leary, R., Crutchley, P, & Fine, A. (2018). Natural language processing of social media as screening for suicide risk. *Biomedical Informatics Insights*, 10, 1–11.

COPS. (n.d.). Law enforcement mental health and wellness (LEMHWA) program resources. Retrieved September 28, 2022, from https://cops.usdoj.gov/lemhwa resources.

Courtney, C., & Russo, C. (2012, March). Combating traumatic stress – the role of CISM teams. Paper presentation for "The Impact of Lethal Situations on Police Stress" panel at the Academy of Criminal Justice Sciences Annual Meeting: New York City, NY.

Courts, L.C., & Mosiniak, S. (2015). Police officers and suicide: An international literature review. *Law Enforcement Executive Forum*, 15(4), 81–96.

Damphousse, K.R. (2008). Voice stress analysis: Only 15 percent of lies about drug use detected in field test. National Institute of Justice. https://nij.ojp.gov/topics/articles/voice-stress-analysis-only-15-percent-lies-about-drug-use-detected-field-test.

Davis, E., & Hyland, S. (2019). Local police departments, 2016: Personnel. Retrieved September 29, 2022, from https://bjs.ojp.gov/content/pub/pdf/lpd16p.pdf.

Dharampal, R., & Ani, C. (2020). The emotional and mental health needs of young carers: What psychiatry can do. *BJPsych Bulletin*, 44(3), 112–120. doi:10.1192/bjb.2019.78.

Don, I., & Brett, G. (2011). Stress and burnout in policing: Does military experience matter? *Policing*, 34(1), 49. http://www.emeraldgrouppublishing.com/products/journals/journals.htm?id=pijpsm.

Donnelly, E., Valentine, C., & Oehme, K. (2015). Law enforcement officers and employee assistance programs. *Policing: An International Journal*, 38(2), 206–220. https://www.emerald.com/insight/content/doi/10.1108/PIJPSM-11-2014-0116/full/html.

Drexler, M. (2013). Guns & suicide: The hidden toll. *Harvard Public Health*. https://www.hsph.harvard.edu/magazine/magazine_article/guns-suicide/.

Du, J., Zhang, Y., Lou, J., Jai, Y., Wei, Q, Tao, C., & Xu, H. (2017). Extracting psychiatric stressors for suicide from social media using deep learning. *BMC Medical Informatics and Decision Making*, 18(43). https://doLorg/10.1186/s12911-018-0632-8.

Durborow, N., Lizdas, K.C., O'Flaherty, A., & Marjavi, A. (2010). *Compendium of state statues and polices on domestic violence and health care*. Family Violence Prevention Fund.

Fahey, R.A., Matsubayashi, T., & Ueda, M. (2018). Tracking the Werther Effect on social media: Emotional responses to prominent suicide death on twitter and subsequent increases in suicide. *Social Science & Medicine*, 219, 19–29.

French, G. (2016, September 14). How to stand up a regional SWAT team. *Police1*. https://www.police1.com/swat/articles/how-to-stand-up-a-regional-swat-team-KWUPpGtCuEtwQhSn/.

Galatzer-Levy, I.R., Brown, A.D., Henn-Haase, C., Metzler, T.J., Neylan, T.C., & Marmar, C.R. (2013). Positive and negative emotion prospectively predict trajectories of resilience and distress among high-exposure police officers. *Emotion*, 13(3), 545–553. doi:10.1037/a0031314.

Gul, Z., & Delıce, M. (2011). Police job stress and stress reduction/coping programs: The effects on the relationship with spouses. *Turkish Journal of Police Studies/Polis Bilimleri Dergisi*, 13(3), 19. http://library.usask.ca/find/ejournals/view.php?id=2670000000156089.

Hyman, M., Dill, J., & Douglas, R. (2018). *The Ruderman white paper on mental health and suicide of first responders*. The Ruderman Family Foundation. https://dir.nv.gov/uploadedFiles/dirnvgov/content/WCS/TrainingDocs/First%20Responder%20White%20Paper_Final%20(2).pdf

International Association of Chiefs of Police. (2019). Peer support as a powerful tool in law enforcement suicide prevention. Retrieved September 28, 2022, from https://www.theiacp.org/sites/default/files/2020-10/244736_IACP_NOSI_PeerSupport_p5.pdf.

International Association of Chiefs of Police. (2017). Breaking the silence on law enforcement suicides. https://cops.usdoj.gov/RIC/Publications/cops-p281-pub.pdf.

Illinois Association of Chiefs of Police. (n.d.). ILACP funeral assistance team manual. https://www.ileas.org/sites/default/files/conference/breakouts/ILACP%20Funeral%20Assistance%20Response%20Team%20Manual.pdf.

Iseselo, M., Kajula, L., & Yahya-Malima, K. I. (2016). The psychosocial problems of families caring for relatives with mental illnesses and their coping strategies: A qualitative urban based study in Dar es Salaam, Tanzania. *BMC Psychiatry*, 16 (146), 146–146. https://doi.org/10.1186/s12888-016-0857-y.

Johnson, O., Papazoglou, K., Violanti, J., Pascarella, J. (Eds.) (2022). *Practical considerations for preventing police suicide: Stop officer suicide*. Springer.

Karaffa, K., Openshaw, L., Koch, J., Clark, H., Harr, C., & Stewart, C. (2015). Perceived impact of police work on marital relationships. *Family Journal*, 23(2), 120. doi:10.1177/1066480714564381.

Katersky, A., & Jacobo, J. (2020, February 18). NYPD creates new approach to prevent officer suicides. *ABC News*. https://abcnews.go.com/US/nypd-creates-approach-prevent-officer-suicides/story?id=69055226.

Keasar, V., Sznitman, S., & Baumel, A. (2022). Suicide prevention outreach on social media delivered by trained volunteers: A qualitative study. *Crisis: The Journal of Crisis Intervention and Suicide Prevention*, doi:https://doi.org/10.1027/0227-5910/a000864.

Klinoff, V.A., Van Hasselt, V.B., & Black, R.A. (2015). Homicide-suicide in police families: An analysis of cases from 2007–2014. *Journal of Forensic Practice*, 17(2), 101. doi:10.1108/JFP-07-2014-0019.

Klugman, J. (2020). Do 40% of police families experience domestic violence? Retrieved September 27, 2022, from https://sites.temple.edu/klugman/2020/07/20/do-40-of-police-families-experience-domestic-violence/.

Kunst, M.J.J., Saan, M.C., Bollen, L.J.A., & Kuijpers, K.F. (2017). Secondary traumatic stress and secondary posttraumatic growth in a sample of Dutch police family liaison officers. *Stress & Health: Journal of the International Society for the Investigation of Stress*, 33(5), 570–577. https://doi-org.ezproxy1.apus.edu/10.1002/smi.2741.

Lambert, E.G., Qureshi, H., Frank, J., Keena, L.D., & Hogan, N.L. (2017). The relationship of work-family conflict with job stress among Indian police officers: a research note. *Police Practice & Research*, 18(1), 37–48. https://doi.org/10.1080/15614263.2016.1210010.

Luxton, D.D., June, J.D., & Fairall, J.M. (2012). Social media and suicide: A public health perspective. *American Journal of Public Health*, 102, S195–S200.

Makin, D. (2016). A descriptive analysis of a problem-based learning police academy. *Interdisciplinary Journal of Problem-Based Learning*, 10(1), 18–32.

Marchand, A., Nadeau, C., Beaulieu-Prévost, D., Boyer, R., & Martin, M. (2015). Predictors of posttraumatic stress disorder among police officers: A prospective study. *Psychological Trauma: Theory, Research, Practice, and Policy*, 7(3), 212–221. doi:10.1037/a0038780.

Mathew, K.J., Pathak, A., Sakshi, R., & Sanku, J.S. (2016). Risk of psychological distress among individuals living with a mentally ill person: A study from a backward state of India and its implications. *Online Journal of Health and Allied Sciences*, 15(4), 6. http://www.ojhas.org/issue60/2016-4-6.html.

McAleer, G. & Schlosser, L. (n.d.). Share opioid use disorders among police and public safety personnel: What law enforcement leaders need to know. *Policechiefmagazine.org*. Retrieved September 24, 2022, from https://www.policechiefmagazine.org/opioid-use-among-police-personnel/.

Mennicke, A.M., & Ropes, K. (2016). Estimating the rate of domestic violence perpetrated by law enforcement officers: A review of methods and estimates. *Aggression and Violent Behavior*, 31, 157–164.

Mills, C., Milloy, J., Carson, J., Bourke, M., & Grillo, R. (2020). *2019 Virginia Public Safety Mental Health Pilot*. 2019 Virginia Pulblic Safety Mental Health Pilot Survey. Retrieved September 23, 2022, from https://vdocuments.site/2019-virginia-public-safety-mental-health-pilot-the-pilot-survey-did-not-ask-respondents.html.

Mueller, A.S. (2017). Does the media matter to suicide? Examining the social dynamics surrounding media reporting on suicide in a suicide-prone community. *Social Science & Medicine*, 180, 152–159.

Olson, A., & Wasilewski, M. (2020, May 6). 9 steps to creating a culture that supports officer mental wellness. *Police1*. Retrieved September 29, 2022, from https://www.police1.com/health-wellness/articles/9-steps-to-creating-a-culture-that-supports-officer-mental-wellness-FIIpjMsmfjf0IWmO/.

Orange County Sheriff's Office. (2017). *Policy and procedure manual*. https://powerdms.com/public/ORCSO/tree/documents/301343.

Orange County Sheriff's Office. (2020). *Policy and procedure manual*. https://powerdms.com/public/ORCSO/tree/documents/301514.

Padyab, M., Backteman-Erlanson, S., & Brulin, C. (2016). Burnout, coping, stress of conscience and psychosocial work environment among patrolling police officers. *Journal of Police and Criminal Psychology*, doi:10.1007/s11896-015-9189-y.

Palo Alto Police Department. (2019). *Palo Alto Police Department Policy Manual*. https://www.cityofpaloalto.org/civicax/filebank/documents/74121.

Patton, C.L., & Fremouw, W.J. (2016). Examining "suicide by cop": A critical review of the literature. *Aggression and Violent Behavior*, 27, 107–120. https://doi.org/10.1016/j.avb.2016.03.003.

Pompili, M., Serafini, G., Innamorati, M., Dominici, G., Ferracuti, S., Kotzalidis, G.D., Serra, G., Girardi, P., Janiri, L., Tatarelli, R., Sher, L., & Lester, D. (2010). Suicidal behavior and alcohol abuse . *International Journal of Environmental Research and Public Health*, 7, 1392–1431.

Queirós, C., Passos, F., Bártolo, A., Faria, S., Fonseca, S. M., Marques, A.J., Silva, C.F., & Pereira, A. (2020). Job stress, burnout and coping in police officers: Relationships and psychometric properties of the Organizational Police Stress Questionnaire. *International Journal of Environmental Research and Public Health*, 17(18), 6718–. https://doi.org/10.3390/ijerph17186718.

Ramchand, R., Saunders, J., Chan Osilla, K., Ebener, P., Kotzias, V., Thorton, E., Strang, L., & Cahill, M. (2019). Suicide prevention in U.S. law enforcement agencies: A national survey of current practices. *Journal of Police and Criminal Psychology*, 34(1), 55–66. https://doi.org/10.1007/s11896-018-9269-x.

Reaves, B.A. (2016). *State and local law enforcement training academies, 2013.* Bureau of Justice Statistics. https://www.bjs.gov/content/pub/pdf/slleta13.pdf.
Remington, K. (2022). Ohio police departments talk polygraphs: Hiring and investigations. Retrieved from https://www.police1.com/police-products/investigation/investigative-software/articles/ohio-police-departments-talk-polygraphs-hiring-and-investigations-Ck0q3VkVLwJRnada/.
Roberts, N.A., Leonard, R.C., Butler, E.A., Levenson, R.W., & Kanter, J.W. (2013). Job stress and dyadic synchrony in police marriages: A preliminary investigation. *Family Process*, 52(2), 271–283. doi:10.1111/j.1545-5300.2012.01415.x.
Robinson, J., Cox, G., Bailey, E., Hetrick, S., Rodrigues, M., Fisher, S., & Herrman, H. (2016). Social media and suicide prevention: A systematic review. *Early Intervention in Psychiatry*, 10, 103–121.
Russell, L.M. (2014). An empirical investigation of high-risk occupations Leader influence on employee stress and burnout among police. *Management Research Review*, 37(4), 367–384. doi:10.1108/MRR-10-2012-0227.
Russo, C. (2014, February 19). Demystifying the background investigation process: What you can expect when applying for a law enforcement job. *In Public Safety.* http://www.policeone.com/investigations/articles/6878088-Demystifying-background-investigations-What-you-can-expect-when-applying-for-a-law-enforcement-job/.
Russo, C.W., & Hunziker, S. (2019, March 4). First responders with psychological injuries must be eligible for workers' compensation, pensions. *In Public Safety.* https://inpublicsafety.com/2019/03/first-responders-with-psychological-injuries-must-be-eligible-for-workers-compensation-pensions/.
Sadulski, J.S. (2017). Managing police stress to strengthen relationships at home. *In Public Safety.* https://inpublicsafety.com/2017/02/managing-police-stress-to-strengthen-\relationships-at-home/
Sadulski, J.S. (2018). How police spouses can manage stress (and why they need to). *Police1.* https://www.police1.com/health-fitness/articles/how-police-spouses-can-manage-stress-and-why-they-need-to-4TieA618BXb1w0M8/.
Sadulski, J.S. (2020). Negative public narrative takes toll on law enforcement. *AMU Edge.* https://amuedge.com/negative-public-narrative-takes-toll-on-law-enforcement/.
Saunders, D.G., Prost, S.G., & Oehme, K. (2016). Responses of police officers to cases of officer domestic violence: Effects of demographic and professional factors. *Journal of Family Violence*, 31(6), 771–784. https://doi.org/10.1007/s10896-0822-2
Schaible, L.M., & Six, M. (2016). Emotional strategies of police and their varying consequences for burnout. *Police Quarterly*, 19(1), 3. doi:10.1177/1098611115604448.
Schlosser, L.Z., & McAleer, G.P. (n.d.). Opioid use disorders among police and public safety personnel: What law enforcement leaders need to know. *Police Chief.* https://www.policechiefmagazine.org/opioid-use-among-police-personnel/.
Siddiqui, S., & Khalid, J. (2019). Determining the caregivers' burden in caregivers of patients with mental illness. *Pakistan Journal of Medical Sciences*, 35 (5), 1329.
Steinkopf, B.L., Hakala, K.A., & Van Hasselt, V.B. (2015). Motivational interviewing: Improving the delivery of psychological services to law enforcement. *Professional Psychology: Research and Practice*, 46(5), 348–354. doi:10.1037/pro0000042.

Stinson, P.M., & Liederbach, J. (2012). Fox in the henhouse: A study of police officers arrested for crimes associated with domestic and/or family violence. *Criminal Justice Policy Review*, 24(5), 601–625.

Teo, A.R., Strange, W., Bui, R., Dobscha, S.K., & Ono, S.S. (2020). Responses to concerning posts on social media and their implications for suicide prevention training for military veterans: Qualitative study. *Journal of Medical Internet Research*, 22(10), 1–10.

The Educational Fund to Stop Gun Violence. (2021, March 2). Statistics. *Prevent Firearm Suicide*. Retrieved September 23, 2022, from https://preventfirearmsuicide.efsgv.org/about-firearm-suicide/statistics/.

U.S. Department of Justice COPS. (2021). Community-oriented policing services, family matters executive guide for developing family-friendly law enforcement policies, procedures, and culture. Retrieved from https://cops.usdoj.gov/RIC/Publications/cops-w0948-pub.pdf.

Violanti, J.M. (2007). Homicide-suicide in police families: Aggression full circle. *International Journal of Emergency Mental Health*, 9(2), 97–104.

Violanti, J.M., Owens, S.L., McCanlies, E., Fekedulegn, D., & Andrew, M.E. (2017). Law enforcement suicide: A review. *Policing: An International Journal*, 42(2), 141–164.

Wolk-Wasserman, D. (1986). Suicidal communication of persons attempting suicide and responses of significant others. *Acta Psychiatrica Scandinavica*, 73, 481–499.

Yanan, W., Lu, Z., Tianhong, H., & Quanquan, Z. (2014). Stress, burnout, and job satisfaction: Case of police force in China. *Public Personnel Management*, 43(3), 325–339 15p. doi:10.1177/0091026014535179.

Zdravkovic, M., Milic, M., Stojanovic, M., & Kostov, M. (2009). Three cases of death caused by shots from blank cartridge. *American Journal of Forensic Medicine and Pathology*, 30(4), 403–406.

9
POLICE SUICIDE IN BRAZIL
What do we know?

Dayse Assunção Miranda and Fernanda Novaes Cruz

Introduction

The Brazilian police forces are globally known for their high levels of lethality, primarily directed toward young individuals from impoverished and black communities (Cano, 2010), and their low level of accountability (González, 2022). Simultaneously, these forces exhibit elevated rates of police lethality. The violent daily reality in some Brazilian cities frequently exposes police officers to conflict situations, occasionally rendering them victims.

Apart from exposure to violence, other factors contribute to the intricacies of police performance in Brazil. Each of the 27 Brazilian states has its own Military Police (MP) and Civil Police (CP). The first is militarized, based on an Armed Forces model, and responsible for ostensive-preventive policing; it is visible on the streets and four times bigger than the Civil Police. The Military Police are more exposed to violent episodes and deaths involving police officers, with the highest number of police officer deaths. The Civil Police are responsible for investigating crimes; they tend to work in police departments and are less often seen on the streets. This separation of Civil and Military police officers creates breakdowns in coordination between the police groups (Sapori, 2018). Both police forces have dual career paths, creating a significant gap between the highest and lowest ranks.

The militarization of the MP is considered one of the legacies of the authoritarian military period experienced in the country between 1964 and 1985. It still maintains a structure and practices related to military values, such as strong obedience and hierarchy; which results in a work

DOI: 10.4324/9781003452379-10

environment marked by fear and punishment (Costa, 2011), aspects that local researchers deem incompatible with the principles of a democratic society.

Although the effects of police work on mental well-being have been indirectly mentioned in several studies concerning Brazilian law enforcement (Minayo and Souza, 2003; Huggins et al., 2006; Constantino et al., 2008), it is only recently that research has focused on police suicides and their related factors.

One of the explanations for the scarcity of investigations concerning the risk of death by suicide in the police profession in Brazil can be attributed to limitations within the available data. The main official source of suicide data in Brazil—as well as of other deaths—is the Brazilian System of Death Registration (SIM–Sistema de Informações de Mortalidade), maintained by the Brazilian Ministry of Health. Previous research has highlighted this source as more reliable to analyse violent deaths than that of the Public Security departments (Murray et al., 2013). SIM data comes from the Brazilian Death Certificates provided by forensic pathologists. The underlying causes of death were coded and edited according to the International Classification of Diseases, Tenth Revision (ICD-10) (SIM DATASUS).

SIM data has two significant limitations. First, the records are not always adequately filled out, which hinders the development of analyses based on some of the victim characteristics, including their occupation. Second, there is a problem of misclassification of the cause of death. Many suicide cases are categorized as accidents or as undetermined causes (Borges et al., 2013). Violanti (1995) attributes this issue to a stigma surrounding death by suicide. In Rio de Janeiro MP, we identified that when an officer commits suicide, his family has less financial support and institutional honors than in other types of death (Cruz et al., 2022).

As a result, some officers attempted to conceal the intention of taking their own lives by engaging in armed conflicts without protection or intentionally causing accidents, aiming to die, whilst providing better financial support for their families (Miranda, 2012). For the same reason, colleagues of suicidal officers conceal information that might clarify the cause of death as suicide. It is common to find cases within the police service categorized as "deaths by firearm" with unknown intention (Miranda, 2012). Such failures can lead to mistaken conclusions not only regarding suicide rates but also their associated factors.

The second source of police suicide data comes from Public Security departments. This data comes from internal police departments. The national collection and publicization of this source are carried out by the Brazilian Public Security Forum (FBSP – Fórum Brasileiro de Segurança Pública). FBSP is an NGO committed to building an environment of reference and technical cooperation in the Public Security field. Every year, FBSP requests official data from each Security Department or equivalent Police Department, based on the Brazilian public information law. This source could be seen as an alternative to SIM data; however, police organizations do not always fulfill data requirements. Many of them do not respond to requests, thus it is believed that these statistics are also underreported.

FBSP data has been published since 2007 in an annual report that includes several crimes and other issues relevant to Public Security. Police suicide was included only in 2018, covering the number of suicides of on-duty civil and military officers per state. Between 2017 and 2022, 497 Brazilian police officers, both civilian and military, took their own lives. These deaths surpass the numbers of officers victimized in confrontations while on duty: during the same period, 316 officers died in such confrontations. These figures highlight an important issue: despite the extremely violent daily challenges faced by these agents, Brazil loses more police officers due to self-inflicted violence than to deaths in confrontation situations (Fórum Brasileiro de Segurança Pública 2018, 2019, 2020, 2021, 2022, 2023).

An alternative dataset is organized by the Instituto de Pesquisa, Prevenção e Estudos em Suicídio (IPPES). Since 2018, IPPES has been monitoring suicide deaths among Brazilian public security professionals through unofficial sources such as news and social media messages. This data is published annually in a Bulletin. This publication displays the suicide figures, the method adopted, and some sociodemographic characteristics of the victims.

TABLE 9.1 Military and Civil Police suicide from 2017 to 2022

	2017	2018	2019	2020	2021	2022
Military Police	53	67	69	52	78	69
Civil Police	21	26	13	13	23	13
Total	74	93	82	13	101	82

Source: Fórum Brasileiro de Segurança Pública (2018, 2019, 2020, 2021, 2022, 2023)

TABLE 9.2 Military and Civil Police homicide on duty from 2017 to 2022

	2017	2018	2019	2020	2021	2022
Military Police	11	69	47	46	15	18
Civil Police	71	12	5	14	7	1
Total	82	81	52	60	22	19

Source: Fórum Brasileiro de Segurança Pública (2018, 2019, 2020, 2021, 2022, 2023).

This data yielded interesting findings. One of them is that some of the suicide deaths were preceded by a homicide. The victims of the homicide were predominantly women with some emotional connection to the suicide victims. Between 2018 and 2021, we found 36 homicides followed by suicides. The study demonstrated that similar to research conducted in other countries, the majority of suicides occurred through the use of firearms, whereas this is not the primary method used for suicides among the Brazilian population (IPPES, 2022).

In addition to the challenges with the available data, Brazilian law enforcement agencies are generally not receptive to research conducted by non-law enforcement scholars. Opportunities for researchers to apply questionnaires or conduct interviews are not often available. These obstacles are faced by researchers not only in the field of mental health but also across other areas.

Suicide and police work

The occupational risk of suicide has been the focus of numerous international empirical studies. Despite the limitations of available death statistics (Stack, 2001), North American and English literatures have sought to investigate the occupational risk and suicide among police officers (Chae and Boyle, 2013; O'Hara and Violanti, 2009; Violanti, 1997; Hem et al., 2001). How can police suicide be explained? Under what conditions do police officers commit suicide? What factors contribute to the unique risk of suicide among police officers compared to other occupational groups? These are some of the questions that underlie the ongoing debate.

Researchers have been arguing for comprehending police suicide as a multifaceted issue encompassing societal, organizational, and individual dimensions. Workplace stress typically encompasses the exposure of these professionals to traumatic situations, stress, and deaths, including suicides; changes in responsibilities and irregular work schedules; subpar equipment; and public mistrust.

Frédéric Deschamps and colleagues (2003) investigated the association between policing, potential stressors, and stress levels within a group of 617 police officers from the French metropolitan force. The study considered groups of officers in distinct institutional positions and concluded that there is a correlation between stress levels, suicide, and police activities.

Links between socio-demographic variables (age and gender), occupational and health characteristics, and stress levels have also been investigated by these researchers. Police officers with the highest levels of occupational stress are those who have more than 15 years on duty, sergeants, officers in administrative roles, individuals who are divorced and over 30 years old, those who lack leisure activities during their free time, and those who do not have hobbies. These findings suggest that occupational stress within the police force arises from both stressful aspects of the profession and from personal life.

J.P. Cummings (1996) conducted research on the determinants of suicide among police officers from eight municipal agencies in Illinois, USA. The author identified an association between police stress and suicide. Regarding organizational factors, some of the indicated aspects include the hierarchical relationship between superior and subordinate officers, high police turnover, ambiguous policies and rules, fear of internal investigations, bureaucracy, and peer pressure.

A group of predictors of police suicide consists of the interaction between alcohol use, drug dependency, age, and mental illness. Kates (2001) found a connection between alcoholism, older age, physical illness, and retirement. The author also identified interactions involving firearms, continuous exposure to death situations, perception of inconsistencies within the criminal justice system, and a negative perception of their public image. In the Detroit Police Department (USA), a strong association with alcohol abuse was identified in 42% of police officers who took their own lives. On the other hand, 33% of them had a diagnosis of psychosis. The research revealed that half of the officers who died by suicide had a history of psychiatric or medical disorders, and many had severe alcohol use problems (Kates, 2001).

Another group of predictors for suicide and occupational risk involves the easy access to lethal methods. Among police officers, the convenient availability of firearms presents a risk factor. Similarly, within professions like physicians, pharmacists, dentists, and nurses, having access to drugs and medications increases the chances of suicide (Alpert and Dunham, 1998; Boxer et al., 1995; Burnett et al., 1992; Wasserman, 1992).

Police culture is also relevant. Officers tend to see things as right or wrong, which makes dealing with stressful situations and other adversities challenging (Violanti, 1997). This culture is reinforced in police training, where police officers are exposed to a socialization process. This black and white thinking guides their lives. Consequently, they face difficulties dealing with different ways of thinking, affecting their personal and work relationships (Violanti, 1997). For these officers, marital separation, retirement, loss of a loved one can be more challenging to handle and may affect their ability to cope.

Violanti (1995) uncovered that social support and trust are two significant factors associated with police suicide within the North American context. Low trust among peers elevates the risk of suicide among police officers. In his own words, "Police officers are more hesitant than the average citizen to get help for emotional problems. Because of their roles, they mistrust many things, and they especially mistrust mental health professionals" (Violanti, 1995, p. 23).

These findings have taught us that, although the existing data are limited, understanding suicidal behavior within the police force requires an interactive analysis of multiple risk factors (Chae and Boyle, 2013). Individual factors (sociodemographic profile, personality traits, interpersonal relationships); organizational factors (work conditions), as well as social factors external to the police environment, are predictors of police suicide that deserve deeper exploration through empirical research on the suicide risk of police officers, compared to distinct occupational groups.

Empirical research in Brazil has also identified a relative weight of certain correlates of occupational suicide. Four of these are frequently cited: demographic factors, organizational factors, facilitative means, and the presence of mental illness. These findings will be presented in the upcoming subsections.

Police suicide in Brazil

When we began this study on police suicide in Brazil, we carried out quantitative and qualitative data collection in different national contexts. Our initial study on occupational risk and suicide among Military Police officers in the state of Rio de Janeiro led to the book *Por que Policiais se Matam?* (Why Do Police Officers Kill Themselves?) in 2016 (Miranda et al., 2016a). The book contributed to bringing academic, political, and institutional visibility to the magnitude of the issue and the profile of police officers who died by suicide in that police force.

At that time, official data showed that suicide within the Military Police in Rio de Janeiro (PMERJ – Polícia Militar do Estado do Rio de Janeiro) was a recurring yet unstable form of victimization. Between 1995 and 2009, 58 on-duty police suicides were registered. Three occurred while officers were working and 55 on days off. On average, there were three suicides per year. The suicide mortality rates in PMERJ for this period varied dramatically, ranging between 0 and 39 deaths per 100,000 inhabitants (Miranda et al., 2016a). The majority of victims were male, married or in stable relationships, evangelical, and held lower-rank positions.

To comprehend the dynamics of these deaths and potential associated factors, we carried out psychosocial autopsies with family members, friends, and colleagues of 26 victims, recorded between 2005 and 2009. These interviews revealed that victims consumed alcohol, took on extra security jobs to supplement their incomes, had a history of using police health services (though not always psychiatric services), and generally were satisfied with working for the police.

Concurrently, as part of the same research, we carried out a survey and an interview with 224 police officers who had suicidal thoughts (22%), had attempted suicide (10%), or did not have thoughts or attempts (control group) (68%). Across all groups, job satisfaction was low, but even lower among officers who had thought about or attempted suicide (Miranda et al., 2016a). This contradiction between the narratives of the victims' families and friends, and those of police officers who had considered or attempted suicide, was evident.

A subsequent study investigated the dimensions and severity of suicidal behavior among professionals in the Military Police across all 27 Brazilian states and found similar patterns to the previous one. This study was based on a questionnaire with 18,007 responses. Results pointed out that: 3.6% of the Military Police officers had attempted suicide, 18% had suicidal thoughts, and 79% did not have thoughts or attempts (control group) (Miranda et al., 2016b).

The authors also concluded that factors associated with suicidal behavior among police officers interact across four levels of analysis: (i) organizational; (ii) situational; (iii) social; and (iv) individual. At the organizational level, the study pointed out dissatisfaction because of the lack of societal support for the police; career advancement difficulties, disciplinary regulations, insufficient specialized training, and limited health services were all associated with suicidal thoughts and acts. Conversely, job satisfaction served as a protective factor against suicidal ideation and attempts. At the situational level, data suggested that higher exposure to direct (lethal and non-lethal) and indirect (lethal and non-lethal) victimization increases the risk of suicidal thoughts and attempts. In terms of the social dimension, researchers observed a high level of mistrust. Regular friendship relationships shield professionals from thoughts and attempts of self-violence. Finally, at the individual level, i.e., the physical and emotional health of the police officer, the study demonstrated that insomnia, "little interest or pleasure in doing work activities," "difficulties for concentrating," "feelings of fear and/or panic," "feeling 'down,' depressed, or hopeless," "feeling tired or having little energy," and "a feeling of failure" were statistically associated with suicidal thoughts and attempts (Miranda et al. 2016b).

These results contributed to the formulation of an ecological model of suicide among Military Police officers. The logic of this model follows the premise that vulnerability to suicidal behaviour among Military Police officers involves four interactive dimensions: (1) organizational; (2) situational; (3) social; and (4) individual. These dimensions are interdependent.

The first dimension encompasses working conditions (professional training, relationships with superiors, work schedules, workplace infrastructure, and available material resources) and organizational factors, such as police subculture, military hierarchy, disciplinary regulations, and officers' beliefs and traditions. The second dimension is situational, encompassing aspects characterizing the risk, loss, and conflicts experienced by Military Police officers. According to Minayo and Souza (2003), risk and security, as perceived by the police, are two intrinsic categories of the police profession. Risk, from the perspective of Military Police officers, is primarily characterized by armed confrontations where they expose themselves and their lives are at stake.

The third dimension is social factors. Relationships and regular contacts established within the police force and the family, as well as participation in activities promoting collective action, can be protective factors against suicidal ideation and suicide attempts. The fourth and final dimension examined pertains to individual aspects. Problems with sleep, fear, lack of energy, and anxiety crises were the risk factors for suicidal thoughts and attempts reported by the surveyed officers.

In 2022, we investigated the applicability of the four dimensions of the ecological model of suicide among agents of the Military Police, Civil Police, and Fire Department of the state of Espírito Santo (SegurançaQPrevine, 2023). The following section presents the results mostly related to the organizational factors of the analyzed cases.

Suicide and mental illness among public safety professionals in Espírito Santo

Espírito Santo is part of the Southeast Region of Brazil, along with the states of São Paulo, Rio de Janeiro, and Minas Gerais. The state is considered small in comparison to its neighbours, with only 3,833,712 inhabitants (IBGE, 2022). In 2022, the intentional violent death rate (29.3) was slightly higher than the national rate (23.3), ranking as the 14th highest rate among the 26 states and the Federal District (Fórum Brasileiro de Segurança Pública, 2023).

Among the general population, Espírito Santo presents a suicide mortality rate (6.2) close to that observed for Brazil (6.5) (SegurançaQPrevine, 2023). Among public safety professionals, between 2013 and 2021, there were 26 suicides, with only two female victims. Twenty were Military Police officers, three were Civil Police officers, and three were Military Firefighters. One of these cases involved a murder-suicide, where a female officer took the life of her boyfriend before taking her own life.

Despite being a small state compared to others in the country, and having relatively lower violence rates than other states, it gained national attention due to a Military Police officer strike that occurred in 2017. In Brazil, Military Police officers are prohibited from going on strike, and to circumvent this prohibition, the spouses of police officers staged blockades in front of police stations in the metropolitan region of the state, blocking the exit of police officers and their vehicles. The movement's demands included salary adjustments, changes in promotion laws, additional payments, better equipment, as well as symbolic requests for the recognition and valorization of their services (Rocha, 2019). During the strike, a sense of fear pervaded the state, and within a few days, there were at least 142 homicides, along with other crimes.

In response to the movement, the state government increased punitive measures outlined in the Federal Constitution, and police officers faced allegations of desertion, abandonment of duty, and disobedience, leading to inquiries and dismissals for disciplinary reasons (Ferro, 2018). Only in 2019 were Military Police officers investigated, prosecuted, or punished for participating in or having their families participate in the protests granted amnesty. These events became fundamental to understanding the psychological distress among Military Police officers of the state. Interviews with the officers from Espírito Santo frequently confirmed this association. The effects of the Strike episode emerged in the accounts even when they were not explicitly included in the interview script.

The research was conducted throughout 2022. We carried out 19 interviews with (i) colleagues who participated in training courses with the victims and/or who were working with the victims before their suicide (12); and (ii) victims' relatives (7). We analyzed 11 suicides among public safety professionals, including 7 Military Police officers, 2 Civil Police officers, and 2 Military Firefighters; therefore, some interviews refer to the same cases. The access to the interviewees was facilitated by the State Public Security Department. The interviews followed a semi-structured script that explored interpersonal, professional, organizational, and situational issues, including the victims' professional trajectory, social relationships, work conditions, and the conditions, circumstances, and motivations for their deaths.

Similar to the research conducted in Rio de Janeiro (2016), we found in Espírito Santo (2023) the combination of individual, social, organizational, and situational risk factors associated with suicide among these officers. It was interesting to observe how different interviewees attributed different motivations to the same case. This fact drew our attention to two issues: firstly, that family or friends, do not always have knowledge of the victim's personal life; and secondly, the risk of attributing a single cause to these phenomena. It is in response to these empirical observations that we have put forth the hypothesis of the multifactorial nature of police suicide (Miranda et al., 2016b). In this work, we will highlight the predictors directly related to police work, factors that have already been defined in the literature as organizational or operational (Shane, 2010).

The distribution of resources and punishments is an important organizational factor in police work. Several authors have examined the topic of distributive justice and organizational justice and their impacts (Wolfe and Nix, 2017; Sun et al., 2018; Peacock et al., 2021). Van Craen (2016) argues that unequal treatment or treatment not based on the right to voice, respect, or accountability can fuel feelings of anger and frustration among agents. In the Brazilian context, even within a militarized institution with strict hierarchical rules, officers identify inequalities in processes even when involving people of the same hierarchical level. The frustration with these perceived unjust processes appeared in many interviews, associated with professional dissatisfaction and sometimes as a trigger for other mental health issues. It is similar to previous studies that had already found a strong relationship between professional dissatisfaction and vulnerability to suicidal behavior (suicidal ideation and suicide attempts) (Miranda et al., 2016a and 2016b).

In Espírito Santo, in one of the analyzed cases, the victim was described by family and friends as a police officer very dedicated to work and a profound connoisseur of internal bureaucracies, including the internal carrier progression process. Despite his dedication to the profession, contrary to the formal regulations, other officers had been promoted ahead of him, fueling a sense of unfairness and impacting his relationship with work. This officer took his own life upon returning from a unit gathering. The relative of another officer also recounted how his brother had been promoted and then "demoted," which had led to profound disappointment and subsequently a depressive condition that worsened until culminating in suicide.

Cruz et al. (2023) demonstrated that disrespectful experiences of Military Police officers in São Paulo during an Administrative Disciplinary Procedure worsened these agents' assessment of their relationship with superiors and the organization. In our research, conducted in Military Police institutions in Rio de Janeiro and Espírito Santo, regarding the relationship between mental health and punishment experiences, we found two distinct perspectives. The first relates to dissatisfaction with punishments considered unjust. These include not only formal punishments but also informal punishments, widely adopted in these institutions, such as transfers to different locations or shifts, which sometimes deeply affect these agents' routines.

The second is related to the fear of being expelled from the institution after an incident of misconduct. Victims fitting this second category are described as "potential problems" from the beginning of their careers. Interviews reveal how certain personality characteristics of the victim are indicated as inappropriate for the expected profile for that role (whether Civil Police, Military Police, or Military Firefighter). In one case, where the officer fit this profile, the trigger for suicide was reported to be involvement in a fight during time off. This officer had inappropriately fired a weapon in a public place. This view of the "problematic officer" tends to assign responsibility for behavior to the individual, while the institution is disregarded. However, the same interviewee, who exhibits traits of the "problematic officer" personality, reflects on how all officers are subject to "becoming a criminal":

> When you enter the police, you never imagine that you could be arrested because you have an impeccable life. And from the moment you enter the police, this fear starts to haunt you, right? This is a huge torment for the police. So, in my case too, I'm not afraid of criminals, I'm afraid of the police. So, this is tormenting. So, leaving the position of being right, of being a police officer, to the position of being a criminal, would be a great shame. So, I've seen some friends, including one just because he went through a very complicated incident, and then they put it in the media that they were wrong, and the weight of society comes around. He called right away to go get his gun because he wanted to kill himself. So, the weight of judgment for someone who's sure they're being judged wrongly is a heavy burden.
>
> *(Military Police Colleague)*

By presenting the tension between "right and wrong" and the shame of being equated with a "criminal," the interviewee reinforces the argument that the formal and informal socialization process within police institutions tends to develop a dichotomous and inflexible mode of thinking. This rigidity sometimes translates into difficulties in assuming multiple social roles, both within internal relationships and in society and their social connections, which is a crucial element for understanding police suicide (Violanti, 1997).

Finally, it is necessary to highlight the consequences of the strike on the personal and professional lives, as well as the mental health, of these agents. Many interviewees reported tensions between following their peers and adhering to the strike or following commanders' orders. Another source of suffering was being confined in police units far from their families. One of the interviewees, who was confined in one of the units, described how the process impacted the mental health of the police officers:

> There were constant threats of punishment. If we stayed there, we could be arrested, charged with a crime, charged with this or that. And on the other hand, we couldn't give in, right? Because the other police units were in the same situation, but yeah, it was a psychological pressure in that sense.
>
> *(Military Police Colleague)*

In two of the analyzed cases, suicide was directly attributed to the strike. In one of them, the relative believed that the officer was not able to "handle the pressure." In the other case, it was pointed out that the transfer of units caused a rupture in social interactions among peers, which contributed to the officer taking their own life:

> (...) we were all very close, not just him, our team used to work together, like I said we went out a lot, right? And because of the strike, everyone was separated, I think he felt that a lot, right? Well, I don't know if he had other friendships, so I think he felt that separation from everyone a lot. So, that's the path I see, I don't know, right, I don't see another reason.
> *(Military Police Colleague)*

The isolation of police officers is one of the themes that has been pointed out in both national literature (Miranda et al., 2016a) and international literature (Violanti, 1997) regarding police suicide. Often these agents have few social networks, and many of them are mediated by work, where they can find people who "truly understand their way of life". In this sense, the interviewee believes that the transfer, by breaking the bonds between peers, contributed to his colleague taking his own life.

In addition to deaths, other effects of the strike reverberate in daily work, even five years later. We identified constant complaints about the loss of autonomy for police officers. According to one of the interviewees, "If before, the military had some autonomy to decide on the policing of their area, after 2017, they no longer had it, they had to follow a schedule." There is an association between the strike and an increase in the control over agents' conduct. According to one of the interviewees, there was a significant increase in disciplinary procedures from that year onwards. In interviews conducted with health professionals, a consensus point was an increase in sick leaves due to mental health issues. Unfortunately, the research did not have access to health data.

In analyzing the organizational aspects present in the interviews carried out in Espírito Santo, our intention was not to attribute the causality of the deaths solely to this dimension. As we previously emphasized, we argue that police suicide is multifactorial. Our goal is to shed direct or indirect light on the organizational themes that emerged in colleagues' and family members' narratives. While some of these factors are similar to the context in Rio de Janeiro and have also been presented in other contexts outside of Brazil, the case in Espírito Santo brings the peculiarity of the strike and its impacts. This case inspires us to reflect on the limitations of policing as it is structured in Brazil, to address not only the demands of society but also those of the police officers themselves.

Conclusion

Despite the violent daily life in Brazilian cities, the country annually loses more police officers to suicide than in confrontations during their work (Fórum Brasileiro de Segurança Pública, 2023).

The limitations of available data mean that we still do not know much about the profile of these victims. We know that police suicide in Brazil is predominantly male, even though police forces are still predominantly male. Developing analyses that compare rates by gender—both in the general population and among police officers—depends on the quality of gender variable availability in records, which is not always available. Based on unofficial data, we also know that firearms were the primary means adopted by public safety professionals to take their own lives (IPPES, 2022). This reinforces the risk exposure that these professionals have due to being armed all the time, even when off-duty or retired.

Empirical and national research confirms that suicide among police officers and its effects are complex and multifactorial issues. Data collected through our studies allowed us to construct the ecological model of police suicide in Brazil, consisting of sociodemographic, organizational, individual, and situational factors (Miranda et al., 2016a, 2016b). The narratives collected in the states of Rio de Janeiro and Espírito Santo revealed that there is no overlap of one factor over the other. On the contrary, the phenomenon of police and firefighter suicide results from the interaction of these associated factors.

In Espírito Santo, as in our previous studies, occupational issues emerge as risk factors associated with police suicide. This relationship presupposes understanding how the everyday work routine can affect the professional's health. Another significant factor is the history of previous attempts. Interviews also showed that professionals may be suffering without seeking help, or if they have sought help, they did not share what was happening with their family or colleagues. Situations like these confirm the existing taboo in institutions regarding the agents' decision to seek help. At the same time, in several interviews, colleagues were able to acknowledge that police work impacts agents' stress and often admitted that these factors affect their own lives. Perhaps the most significant conclusion in this aspect is that the taboo still exists, and police officers suffer emotionally alone.

The study in Espírito Santo highlights the need for the adoption of fair procedures, established through clear rules and procedures, and respectful treatment in internal and external relationships. This applies both to the distribution of resources and to punishments or rewards; injustices in the promotion process are the most cited factors in relation to the psychological distress of these professionals. This situation suggests how the lack of career advancement opportunities, lack of professional recognition (from superiors), and a sense of devaluation by society affect the mental health of these professionals. We conclude, then, that promotions and facing punishment processes can contribute to the process of psychological distress in this occupational group.

In Rio de Janeiro, we found more narratives of the relationship between exposure to victimization situations and suicidal behavior than in Espírito Santo, which may be related to the more violent daily life in the former capital. At the same time, we also found in the narratives of colleagues of police victims that the feelings after witnessing a violent death influenced the decision-making process within and outside the professional's work. Our studies did not seek to examine the effects this exposure has on the psyche of police officers. However, it can be assumed that exposure to violent death and human suffering produces a negative emotional impact experienced differently by each person. The trauma caused by death can bring about pain that leads the individual to believe that the solution to their problems would be to take their own life. Here is another issue to be investigated.

Despite the efforts presented throughout this work, understanding the suicide of public safety professionals in Brazil still requires new studies and research. It is necessary to improve the quality of available data, investigate whether there are state or police force differences, and deepen the analysis of the presence and absence of risk and preventive factors. At the same time, we hope that what we already know will help guide the development of evidence-based prevention actions, as this is still a long path to take.

References

Alpert, G.P., Dunham, R.G. *Policing Urban America*. New York: Waveland, 1998.

Boxer, P.A., Burnett, C.A., Swanson, N.Suicide and Occupation: A Review of the Literature. *Journal of Occupational and Environmental Medicine*, 37 (4), 442–452, 1995.

Burnett, C.A., Boxer, P.A., Swanson, N. *Suicide and Occupation: Is there a Relationship?* American Psychological Association, National Institute for Occupation Health Conference, Washington, DC, 1992.

Borges, D. et al. Mortes violentas no Brasil: uma análise do fluxo de informações. In *Pensando a Segurança Pública, volume 1*. 1st edn, 329–409. Brasília: Ministério da Justiça, 2013.

Cano, I. 2010. Racial Bias in Police Use of Lethal Force in Brazil. *Police Practice and Research*, 11 (1), 31–43, 2010. doi:10.1080/15614260802586350.

Chae, M., Boyle, D.Police Suicide: Prevalence, Risk, and Protective Factors. *Policing: An International Journal of Police Strategies & Management*, 36, 91–118, 2013.

Cummings, J. P.Police Stress and the Suicide Link. *Journal Police Chief*, 63 (10), 85–96, 1996.

Constantino, P., Souza, E.R., Minayo, M.C.D.S. *Missão prevenir e proteger: condições de vida, trabalho e saúde dos policiais militares do Rio de Janeiro.* 1st edn. Rio de Janeiro: Fiocruz, 2008.

Costa, A.T.M.Police Brutality in Brazil: Authoritarian Legacy or Institutional Weakness? *Latin American Perspectives*, 38 (5), 19–32, 2011. doi:10.1177/0094582X10391631.

Cruz, F.N, Miranda, D., Rastrelli, A.N.Luto por suicídio e posvenção na polícia militar. *Revista Brasileira de Segurança Pública*, 16 (3), 1413v, 2022 doi:10.31060/rbsp.

Cruz, F.N., Oliveira, A.R., Castelo Branco, F., Cubas. V.O.The Impact of Administrative Disciplinary Proceedings on Military Police Officers in São Paulo. *Policing: A Journal Of Policy And Practice*, 17 (August), 1–15, 2023. doi:10.1093/police/paad046.

Deschamps, F., Paganon-Badinier, I., Marchand, A., Merle, C.Sources and Assesssment of Occupational Stress in the Police. *Journal of Occupational Health*, 45, 358–364, 2003.

Kates, A.R. *CopShock: Surviving Posttraumatic Stress Disorder (PTSD)*. New York: St. Martin's, 2001.

Ferro, P.L. *Polícia Militar do Espírito Santo: uma abordagem histórica, social e psicológica, sobre a formação e a violência.* PUC São Paulo, 2018. Available at: https://tede2.pucsp.br/bitstream/handle/21436/2/Pedro%20Luiz%20Ferro.pdf

Fórum Brasileiro de Segurança Pública. 2018. *12° Anuário Brasileiro de Segurança Pública*. São Paulo.

Fórum Brasileiro de Segurança Pública. 2019. *13° Anuário Brasileiro de Segurança Pública*. São Paulo.

Fórum Brasileiro de Segurança Pública. 2020. *14° Anuário Brasileiro de Segurança Pública*. São Paulo.

Fórum Brasileiro de Segurança Pública. 2021. *15° Anuário Brasileiro de Segurança Pública*. São Paulo.

Fórum Brasileiro de Segurança Pública. 2022. *16° Anuário Brasileiro de Segurança Pública*. São Paulo.

Fórum Brasileiro de Segurança Pública. 2023. *17° Anuário Brasileiro de Segurança Pública*. São Paulo.

González, Y.M. *Authoritarian Police in Democracy: Contested Security in Latin America.* New York: Cambridge University Press, 2022. doi:10.1002/polq.13402.

Hem, E., Berg, A.M., Ekeberg, Ø. Suicide in Police—A Critical Review. *Suicide and Life-Threatening Behavior*, 31(2), 224–233, 2001.

Huggins, M., Haritos-Fatouros, M., Zimbardo, P.G. *Operários da violência: Policiais torturadores e assassinos reconstroem as atrocidades brasileiras.* Brasília: Editora UnB, 2006.

IBGE (Instituto Brasileiro de Geografia e Estatística). *Censo Brasileiro de 2022.* Rio de Janeiro: IBGE, 2022.

IPPES (Instituto de Pesquisa, Prevenção e Estudos em Suicídio). *Boletim de notificação de mortes violentas intencionais e tentativas de suicídio entre profissionais de segurança pública no Brasil,* 2022. Available at: https://ippesbrasil.com.br/wp-content/uploads/2022/12/Boletim-IPPES-2022-VF.pdf.

Minayo, M.C. de S., Souza, E.R. *Missão investigar: entre o ideal e a realidade de ser policial.* Rio de Janeiro: Garamond, 2003.

Miranda, D. *Suicídio e risco ocupacional: A condição do policial militar do estado do Rio de Janeiro.* Partial report, CNPq, 2010.

Miranda, D. *Risco ocupacional: A condição do policial militar do Estado do Rio de Janeiro*. Final report. CNPq, 2012.

Miranda, D. et al. *Por que os policiais se matam? condições de vida, trabalho e saúde dos policiais militares do Rio de Janeiro*. Rio de Janeiro: Mórula, 2016a.

Miranda, D. et al. O comportamento suicida entre profissionais de segurança pública e prevenção no Brasil. *Pensando a Segurança Pública*, 6, p. 51, 2016b. Available at: http://www.justica.gov.br (Accessed: 20 August 2020).

Murray J., Cerqueira D.R., Kahn T.Crime and Violence in Brazil: Systematic Review of Time Trends, Prevalence Rates and Risk Factors. *Aggression and Violent Behavior, 18* (5), 471–483, 2013. doi:10.1016/J.AVB.2013.07.003.

O'Hara, A.F., Violanti, J.M.Police Suicide: Web Surveillance of National Data. *International Journal of Emergency Mental Health*, 11 (1), 17–23, 2009.

Peacock, R.P. et al. External Procedural Justice: Do Just Supervisors Shape Officer Trust and Willingness to Take the Initiative with the Public? *International Criminal Justice Review*, 1–20, 2021. doi:10.1177/1057567721996790.

Rocha, G.D. *Quando as armas do Leviatã se voltam contra si: a greve da Polícia Militar do Espírito Santo de fevereiro de 2017*. Universidade Federal do Estado do Espírito Santo, 2019.

Sapori, L.F.The Dual Civil and Military Models for Policing in Brazil. In: Riccio, V; Skogan, W.G. *Police and society in Brazil*. New York: Routledge, 29–42, 2018.

Shane, J.M.Organizational Stressors and Police Performance. *Journal of Criminal Justice*, 38 (4), 807–818, 2010. doi:10.1016/j.jcrimjus.2010.05.008.

Stack, S.Occupation and Suicide. *Social Science Quarterly*, 82 (2), 384–396, 2001.

SegurançaQPrevine no Espírito Santo. *Segurança Pública e Defesa Social do Espírito Santo*. Final report, 2023.

Sistema de Informações de Mortalidade (SIM). Coordenadoria do Sub-sistema de Mortalidade. Available online at: http://tabnet.datasus.gov.br/tabdata/sim/dados/cid9/docs/intro.pd.

Sun, I.Y. et al. Internal Procedural Justice, Moral Alignment, and External Procedural Justice in Democratic Policing. *Police Quarterly*, 21 (3), 387–412, 2018. doi:10.1177/1098611118772270.

Van Craen, M.Understanding Police Officers' Trust and Trustworthy Behavior: A Work Relations Framework. *European Journal of Criminology*, 13 (2), 274–294, 2016. doi:10.1177/1477370815617187.

Violanti, J.M.The Mystery Within, Understanding Police Suicide. *FBI Law Enforcement Bulletin*, pp.19–23, 1995.

Violanti, J.M.Suicide and the Police Role: A Psychosocial Model. *Policing: A Journal of Policy and Practice*, [S. l.], 4, 698–715, 1997.

Wasserman, I.M.Economy, Work, Occupation and Suicide. In: Maris, R.; Berman, A.; Maltsberger, J.; Yufit, R. (eds). *Assessment and Prediction of Suicide*. New York: Guilforf, 520–539, 1992.

Wolfe, S.E. and Nix, J.Police Officers' Trust in Their Agency: Does Self-Legitimacy Protect Against Supervisor Procedural Injustice? *Criminal Justice and Behavior*, 44 (5), 717–732, 2017. doi:10.1177/0093854816671753.

10
PTSD

Is it pension worthy

Charles Russo and Stephanie Myers-Hunziker

As first responders, public safety personnel, law enforcement officers, firefighters, paramedics and emergency medical technicians often experience traumatic events. Typically, they encounter such events while in the middle of working their normal shifts (Regambal et al., 2015). They see, hear, smell and taste things that most only read about. First responders might receive cuts, bruises, broken bones, torn ligaments and tendons, loss of limbs/sight/hearing, paralysis, etc. Due to these physical injuries, they may be unable to function as they did prior to the traumatic event. As a result, they may need to retire altogether from their profession. Others may be forced to return to work before they are ready.

Aside from the potential reality of physical injury, some first responders experience wounds that are not readily observable. According to the National Institute of Mental Health, an individual who has experienced a traumatic event might suffer from posttraumatic stress disorder (PTSD) (National Institute of Mental Health, 2016). As one might surmise, some first responders may experience more than one traumatizing event across their professional career. While the injuries caused by posttraumatic stress may not be visible, they can be impactful and life changing. The National Institute of Mental Health (2016) notes that PTSD might be diagnosed if a person has, within the past month, experienced at least one re-experiencing symptom (i.e. flashbacks), at least one avoidance symptom (i.e. avoiding places or feelings), at least two arousal and reactivity symptoms (i.e. easily startled, difficulty sleeping), and at least two cognition and mood symptoms (i.e. feeling guilt or self-blame). For

DOI: 10.4324/9781003452379-11

example, individuals who may be suffering from posttraumatic stress may be easily startled and then transported back to the moment they experienced the traumatic episode. They may actively avoid anything or any place that reminds them of the trauma and mentally be blaming themselves for not being able to do more to help others. Certain sights, sounds and smells might be triggers for these stressful reactions, which might be accompanied by an accelerated heartbeat, disturbing images in the mind, perspiration, and dilated pupils; to name but a few possibilities.

Most of those experiencing these physical reactions, known as posttraumatic stress (a normal reaction to an abnormal event), can continue with only a minor disruption at work. The respective reactions might completely dissipate over time. For others, those certain sights, sounds, smells and tastes are accompanied by long term debilitating reactions, known as posttraumatic stress disorder (PTSD), that make them unable to continue with normal work tasks. This might continue for an uncertain amount of time. Sometimes a person may not ever be able to return to life as it was before the stressful event occurred. A hallmark of posttraumatic stress disorder is that the person first be exposed to a stressful and life-threatening event and to then have "three distinct types of symptoms consisting of a re-experiencing of the event, avoidance of reminders of the event, and hyperarousal for at least one month" (Yehuda, 2002, p. 109). The reality is that those suffering usually do so in silence. For those first responders who return to work too early, the possibility exists for them to react not based on the situation at hand; instead, the first responder may overreact or underreact to a given situation. This could place them as well as others in harm's way.

Pension eligibility and workers' compensation

For those who experience physical injuries that prohibit them from continuing in their professions, medical disability pensions and workers' compensation are often available to provide them a sense of financial security for their uncertain future. However, for those who experience PTSD, medical disability pensions and workers' compensation may not be in their future. Unable to continue in their professions and possibly the "normal" life they had prior to the traumatic event, these individuals may be further traumatized by the lack of resources and financial support for these permanent injuries that cannot be seen by others. Some may even feel they have no choice but to return to work even though they may not be ready psychologically.

Those who seek pensions and disability based solely on psychological trauma face an uphill battle. Much of the pension and workers' compensation language addresses physical injury, not psychological harm. Absent physical injury, public safety personnel unable to perform in their profession due to a psychological injury have been left with a very uncertain future. While individual cases have been progressing through our court and appeals systems, discussions at various state and local levels have begun to examine the question… is PTSD worthy of pension benefits and workers' compensation?

Examples of recent traumatic events: Sandy Hook Elementary School

While clearing rooms at Sandy Hook Elementary School, in Newton, CT, shortly after the shooter killed himself, Officer Bean entered classrooms where 20 children had been shot. Since that day, Officer Bean has not returned to work and has been out on long term disability for PTSD, which Newton's insurance policy caps at two years of benefits. Bean's chief tried to fire him six months after the incident as Bean was unable to return to work. When this information became public, the termination order was rescinded due to the public outcry. As Bean was coming upon the end of Newton's two years of long term disability, Bean and his union filed a grievance to continue disability payments. The Connecticut State Board of Mediation and Arbitration ruled that Newton must pay Bean 50% of his salary until his retirement date at which time he can then collect his pension. Newton Police Department calculates the 11 years of payments until Bean's retirement date will amount to $380,797 (Altimari, 2015).

Pulse night club shooting, Orlando, FL

Law enforcement officers who responded to the 2016 Pulse terror attack struggled to gain compensation after the incident in Orlando. First responding officers such as Gerry Realin and Omar Delgado, who were suffering from PTSD due to their work at the Pulse night club but with no accompanying physical injuries, feared that their agencies, Orlando Police Department and Eatonville Police Department respectively, might stop paying their salary at any time – leaving them unable to support their families. These officers had even resorted to GoFundMe accounts and seeking help, unsuccessfully, from the One Orlando Fund that distributed $29.5 million to the Pulse victims (Robles, 2016; Sutton, 2016). As these officers were not inside the club once the shooting started, they were deemed ineligible to receive disbursements from the One Orlando Fund. Suffering from PTSD, knowing that at any time their salaries could cease, and without the availability of workers' compensation for future professional treatment and financial security, these officers feared being revictimized by the system. At the time, Florida was one of several states that did not provide workers compensation for first responders that had been diagnosed with PTSD but are without any physical injury (Harris, 2017; Wise & Beck, 2015).

Progress at the state level

Since the Pulse nightclub shooting Florida's then Governor Rick Scott signed, in 2018, into law a bill that would allow for workers compensation for first responders with PTSD. What one can infer from Florida Senate Bill (376) is that there are specific qualifying events, exposures, and a diagnosis needed for a valid workers' compensation claim. While the new law focuses on qualifying events and compensable claims, it also requires agencies that employ first responders "to provide educational training related to mental health awareness, prevention, mitigation, and treatment" (Florida Department of Financial Services, 2022).

Another state leading the way in terms of change is Minnesota. In 2018 the Minnesota Legislature passed a bill that effectively amended the workers' compensation statute to provide an evidence based presumption for post-traumatic stress disorder in first responders (Minnesota Counties Intergovernmental Trust, 2023). There are several steps required to process a claim of PTSD in the state of Minnesota, but the legislature has made the process more streamlined for workers' compensation; the jury is still out on pension.

When these types of bills are introduced in any state, lawmakers likely worry about the projected costs for the state. It is hard to project an accurate financial analysis of the proposed changes at this time. Despite the uncertainty, we are seeing a trend on a state by state basis where benefits are considered for first responders with PTSD.

Employers want an objective test

Police officers still face an uphill battle when trying to collect workers' compensation absent physical injury. Claims based solely on PTSD have proven challenging to all involved – employees, employers and administrators alike. As there is no objective testing to demonstrate PTSD, such as for other illnesses or diseases like diabetes, heart conditions, lung issues, etc., findings can appear to be subjective. For example, as bills are introduced in different states, we have seen a call for varying *standards of proof* of a PTSD diagnosis. The different bills that were proposed in Florida contained one bill that called for the evidence of a PTSD diagnosis to be by a "preponderance of the evidence" standard while another called for a "clear and convincing evidence" standard (Harris, 2017). Couple the subjectivity of the diagnosis with the absence of physical signs of a disability, many have a difficult time "believing"

PTSD can be a career ending condition (Robinson, 2014). Some point to the overall lack of reliance on the field and study of psychology when creating workers' compensation legislation (Wise & Beck, 2015). There is no question that psychology is an established field of scientific study. It would behoove the workers' compensation field to turn to research to inform their practices as it relates to treating first responders and their mental readiness to return to work after experiencing a traumatic event.

Differences among the states

One recent categorization of states in terms of how they handle claims of mental illness and PTSD without physical injury found that 15 states refuse to award any compensation for PTSD claims under any circumstances (Category One) (Robinson, 2014).

Category Two included 15 states that allow for PTSD claims if the stimulus causing the PTSD, the event(s), was "unusual". States' decisions regarding the definition seem to revolve around "unusual" based on the individual's position/occupation. This could prove a bit ambiguous for public safety personnel in that they are expected to deal with the "unusual" on a regular basis. Category Three consists of 5 states that will award PTSD claims if the stimulus causing the PTSD was "sudden". Category Four is comprised of 3 states where PTSD claims are compensable whether or not "unusual" or "sudden". The remaining 12 states do not fall into one category or another due to inconsistent PTSD rulings.

One example, the state of Illinois fell into Category Two; where PTSD claims are compensable if the event was unusual. In the case of an Illinois fire lieutenant who was in command of fighting a house fire that resulted in the death of a firefighter, this incident was deemed unusual and the lieutenant's PTSD claim was found to be compensable. Requiring fire personnel

TABLE 10.1 PTSD without physical injury compensation

Classification	No. of states	General rule
Category 1	15	Will not award any money for any type of PTSD claim without physical injury.
Category 2	15	Will only award money if the qualifying event was "unusual"
Category 3	5	Might award money if the qualifying event was "sudden"
Category 4	3	Will award money for PTSD claims
Category 5	12	These states do not fall into any category due to uncertainty of rulings.

on that incident to be cleared by a mental health professional before being allowed to return to work strengthened the view that the event was traumatic and unusual (Robinson, 2016).

Florida fell into Category One when the data were released. At the time PTSD was not recognized as a work-related injury. In fact, Florida State Statue (FSS) 440.093 specifically excluded what it categorized as mental and nervous injuries. The Florida statue stated,

> A mental or nervous injury due to stress, fright, or excitement only is not an injury by accident arising out of the employment. Nothing in this section shall be construed to all for payment of benefits under this chapter for mental or nervous injuries without an accompanying physical injury requiring medical treatment. A physical injury resulting from mental or nervous injuries unaccompanied by physical trauma requiring medical treatment shall not be compensable under this chapter.
> (FSS 440.993, 2017)

Since that time, with the signing of SB376 in 2018, Florida has really taken a step forward in support of first responders with PTSD by allowing benefits in some instances.

Likewise, Wise and Beck (2015) examined the implications of workers' compensation practice and policy related to work related trauma and PTSD across states. They discovered that despite "considerable empirical knowledge about trauma and PTSD, a gap exists with respect to laws undergirding workers' compensation (WC) insurance coverage for work-related mental health injuries" (p. 500). They too found that workers' compensation laws vary greatly from state to state and vary greatly in coverage depending on physical injury to psychological injury. Wise and Beck (2015) observed the "lack of reliance on psychological science in scripting legislation and determining WC benefits" (p. 500). They categorized public safety worker compensation systems in three categories as physical-physical injuries, physical-mental injuries and mental-mental injuries. Only one (1) state, Montana, covers only physical-physical injuries. Sixteen states were categorized states that cover as physical-mental injuries as well as physical-physical injuries. Nineteen other states were categorized as states that cover mental-mental injuries as well as physical-physical injuries. Eighteen states provide coverage if the mental cause is found to be extraordinary, unusual and/or outside the individual's scope of a typical experience.

Among states categorized as physical-mental states, disparities were noted in case law bringing into question a definitive classification of that state. While consistency among states is apparent regarding physical injury, coverage of psychological injury will be dependent on the location of the incident/event.

TABLE 10.2 Workers' compensation coverage category of injuries

Workers' compensation coverage category of injuries (Cause of injury – result of injury)	Number of states with coverage (including Washington, D.C.)
Physical-physical	51
Physical-mental	16
Mental-mental	19
Extraordinary/unusual	18

When psychological injury is covered to some extent, language in worker compensation policy fails to mimic that found in psychological science. This leads to uncertainty and confusion when attempting to determine necessary psychological injury benefits.

A more recent review of individual states' approaches to PTSD and the awarding of benefits reveals only a slightly different picture. A report prepared by a large Atlanta based workers' compensation law firm shows a trend toward supporting more claims state by state (Gerber and Holder Law Firm, 2023). A 2019 report published by the National Council on Compensation Insurance shows that "at least 26 states considered new legislation addressing workers' compensation coverage for PTSD and other 'mental-only' injuries for first responders" (NCCI Inc., 2019, p. 4). According to this report, in 2019 at least "eight states (Connecticut, Idaho, Louisiana, Nevada, New Hampshire, New Mexico, Oregon, and Texas) passed legislation addressing benefits for first responders with PTSD" (NCCI Inc., 2019, p. 4). This shows further support for a trend toward supporting police officers and other first responders.

Previous research

The mental health and overall wellbeing of police officers, fire fighters, and other first responders is an important area of study. As such, several researchers have undertaken studies that highlight the presentation of psychological stress and the overall impact of such stress that can occur in response to critical or traumatic events experienced while on the job. Studies tend to support the idea that when compared to first responders that have not experienced a traumatic event, those that have experienced at least one are much more likely to present with symptoms of PTSD (Robinson et al., 1997; Corneil et al., 1999; Pietrzak et al., 2014). Yehuda (2002) notes that the factors that contribute to the "intensity of the response to a psychologically traumatic experience include the degree of controllability, predictability, and perceived threat; the relative success of attempts to minimize injury to self or others; and actual loss" (p. 109).

In a study of 100 suburban police officers exploring the relationship between job related stressors and PTSD researchers reported a statistically significant relationship between exposure to duty related stress and symptoms of PTSD (Robinson et al., 1997). One issue worth noting when comparing research is the different definitions of what qualifies as a "stressor" and the definition of a traumatic event. Again, the subjectivity of these terms may be a hold up for workers' compensation legislation. A hard and fast rule is always preferred when making funding decisions. Having said that, several researchers have confirmed that exposure to life and death threats showed the strongest correlation to PTSD (Robinson et al., 1997; Yehuda, 2002; Pietrzak et al., 2014). In addition, younger officers, having 11 years or fewer in law enforcement experience, displayed PTSD symptoms at a higher rate than more experienced officers (Robinson et al., 1997). Researchers speculated that the younger officers have not yet developed successful coping mechanisms for stressful occurrences – thus perhaps the older and more experienced officers fared better.

In an examination of internal and external risk factors for posttraumatic stress symptoms of Netherlands police officers from five of the seven largest police agencies in that country, researchers identified 37 critical police incidents in the country and then informed police personnel of those agencies the purpose of their study (Carlier et al., 1997). Personnel were then notified that they could participate in the study whenever they experienced a work related critical incident. Several officers, 262 in all, volunteered for the study. Although there are obvious selection biases here, it is important to note that posttraumatic stress symptoms were detected in 34% of the participants, and that actual PTSD was detected in 7% of the sample. Researchers noted that emotional or mental exhaustion at the time of trauma was highly correlated to posttraumatic stress symptoms. This exhaustion is frequently experienced among personnel who respond to traumatic incidents such as the Pulse terror event in Orlando, Florida and the Sandy Hook Elementary School shooting incident in Newton, Connecticut. Many first responders spend hours on scene after the neutralization of the threat occurs.

PTSD has the potential to impact all public safety professionals; not only police officers. Corneil et al. (1999) examined urban firefighters in two countries, the United States and Canada, to determine the risk of PTSD amongst their ranks. Researchers utilized a 15 item measure of posttraumatic stress symptomology. Both United States and Canadian samples presented with similar rates of PTSD. Some 90% of the US sample and 85% of the Canadian sample reported at least one traumatic incident exposure within the past year and both had "high odds ratios for PTSD due to the work strain variable" (p. 139). PTSD experienced by US and Canadian firefighters was reported as four to six times greater than that of US crime victims. Similarly, in a study of 400 plus German firefighters more than 18% met the diagnostic criteria for PTSD (Wagner et al., 1998). These researchers distributed the General Health Questionnaire (GHQ) to 402 firefighters in the German state of Rheinland-Pfalz. Experiencing distressing missions and longer time as a firefighter correlated highest to PTSD from the sampled population. German firefighters with PTSD expressed higher levels of traumatic stress, substance use and body complaints compared to fellow firefighters without PTSD. All are symptoms not associated with physical injury and thus in many US states would not make these firefighters eligible for workers' compensation benefits.

Research also shows that officers with more experience (Robinson et al., 1997) are less likely to experience long term PTSD. Also, at least one study shows that police officers, compared to other types of first responders, were less likely to experience PTSD. This is likely due to the amount of training and preparedness they get on the job (Pietrzak et al., 2014).

Can/should more of this risk management be put into motion to help prevent PTSD?

Summary and discussion

A review of the literature demonstrates that posttraumatic stress is a problem for some first responders who answer calls for service to a traumatic incident. Not everyone is affected in the same way. Research suggests that most will have symptoms of re-experiencing, avoidance, and hyperarousal initially following the trauma – but that this will dissipate over time (Kearns et al., 2012). These responders may return to work immediately or after brief time off for treatment. For others, however, their symptoms persist and cause impairment in functioning (Kearns et al., 2012). Their psychological injuries may lead to a PTSD diagnosis and may require substantial time for treatment. Some may never return to work or a normal life.

Public service agencies and state workers' compensation funds appear to be in the beginning stages of understanding how to best manage those that suffer from PTSD but have no visible physical injuries. Understanding their entitlement to benefits and how to contend with psychological injury is no easy task. Here are a few of what appear to be the foremost points of contention:

1. *Estimates of those affected* – Questions remain as to how many public safety workers that respond to trauma are likely to be diagnosed with PTSD. There are no commonly accepted estimates. Figuring out what employers and insurance companies can expect in terms of the number of claims is important for budgeting purposes.

2. *Objective tests and standards of evidence* – As discussed above, there are differences of opinion when diagnoses are discussed. Some argue for a preponderance of the evidence standard while others argue for a clear and convincing standard of evidence to support a diagnosis. Whatever is decided, questions are then going to be raised about what these standards mean and how they can translate to an objective test. What level of evidence should be required for a clinical diagnosis that would lead to awarding benefits to those affected?
3. *Associated costs and length of coverage* – Once a person is diagnosed with PTSD resulting from a work related episode, then real time estimates need to be made about the costs associated with awarding coverage. Workers' compensation is typically paid by the employer's insurance company. Questions remain about what these costs will mean to insurance companies and the agencies of employment.
4. *Length of coverage* – Decisions need to be made about the length of coverage and the costs associated with that coverage. Substantive discussions and decisions are needed about how long any awarded coverage should last.
5. *The potential consequences of not offering extended benefits* – One concern is that people need to support themselves and their families. What is likely to happen when a first responder that has PTSD is not awarded assistance and benefits is that he or she is likely to return to work before they are psychologically ready to do so. The danger in this reality is that this may place others and that responder in harm's way.
6. *Perceptions of public safety agency heads and administrators are largely unknown* – Do these individuals support the award of disability pensions and workers' comprehension benefits absent of physical injury? If an individual suffers from PTSD but is unable to obtain workers' compensation and/or a disability pension from the agency, what do agency heads and administrators believe should occur?

Studies clearly show that PTSD is being diagnosed among first responders having experienced a traumatic event at work. More research is needed into the legal obligations of these agencies that hire professionals and send them into dangerous situations. Currently we appear to have more questions than answers as to how best to help first responders who are suffering.

References

Altimari, D. (2015, May 21). Newtown must pay $380,000 to officer with PTSD. *Hartford Courant*. http://www.courant.com/news/connecticut/hc-sandy-hook-officer-bean-20150521-story.html

Carlier, I., Lamberts, R., & Gersons, B. (1997). Risk factors for posttraumatic stress symptomatology in police officers: A prospective analysis. *The Journal of Nervous and Mental Disease*, 185(8), 498–506.

Corneil, W., Beaton, R., Murphy, S., Johnson, C., & Pike, K. (1999). Exposure to traumatic incidents and prevalence of posttraumatic stress symptomology in urban firefighters in two countries. *Journal of Occupational Health Psychology*, 4(2), 131–141.

Florida Department of Financial Services. (2022). *Education training materials.* https://www.myfloridacfo.com/Division/wc/Employer/PTSD/.

Gerber and Holder Law Firm2023. *Work-related PTSD: A state-by-state breakdown of workers' compensation laws.* https//www.gerberholderlaw.com/workers-comp-ptsd-by-state.

Harris, D. (2017, February 27). Proposed bills would cover first responders that have PTSD. *Orlando Sentinel.* http://www.orlandosentinel.com/news/breaking-news/os-gerry-realin-ptsd-bill-20170223-story.html

Kearns, M.C., Ressler, K.J., Zatzick, D., & Rothbaum, B.O. (2012). Early interventions for PTSD: A review. *Depression and Anxiety*, 29(10), 833–842. doi:10.1002/da.21997.

Minnesota Counties Intergovernmental Trust (2023). Workers' compensation PTSD presumption, benefits change (2019). http:www.mcit.org/news/workers-compensation-ptsd-presumption-benefits-change/.

NCCI Inc. (National Council on Compensation Insurance) (2019). *Regulatory and Legislative Trends Report.* II_Regulatory-Legislative-Trends2019.pdf (ncci.com)

National Institute of Mental Health (2016). *Posttraumatic stress disorder.* https://www.nimh.nih.gov/health/topics/post-traumatic-stress-disorder-ptsd/index.shtml#part_145373

Pietrzak, R.H., Feder, A., Singh, R., Schechter, C.B., Bromet, E.J., Katz, C.L., ... Southwick, S.M. (2014). Trajectories of PTSD risk and resilience in World Trade Center responders: An 8-year prospective cohort study. *Psychological Medicine*, 44 (1), 205–219. doi:http://dx.doi.org.ezproxy1.apus.edu/10.1017/S0033291713000597.

Regambal, M.J., Alden, L.E., Wagner, S.L., Harder, H.G., Koch, W.J., Fung, K., & Parsons, C. (2015). Characteristics of the traumatic stressors experienced by rural first responders. *Journal of Anxiety Disorders*, 34, 86–93. doi:10.1016/j.janxdis.2015.06.006.

Robles, F. (2016, October 27). Orlando officers grapple with trauma and red tape after massacre. *The New York Times.* http://www.nytimes.com/2016/10/28/us/orlando-shooting-police.html?_r=0

Robinson, H., Sigman, M., & Wilson, J. (1997). Duty-related stressor sand PTSD symptoms in suburban police officers. *Psychological Reports*, 81, 835–845.

Robinson, T.A. (2014, June 21). The post-traumatic stress disorder dilemma for workers' compensation claims. *LexisNexis Workers' Compensation eNewsletter.* https://www.lexisnexis.com/legalnewsroom/workers'-compensation/b/recent-cases-news-trends-developments/archive/2014/06/21/the-post-traumatic-stress-disorder-dilemma-for-workers'-compensation-claims.aspx?Redirected=true

Robinson, T.A. (2016, August 4). Illinois: Fire lieutenant entitled to benefits for PTSD following fatal fire. *LexisNexis Workers' Compensation eNewsletter.* https://www.lexisnexis.com/legalnewsroom/workers'-compensation/b/recent-cases-new

s-trends-developments/archive/2016/08/04/illinois-fire-lieutenant-entitled-to-bene fits-for-ptsd-following-fatal-fire.aspx?Redirected=true

Sutton, F. (2016, August 19). Orlando police officer has PTSD; could lose everything because of state loophole. *WFTV*. http://www.wftv.com/news/local/orlando-poli ce-officer-has-ptsd-could-lose-everything-because-of-state-loophole/426684791

Wagner, D., Heinrichs, M., & Ehlert, U. (1998). Prevalence of symptoms of post-traumatic stress disorder in German professional firefighters. *The American Journal of Psychiatry*, 155(12), 1727–1732.

Wise, E. & Beck, J. G. (2015). Work-related trauma, PTSD, and workers' compensation legislation: Implications for practice and policy. *Psychological Trauma: Theory, Research, Practice, and Policy*, 7(5), 500–506.

Yehuda, R. (2002). Post-traumatic stress disorder. *The New England Journal of Medicine*, 346(2), 108–114. https://search-proquest-com.ezproxy1.apus.edu/doc view/223945286?accountid=828

11
ADDICTIVE HYPERVIGILANCE AND UNCONTROLLED POLICE USE OF FORCE

Jesse Cheng

Introduction

Over 30 years ago, Dr. Kevin Gilmartin – a former hostage negotiator, and a highly respected figure within the U.S. law enforcement community – published a paper in a collection of articles for the Federal Bureau of Investigation (Gilmartin, 1986). Drawing from his deep clinical experience as a police psychologist as well as over a decade of interviews with officers, the article presented the concept of "hypervigilance" as a survival mechanism in a profession filled with peril. Gilmartin's thoughts proved to have broad appeal among law enforcement practitioners. Indeed, the ideas he developed there would later form the basis for his bestselling mental health guide for officers and their families (Gilmartin, 2002).[1] In this theoretical chapter, I present a close reading of Gilmartin's article to suggest that his work contained the seeds of what I call a hypothesis of "addictive hypervigilance." This hypothesis posits that a behavioral addiction to hypervigilance may be contributing causal factors to some instances of uncontrolled police use of force. This chapter lays out the conceptual outlines of the hypothesis, and then suggests a preliminary approach for addressing addictive hypervigilance and its repercussions.

Stated more precisely, a hypothesis of addictive hypervigilance proposes that officers can develop a behavioral addiction to a reactive, fight-or-flight physiological state that promotes the misperception of threats, impairing affected officers' ability over time to exercise appropriate restraint in the use of force. This hypothesis is a combination of three separate propositions – the first two drawn directly from Gilmartin's analysis, the third deduced as a logical consequence. First, hypervigilance promotes the misperception of threats. Second, hypervigilance can constitute a behavioral addiction. Third, and consequently, as officers overestimate threats and increasingly lose self-control in pursuit of the rush state, addiction to hypervigilance impairs the ability over time to exercise appropriate restraint in the use of force. The sections below elaborate on each of these propositions in turn.

To be clear, the hypothesis of addictive hypervigilance presented here is based solely on my interpretation of Gilmartin's work and the supporting literature. The hypothesis has not been subject to empirical testing. But should it prove valid, this chapter again takes its cue from Gilmartin in suggesting that hypervigilance's fear-based, on-guard mentality be modulated through the deliberate cultivation of other professional roles. To be clear, again, this tentative recommendation remains purely conceptual in nature, responding as it does to a still-untested hypothesis. The general approach raised here, however, would align with emerging visions to reorient policing practice in the U.S. The discussion and recommendations section explores these thoughts.

Background: The experience of hypervigilance

Gilmartin's explanation of hypervigilance begins with street officers' adoption of a particular "perceptual set" – a specific mental orientation that shapes their interpretation of the surrounding environment and how to respond to it. Under the hypervigilant perceptual set, officers embrace the mentality that in a hostile world filled with unknown dangers, caution requires a mode of heightened alert in encounters with the public. Practitioners are to interpret "most aspects of their environment as potentially lethal" (Gilmartin, 1986: 445). From their earliest days of training and through field experiences on the job, officers learn that they must never stop assessing their surroundings, and that "even the most innocuous situations need to be processed" (Gilmartin, 1986: 446). In fact, Gilmartin contends that it is this on-guard mindset that empowers officers to protect innocent people and themselves, enabling quick action against threats that laypeople will fail even to perceive.

In addition to this anticipatory mental component, hypervigilance involves a series of "physiological consequences" that include "a feeling of energization, rapid thought pattern, and a general speeding up of the physical and cognitive reactions" (Gilmartin, 1986: 446). These behaviors are themselves the result of "elevated innervation of the sympathetic branch of the autonomic nervous system": a fight-or-flight response (Gilmartin, 1986: 446). Officers find themselves, literally, in survival mode. Their senses feel sharp; their minds race, poised to instantly set their bodies in motion at even the subtlest sign of danger. Thus, the hypervigilant mentality, which practitioners are conditioned through their training and experience to view as essential for survival, produces an actual survival response that manifests in their very physiology.

The hypervigilant officer invokes this heightened state while on street duty, regardless of whether genuine threats ever materialize. Consequently, "the officer is altering his physiology daily [even] without being exposed to significantly threatening stressor situations" (Gilmartin, 1986: 446). As Gilmartin pointed out, officers themselves reveal some awareness of the physiological imprint of these changes in the observation that "cop work gets in the blood" (1986: 445). And this bodily transformation becomes a habitual aspect of the job – a daily routine that comes with rolling out for patrol and responding to calls.

The combination of mind–body experiences that make up hypervigilance creates a powerful emotional bond between officers. The heightened state produces a "feeling of energy, wit, and comradery" among members of the force, fed by a group survival instinct in the face of unpredictable dangers (Gilmartin, 1986: 447). In turn, this process of bonding and in-group identity formation reinforces the positive sensations that attend the hypervigilant mode. Practitioners strongly associate these invigorating feelings with the workplace, their fellow officers, and their collective professional role as protectors of public safety. But Gilmartin cautioned that this artificially elevated state while on the job comes with a price: a sustained crash once the officer clocks out. Here, Gilmartin referred to the apathy, physical exhaustion, and emotional detachment all too familiar to members of police families. The misunderstandings and conflicts that result with these loved ones ironically often drive street officers into even deeper time and emotional investments in their professional role, at the expense of wider relationships and social identities. It was these downstream effects of hypervigilance that Gilmartin later explored in his mental health guide for the profession.

As important as these insights on personal relationships were, I submit that Gilmartin's analysis also presented fascinating hints about the effects of hypervigilance on police work itself. More specifically, I suggest that the mental and physical processes of hypervigilance may facilitate the resort to uncontrolled force by bodies that are continuously primed for fight or flight. Gilmartin's paper raises two aspects of hypervigilance that support this possibility: first, hypervigilance's promotion of the misperception of threats, and second, the addictive nature of hypervigilance's rush-like physiological state.

Proposition 1: Hypervigilance promotes the misperception of threats

In one of the most provocative lines in his article, Gilmartin observed, "The social consequence of a perceptual set of hypervigilance and its consequence of over-interpreting the environment as potentially lethal would be a loss of capacity to discriminate which situations are in themselves genuinely dangerous" (1986: 446). By thinking of themselves as perpetually vulnerable to danger, street officers fall prone to seeing threats where none may exist. For Gilmartin, however, this is exactly the point of officer safety as well as good policing. The practitioner can always discard false positives – but the consequence of having no positives at all is that members of the public, and officers themselves, are deprived of the protection afforded by mindful vigilance. In his mental health guide, Gilmartin later declares that if officers are to return to their families at the end of the day, embracing hypervigilance is simply common sense: as the saying goes, better safe than sorry (2002: 34). In this regard, Gilmartin's conceptualization of hypervigilance appears to reflect what Stoughton has described as a fear-based policing mentality that "treat[s] every individual...as an armed threat and every situation as a deadly force encounter in the making" (2015: 228).[2]

Gilmartin noted that this "pseudo-paranoia" reinforces the in-group bonding between line-duty officers even as it breeds mistrust toward others (1986: 447). Even supervisory-level officers merit suspicion: the "hair trigger of autonomic reactiveness...leads to second guessing and potentially misinterpreting any management directive" (Gilmartin, 1986: 447). But the importance of threat misperception plainly goes beyond officer mental health and managerial politics. As Gilmartin added, hypervigilance results in "a loss of capacity to discriminate which citizens are genuinely threatening to the officer's safety and which are not" (1986: 448). In short, hypervigilance directly impacts how officers observe and interpret behavior in police–civilian encounters on the streets.

The potential repercussions for officer use of force are notable. Gilmartin stated that the hypervigilant mindset "only increase[s] the effect of any single stressor to place the individual into an adaptation stress reaction. The perceptual set creates highly fertile ground for specific stressor exposure to have major consequences" (1986: 446). One distinguishing characteristic of street-level law enforcement is, precisely, the practitioner's ongoing exposure to potential stressors. When officers have primed their physiology for tripwire alert in the hypervigilant mode, those "major consequences" that Gilmartin mentioned would involve if not escape, then force. And officers in the U.S. have long been conditioned to believe that the assertion of authority through threat containment is the preferred option over retreat (Rubinstein, 1973; Brown, 1988).

The threat misperception that results from hypervigilance is especially crucial in light of the effects of stress on rational decision making. Gilmartin's analysis accords with research showing that chronically elevated stress hormones are associated with a tendency to evaluate stimuli as threatening (Sapolsky, 2000; Korte, 2001). Moreover, it has long been documented that when stressed individuals engage in quick decision making, they will frequently rely on mental shortcuts that increase the likelihood of inaccurate judgments. Such "heuristics" include the uncritical resort to habitual frames of interpretation, overreliance on intuition over reason, and failure to reassess first impressions (Tversky and Kahneman, 1974). Officers are trained to embrace the mindset that "all the unknowns are *potentially* lethal unknowns until proven otherwise" (Gilmartin, 2002: 34). When subjected to immediate stressors, however, hypervigilant practitioners often will not be predisposed to await proof of the counterfactual. Indeed, the very premise of fear-based hypervigilance – the reason why the officer must maintain the edge in even the most innocuous situations – is that any unnecessary hesitation could spell the difference between life or death.

These considerations point to a possibility that could be of vital importance in understanding instances of inappropriate police force. If not exercised properly, hypervigilance may lead to the overzealous suppression of threats that in fact do not exist.

Proposition 2: Hypervigilance can constitute a behavioral addiction

According to Gilmartin, the heightened energy, sharpened perceptions, and sense of situational readiness that come with hypervigilance make for an alluring experience. At the beginning stages of their career, recruits will often find these physical sensations "enjoyable," motivating them to approach their work "with an almost recreation seeking attitude" (Gilmartin, 1986: 446). Later in their professional lives, "the stress reaction and the physiologically elevated states are the very short term rewards that either keep people in law enforcement or, once having left, motivate them to seek a career re-entry" (Gilmartin, 1986: 445). Gilmartin also depicted the inevitable crash at the end of the shift as an "off-duty depression" that stands in contrast with the "street-high" of the job (1986: 447).

Gilmartin's language strongly implies an addictive quality to the rush-like effects of hypervigilance. This is significant given that at the time of the article's writing, academic and clinical conceptualizations of addiction focused primarily on chemical dependence resulting from the ingestion of substances. By contrast, the most recent versions of the *Diagnostic and Statistical Manual of Mental Disorders* (DSM-5-TR) and the *International*

Classification of Diseases (ICD-11) – both updated in 2022 – reflect the current scientific consensus that addiction can include the pursuit of activities without the use of psychoactive drugs.[3] A growing body of studies has been pushing for more precise understandings of a variety of activity-based addictions, including internet use, sex, overeating, and pornography consumption (Rosenberg and Feder, 2014). And with increased attention to the neurobiology of human behavior, research has further revealed that chronic drug use shares similarities with behavioral addiction in their activation of specific brain regions and rewiring of neural pathways (Grant et al., 2006).

The framework of hypervigilance as compulsive, addictive behavior appears to align with current research in several additional respects. First, in his mental health guide, Gilmartin observes that the hypervigilant state "feels rather good physically – at least for the first few years of a law enforcement career" (2002: 40). This remark, hinting at the eventual decline of the pleasurable rush, may reflect another significant characteristic of hypervigilance as behavioral addiction. An influential paper has argued that the development of addiction is marked by a shift in neurological processes from "liking" the high to merely "wanting" it (Berridge and Robinson, 2016). Whereas the former involves chasing the rush because it is actually pleasurable, the latter speaks to the more workmanlike, compulsion-oriented motivation to pursue the object of addiction. The pleasure of the high eventually becomes secondary to the need to continually feed the habit – and this transition from liking to wanting is reflected in the activation of different brain circuitry. The decreasing pleasure that Gilmartin saw in hypervigilant officers is consistent with other research showing that over time, addicts become motivated less by positive reinforcement and more by the avoidance of unpleasant craving or withdrawal symptoms (Volkow et al., 2016).

Second, Gilmartin has pointed out similar mental health challenges between law enforcement and the military, both of which involve "total immersion into a culture of potential risk" (2002: 71). In fact, not long after Gilmartin published his paper on officer hypervigilance, researchers began reporting on war veterans who craved and sought out repeated experiences of "combat addiction" or "combat rush" – an excitatory bodily state routinely followed by a prolonged period of depressive symptoms (Grigsby, 1991; Solursh, 1989). In a recent study of active-duty service members, investigators have proposed the idea of "addictive combat attachment," defined as "a pattern of habitually engaging in combat-related experiences for considerable amounts of time, accompanied by feelings of excitement or euphoria and physiological hyperarousal, with impairment in social or occupational functioning" (Campbell et al., 2016: 1171–1172).

This phenomenon is expressly presented to be addictive in nature, and includes the core feature of behavior-based addiction – the continued pursuit of the addictive activity despite adverse consequences (Rosenberg and Feder, 2014). Consistent experiences across the respondents included gravitation toward the rewarding aspects of combat, such as the sensations associated with threat confrontation and feelings of camaraderie with fellow soldiers; symptoms of tolerance or withdrawal, with the increasingly compulsory need for more frequent and intense physiological arousal; "drifting" into a default mode of combat readiness without conscious awareness; and the swing between combat highs and depressive lows. Here, again, are potential parallels with Gilmartin's sympathetic arousal of the autonomic nervous system, plus the reinforcement of an in-group culture in response to perceived dangers.

Finally, in a co-authored work, Violanti has offered a consistent interpretation of Gilmartin's work, analytically connecting hypervigilance with addictive behaviors rooted in psychological trauma (Paton et al., 1999).[4] Drawing from the literature on trauma, Violanti noted that officers who are continuously exposed to violent events may undergo "addiction to traumatic re-exposure" (van der Kolk and Greenberg, 1987), whereby individuals become drawn to the kinds of stimulating encounters that produced their trauma. Violanti then addressed Gilmartin's paper on hypervigilance, suggesting that by internalizing the hypervigilant perceptual set, an officer with a history of trauma could continue to self-activate the rush associated with high-risk encounters without needing the immediate presence of traumatic stimuli to trigger it.

Importantly, Violanti and his coauthors explicitly described Gilmartin's paper as an analysis of adrenaline "addiction," even though Gilmartin himself never used the word (Paton et al., 1999: 81). Violanti's insights raise the possibility that hypervigilance and psychological trauma have interrelated addictive qualities that exacerbate the other, with possibly connected or overlapping neurobiological processes. When the hypervigilance addict seeks out high-risk, potentially traumatic encounters, the self-fulfilling prophecy of violence may feed the compulsion to maintain extreme levels of heightened alert. This, in turn, may motivate the continued search for the next opportunity for potentially traumatic encounters. Thus, the addiction to hypervigilance, originating in conditioning processes from the earliest days of training, may facilitate the addiction to traumatic re-exposure, developed through actual encounters on the streets.[5]

Proposition 3: Addiction to hypervigilance impairs the ability over time to exercise appropriate restraint in the use of force

Taken together, the two aspects of hypervigilance addressed above – its promotion of threat misperception, and its potential manifestation as behavioral addiction – logically suggest that addiction to hypervigilance may compromise officers' ability to appropriately apply force. Addictive hypervigilance compels affected practitioners to chase a physiological state of tripwire arousal that predisposes them to increased perceptual error. In this heightened fight-or-flight state, officers are prone to oversimplified assessment of the environment through mental shortcuts. Over time, as affected practitioners develop tolerance to addictive behavior and seek escalating stimulus levels, they lose the incentive, ability, and self-control to calibrate the dials of physiological arousal. With higher frequency and intensity, the officer's neurobiology is locked and loaded to over-preemptively detect threats at every turn. Affected practitioners, instead of screening out false positives in the name of restraint, are oriented to detect positives to act on in pursuit of the rush. The culmination of these factors is the significantly increased risk that in civilian interactions, officers will prematurely react to nonexistent dangers. In so doing, they are also more likely to apply force that is unnecessary or disproportionate to the circumstances. Officers' aroused behavior, finally, may provoke actual aggression from community members, creating high-risk encounters that were initially avoidable, but that end up affirming the threat hypersensitivity in a self-perpetuating cycle.

Discussion and recommendations

To summarize, the addictive hypervigilance hypothesis proposes that officers can develop a behavioral addiction to a reactive, fight-or-flight physiological state that promotes the misperception of threats, impairing affected officers' ability over time to exercise appropriate restraint in the use of force. My analysis above drew from Gilmartin's classic work to articulate the first two propositions built into the hypothesis – the proposition that hypervigilance promotes the misperception of threats, and the proposition that hypervigilance can constitute a behavioral addiction. Taken together, these first two propositions lead to the third. As officers overestimate threats and increasingly lose self-control in pursuit of the rush state, addiction to hypervigilance impairs the ability over time to exercise appropriate restraint in the use of force.

I again underscore the fact that the hypothesis of addictive hypervigilance remains untested. But if its validity is conceptually plausible, Gilmartin's insights as a mental health clinician would assume even more urgency in this light. Gilmartin clearly believed that self-control over the hypervigilant state is not just possible, but necessary for officer well-being. When Gilmartin warned about "pseudo-paranoia" and the misperception of threats, he remarked that overinvestment in the job, and the extended hypervigilance that comes with it, "can lead to a pathological interpersonal and intrapersonal mode of interacting if other social roles are not of major importance in the officer's life" (1986: 446). Therefore, he urged that when off duty, officers should mindfully "practice perceptual sets" involved in other social roles (spouse, parent, friend, hobbyist), intentionally developing and activating these other aspects of self-identity as "a form of reality testing" (Gilmartin, 1986: 448). Through the intentional cultivation of multiple mentalities, officers can develop the ability to balance different roles and perceptual sets to more accurately gauge threat levels that lie beyond law enforcement's inner circle. In short, well-adjusted officers train themselves to have the self-control to invoke various mindsets as appropriate so that they are not viewing everyone, including their loved ones, with the on-guard mentality of a street cop.

Again, Gilmartin was writing as a clinician concerned about overcoming extreme in-group identity formation and resistance to wider social relationships and supports. I would tentatively suggest, however, that the need for self-control over multiple mindsets can also apply to the practitioner's exercise of hypervigilance when interacting with the public while on duty. Gilmartin urged that officers remain hypervigilant on the streets at all times. And yet, the proper degree of hypervigilance – how dialed up officers should permit their body's level of fight-or-flight arousal to be – must surely depend on the situation. Although his paper was not explicit on this point, Gilmartin likely would not endorse a full-throttle fight-or-flight mode for every encounter with the public. A more effective recommendation, consistent with so many other aspects of the street officer's job, might be to employ discretion when activating suitable levels of the hypervigilant state. As a mental orientation, hypervigilance can be modulated based on a more grounded evaluation of the threats presented by the practitioner's surroundings, actual knowledge, and enforcement objectives. There is a difference, for instance, between conducting routine traffic patrols versus responding to an active shooter call. Underlying this more rationally deliberative practice is the officer's constant awareness that other, less reactionary perceptual sets may be better-suited for different situations.

Gilmartin has advised that in balancing the job of policing with other aspects of life, the goal is "not so much turning off police work as *turning on* something different" (2002: 112). Within police work itself, this recommendation similarly may be sensible with respect to hypervigilance. If officers do in fact realize that full-fledged fight-or-flight mode is not an optimal mindset every moment they engage with the community, it is perhaps because they intuitively recognize that true situational readiness requires the capacity to maneuver between counterbalancing perceptual sets. Practitioners have the benefit of selecting from an array of other professional roles and mentalities that can be cultivated through experience and training – for example, those of the fair and legitimate figure of authority (Mazerolle et al., 2013); the mental health-informed first responder (Wood and Watson, 2016); the time-buying negotiator, which itself can entail multiple roles (Rogan et al., 1997); the ethical investigator who gathers evidence with integrity (Miller and Gordon, 2014); or even, as Gilmartin would urge, the willing recipient of compassion and self-care. While officers can switch on a baseline level of hypervigilance when on duty, the degree of the heightened state applied in different encounters can vary based on how practitioners choose to modulate it with these various perceptual sets. In fact, I would submit that an expanded practice of role modulation plays an indispensable part in conflict *de*-escalation – one of the most fundamental of law enforcement skills.

In seeking to prevent addiction to hypervigilance and the uncontrolled use of force that may follow, the mastery of role modulation would require that agencies carefully outline and develop multiple roles specific to their needs. Definition of these roles would be supported with clearly articulated ethical values and associated with concrete situational contexts. The officer's facility in navigating between this array of roles would be cultivated through training, and then consistently reinforced through robust incentive and accountability structures once on the job.

Given that the addictive hypervigilance hypothesis remains untested, any thoughts on how to address addictive hypervigilance remain speculative. An expanded practice of role modulation, however, would align well with collaboratively defined visions of the policing profession advanced in recent years in the U.S. Role modulation requires equipping officers with a broader social-emotional toolkit for confronting the hard complexities of community relationship-building (President's Task Force on 21st Century Policing, 2015). It is premised on the need for officers to distinguish truly perilous situations from those in which deliberative thinking is to be prioritized (Police Executive Research Forum, 2016). Instead of fixating solely on asserting control over others in the lockdown of threats, role modulation emphasizes disciplined *self*-control with the recognition that reactive antagonism threatens officer safety in the long run (Rahr and Rice, 2015; Stoughton, 2015). And in clarifying the multiple mindsets that are to be activated with situational discretion, this approach underscores that some circumstances may call for roles that are best fulfilled by others adjacent to law enforcement who can offer different sets of expertise (United States Conference of Mayors, 2020).

Conclusion

This chapter has drawn from Gilmartin's work to present a hypothesis of addictive hypervigilance. Further conceptual and empirical exploration of this hypothesis is encouraged to evaluate the possibility of addictive hypervigilance as a contributing causal factor to some instances of uncontrolled police use of force. The chapter also developed Gilmartin's clinical recommendations to tentatively propose an expanded practice of role modulation that may be essential for addressing the problems associated with addictive hypervigilance, should the hypothesis find empirical support. Finally, the chapter suggested that an expanded practice of role modulation would have benefits that accord with recently articulated visions of the profession in the U.S.

Notes

1 In the U.S., several works by Gilmartin are considered essential reads within the profession. See https://thinbluelinefoundation.org/managing-job-stress.
2 Stoughton, a law professor who is himself a former police officer, states that under the "warrior" mentality that has dominated U.S. law enforcement practices, "officers don't learn to be vigilant, attentive, cautious, alert, and observant just because it's fun. They do so because they are afraid...For Warriors, hypervigilance offers the best chance for survival" (2015: 227–228).
3 Both manuals classify gambling disorder as addiction; the ICD-11 also includes gaming disorder.
4 This work updates and expands on a prior article sole-authored by Violanti (1997).
5 The nexus between hypervigilance and psychological trauma is a longstanding one. Since the third revised edition of the DSM, trauma has been diagnostically linked with a tendency toward "hypervigilance" – a symptom of heightened arousal (American Psychiatric Association, 1987). Although no versions of the manual expressly define hypervigilance, trauma investigators have understood the concept as "a cognitive, physiological, and behavioral pattern in which an individual either responds to neutral or ambiguous stimuli as if they were threatening or is enhanced in his or her detection and reaction to threatening or threat-related stimuli" (Kimble et al., 2013: 1673). This definition of hypervigilance appears consistent with Gilmartin's formulation in the policing context.

References

American Psychiatric Association (1987) *Diagnostic and Statistical Manual of Mental Disorders* (3rd edn, text rev.). Washington. DC: American Psychiatric Association.
Berridge KC and Robinson TE (2016) Liking, wanting and the incentive-sensitization theory of addiction. *American Psychologist* 71 (8): 670–679.
Brown MK (1988) *Working the Street: Police Discretion and the Dilemmas of Reform* (2nd edn). New York: Russell Sage Foundation.

Campbell MS, Ryan M, Wright D, Devore MD and Hoge CW (2016) Postdeployment PTSD and addictive combat attachment behaviors in US military service members. *American Journal of Psychiatry* 173 (12): 1171–1176.

Gilmartin KM (1986) Hypervigilance: A learned perceptual set and its consequences on police stress. In: Reese JT and Goldstein HA (eds) *Psychological Services for Law Enforcement*. Washington, DC: US Government Printing Office, pp. 445–448.

Gilmartin KM (2002) *Emotional Survival for Law Enforcement: A Guide for Officers and Their Families*. Tucson, AZ: E-S Press.

Grant JE, Brewer JA and Potenza MN (2006) The neurobiology of substance and behavioral addictions. *CNS Spectrums* 11 (12): 924–930.

Grigsby J (1991) Combat rush: Phenomenology of central and autonomic arousal among war veterans with PTSD. *Psychotherapy* 28 (2): 354–363.

Kimble MO, Fleming K and Bennion KA (2013) Contributors to hypervigilance in a military and civilian sample. *Journal of Interpersonal Violence* 28 (8): 1672–1692.

Korte SM (2001) Corticosteroids in relation to fear, anxiety and psychopathology. *Neuroscience & Biobehavioral Reviews* 25 (2): 117–142.

Mazerolle L, Antrobus E, Bennet S and Tyler TR (2013) Shaping citizen perceptions of police legitimacy: A randomized field trial of procedural justice. *Criminology* 51 (1): 33–63.

Miller S and Gordon IA (2014) *Investigative Ethics: Ethics for Police Detectives and Criminal Investigators*. Hoboken, NJ: Wiley-Blackwell.

Paton D, Violanti J and Schuckler E (1999) Chronic exposure to risk and trauma: Addiction and separation issues in police officers. In: Violanti JM and Paton D (eds) *Police Trauma: Psychological Aftermath of Civilian Combat*. Springfield, IL: Charles C. Thomas, pp. 78–87.

Police Executive Research Forum (2016) *Guiding Principles on Use of Force*. Washington, DC: Police Executive Research Forum.

President's Task Force on 21st Century Policing (2015) *Final Report of the President's Task Force on 21st Century Policing*. Washington, DC: Office of Community Oriented Policing Services.

Rahr S and Rice SK (2015) From warriors to guardians: Recommitting American police culture to democratic ideals. *New Perspectives in Policing Bulletin*. Washington, DC: US Department of Justice, National Institute of Justice.

Rogan RG, Hammer MR and Van Zandt CT (eds) (1997) *Dynamic Processes of Crisis Negotiation: Theory, Research, and Practice*. Westport, CT: Praeger.

Rosenberg KP and Feder LC (eds) (2014) *Behavioral Addictions: Criteria, Evidence and Treatment*. London: Elsevier.

Rubinstein J (1973) *City Police*. New York: Farrar, Straus and Giroux.

Sapolsky RM (2000) Glucocorticoids and hippocampal atrophy in neuropsychiatric disorders. *Archives of General Psychiatry* 57 (10): 925–935.

Solursh LP (1989) Combat addiction: Overview of implications in symptom maintenance and treatment planning. *Journal of Traumatic Stress* 2 (4): 451–462.

Stoughton S (2015) Law enforcement's "warrior" problem. *Harvard Law School Forum* 128: 225–234.

Tversky A and Kahneman D (1974) Judgment under uncertainty: Heuristics and biases. *Science* 185(4157): 1124–1131.

United States Conference of Mayors (2020) *Report on Police Reform and Racial Justice*. Washington, DC: United States Conference of Mayors.

van der Kolk BA and Greenberg MS (1987) The psychobiology of the trauma response: Hyperarousal, constriction, and addiction to traumatic re-exposure. In: van der Kolk BA (ed.) *Psychological Trauma*. Washington, DC: American Psychiatric Press, pp. 63–87.

Violanti JM (1997) Residuals of police occupational trauma. *Australasian Journal of Disaster and Trauma Studies* 1997 (3). Available at: https://www.massey.ac.nz/~trauma/issues/1997-3/violant1.htm (accessed 29 January 2021).

Volkow ND, Koob GF and McLellan AT (2016) Neurobiologic advances from the brain disease model of addiction. *New England Journal of Medicine* 374 (4): 363–371.

Wood JD and Watson AC (2016) Improving police interventions during mental health-related encounters: Past, present and future. *Policing and Society* 27 (3): 289–299.

12

THE LAW ENFORCEMENT WORKFORCE CRISIS

Developing targeted recruitment and retention strategies for future generations

Nicole Cain

Introduction

Recruitment and retention of police officers is a consistent challenge facing law enforcement leaders. Low pay, antiquated hiring practices, increases in resignations and retirements, negative public perception, exposure to chronic stress and trauma, and increasing responsibilities of police officers are contributing to the decline in the number of police applicants (Cain, 2019a; Donohue, 2022; Morrison, 2017). Furthermore, military call-ups, rising levels of illicit drug use, obesity, outdated grooming standards, and the accumulation of excessive debt have lessened the qualified applicant pool (Morrison, 2017; Police Executive Research Forum, 2023). Another contributing factor is the exit of baby boomers from the workforce. This generation of law enforcement officers generally remained at the same police organization for the duration of their career. Their departure marks the loss of experience and institutional knowledge and a vital component of on-the-job training for the next generation of officers. Changing generational preferences impact law enforcement in two ways; younger workers are less likely to remain in any one profession, and they are less inclined to enter policing at all (Donohue, 2022; Police Executive Research Forum, 2023). As the number of millennials in the workforce grows, law enforcement leaders must understand the intrinsic motivators of this generation and develop targeted recruitment and retention strategies.

Background of the study

The purpose of this research study was to understand the differences between generational cohorts and specifically the millennial generation's motivation for entering and remaining in the law enforcement profession, as well as their satisfaction with their career choice. Identifying hygiene and motivational factors for millennial police officers will assist law enforcement leaders in developing strategic recruitment and retention efforts.

The United States has approximately 17,541 state and local law enforcement agencies, which employ approximately 788,000 police officers (Gardner & Scott, 2022). According to the Bureau of Justice Statistics (2022), from 1996 to 2018, the number of full-time sworn officers per 100,000 citizens decreased 4% from 250 to 241 (Gardner & Scott, 2022; Goodison, 2022). Law enforcement positions are remaining vacant and fewer people are attracted to the profession (Donohue, 2022). A survey conducted by the Police Executive Research Forum (PERF) of 411 police departments in the United States found that 29% of police officers who voluntarily resigned from their job had been employed less than a year, and another 40% had been employed fewer than five years (PERF, 2019). PERF conducted another survey in 2023 to better understand current status of law enforcement staffing. The survey found that total sworn staffing numbers decreased 4.8% from January 2020 to January 2023. The number of sworn officers hired decreased significantly in 2020 then increased 35% in 2022. Additionally, there were 47% more resignations in 2022 than in 2019, and there were 19% more retirements in 2022 than in 2019 (PERF, 2023). Ultimately resignations and retirements are outpacing hiring.

The Center for State and Local Government Excellence (2018) surveyed 337 state and local governments to identify workforce trends. The researchers found that 82% of the respondents considered recruitment and retention their highest priority, and 27% identified policing as the most difficult position to fill (Center for State and Local Government Excellence, 2018).

Insufficient staffing levels impact the quality of service provided to the community as well as the performance, productivity, and morale of officers within the law enforcement organization (Northup, 2018). Northup (2018) found that a workforce shortage "leads to an overworked workforce, which, in turn, leads to police officer fatigue" (p. 22). Studies have shown that police officer fatigue increases the overuse of sick time, accidental on-duty injuries, and the number of citizen complaints. Furthermore, officers expected to work longer hours to compensate for the workforce deficiency commonly experience health issues such as increased stress, sleep-deprivation, cardiovascular disease, and musculoskeletal disorders (Northup, 2018).

Millennials are currently the largest cohort (35%) participating in the United States work force (Fry, 2018). Understanding how millennials differ from previous generations in their "communication styles, technology needs, professional development preferences, workplace expectations, compensation and benefit needs, and desired leadership styles" can assist law enforcement leaders in developing targeted recruitment tactics (Kapoor & Solomon, 2011, p. 308).

Literature review

According to a review of the literature, three leading factors impact the ability for police leaders to attract and retain candidates: a strong economy, the perception of increased danger associated with policing, and the poor image of policing (Maciag, 2018; Meese & Malcolm, 2018; Morrison, 2017; Northup, 2018; PERF, 2019). The pool of qualified law enforcement applicants decreases when unemployment rates are low and the economy is healthy because people are less inclined to enter dangerous, low paying careers during economic growth (Morrison, 2017). Law enforcement officers are continuously exposed to highly charged, negative or violent situations. The continuous exposure to violence and trauma increases the risk that police officers will experience stress, anxiety, depression, post-traumatic stress disorder (PTSD), and suicide (Chopko et al., 2015). Although the suicide rates fluctuate year to year, in general police officers commit suicide at a higher rate than the civilian population (Ramchand et al., 2018). Lastly, the public's perception of law enforcement has deteriorated over the past decade negatively impacting law enforcement's ability to recruit members of their respective communities to the profession (Meese & Malcolm, 2018). Police encounters with citizens, especially those involving the use of force, are often highly publicized; consequently, public scrutiny about law enforcement operations, accountability, training, and organizational culture is increased (Meese & Malcolm, 2018). The social media platform provides a global medium for citizens to share their opinions about their interaction with police officers (Meese & Malcolm, 2018). Improving community and police relations is fundamental to the development of effective recruitment and retention strategies (Meese & Malcolm, 2018).

The United States workforce is comprised of multiple generational cohorts, and their respective preferences impact the job market as well as individual organizations that employ them. Generational differences influence organizational effectiveness in the following areas: recruiting and retention, motivation, communication, productivity, change management, and team building (Arrington & Dwyer, 2018; Lyons et al., 2015; Murray, 2011). Leaders are tasked with managing diverse generations within the workforce and should recognize the goals, values, and beliefs of each generation to achieve organizational success (Arrington & Dwyer, 2018). Generational research indicates that millennials differ greatly from Baby Boomers and Generation X. Jensen and Graves (2013) indicated in their research that millennials prefer a decentralized organizational structure composed of several teams, because it fosters increased collaboration and open communication that is typically hindered by a bureaucratic rank structure. Millennials favor transformational leaders who allow them to participate in decision-making, utilize their critical thinking skills, encourage personal growth, and provide immediate feedback. Millennials embrace technology, service, and teamwork and desire training and educational opportunities (Benson & Brown, 2011). A survey conducted in 2022 of 1,003 state and local government employees found that workers under the age of 40 considered work/life balance 56%, quality of supervisor (43%), and potential for career advancement (42%) as the major factors that attracted them to their current job (Liss-Levinson & Young, 2023).

The limited pool of police applicants exists, in part, because millennials are not attracted to the law enforcement profession as they had been in previous generations (Morrison, 2017). As police officers from the baby boomer and Generation X generations retire, millennials will need to fill their positions. The recruitment process of law enforcement officers is one of most fundamental steps in maintaining and operating a successful law enforcement organization. Evaluating an organization's current qualifications, like minimum age requirements, education requirements, residency requirements, and physical fitness standards, as well as their disqualifiers, like past drug use, minor arrests, visible tattoos, and poor credit history, is beneficial to determine if the standards are still appropriate (Morrison, 2017). The hiring and selection process for law enforcement officers varies from agency to agency, but it is often lengthy, cumbersome, and unappealing to millennials (Donohue, 2022; PERF, 2023).

Information from the review of the literature demonstrates that the crises are affecting law enforcement organizations of every size across the United States. To ensure the future of policing, law enforcement leaders must recognize generational differences and develop strategies to recruit and retain new generations' officers (Arrington & Dwyer, 2018; Wiedmer, 2015). Law enforcement leaders must target, recruit, hire, and retain officers who possess skill sets compatible with their agencies and community demographics to provide efficient service delivery and ensure the longevity of their organization (Meade, 2016).

Overview of methodology

The research design and methodology for the study was broadly non-experimental, quantitative, and more specifically, survey research. The study's proposed research questions were addressed broadly using a variety of descriptive, associative, predictive, and inferential statistical techniques. Frequency counts (n), measures of central tendency (mean scores), and variability (standard deviation) represented the primary descriptive statistical techniques used in the six research questions.

The judgment phase of the establishment of the survey instrument's content validity was executed through a content analysis of Herzberg's theory, specifically focusing upon work environmental factors and activities broadly described as *hygiene factors* (salary, benefits, career advancement, and work schedule) and *motivational factors* (sense of mission, professional respect, and removing criminal influence). The agreed upon themes based upon Herzberg's theory by the subject matter experts formed the basis of item development for the study's research instrument.

The study's sample was broadly non-probability by sampling type, purposive in nature and convenient. The sample of study participants were identified through access to a master list of 240 sworn law enforcement officers at a mid-sized agency in central Florida. The population sampled for participation in the study was an aggregate of 240 potential participants.

This study's researcher-constructed survey instrument was initially used in a pilot study to determine internal consistency. The study's research instrument format was comprised of four demographic questions and 11 five-point Likert scale items in which 5 represented the strongest agreement with the item and 1 represented the strongest disagreement with the item. The study's piloted survey was created and distributed to 36 randomly selected sworn members at a mid-sized agency in central Florida through the online survey tool SoGoSurvey. The internal consistency of participant responses ($n = 26$) in the pilot study was high ($\alpha = .82$). The researcher-constructed instrument ($\alpha = .82$; $p < .001$) exceeded the expected level ($\alpha = .70$). No adaptations were made to the piloted survey. The survey results from the piloted survey were included in the data analysis.

Research questions, analysis, and results

This study examined current law enforcement officers' hygiene and motivational factors for choosing a career in law enforcement and their satisfaction with their career choice. Each participant was categorized into a generational cohort (baby boomer, Generation X, or millennial) based on their year of birth. Based on the review of the literature, the generational groupings were established as follows: participants who were 23–38 years of age were classified as millennials ($n = 37$); participants who were 39–54 years of age were classified as Generation X ($n = 55$); and participants who were 55–73 years of age were classified as baby boomers ($n = 7$). Baby boomer participants were not included in the analysis.

Analysis by research question

In research questions one, two, and three, the single sample t test was used to assess the statistical significance of participant response in the first portion of the question. The alpha level of $p < .05$ represented the threshold for statistical significance of finding. Cohen's d was used to assess the magnitude of effect (effect size). Cohen's parameters of interpretation of effect sizes was employed for comparative purposes. In the second portion of research questions one through six, the t test of independent means was used to assess the statistical significance of difference in mean scores between the participant groups being compared to millennials.

The alpha level of $p < .05$ represented the threshold for statistical significance of question finding. The assumptions of normality and homogeneity of variances was assessed using the Shapiro-Wilk test and the Levene test respectively. Values of $p > .05$ were indicative of both assumptions having been satisfied. Cohen's d, or an alternative effect size measure (Hedges g; Glass') was used to assess the magnitude of effect (effect size). Cohen's parameters of interpretation of effect sizes were employed for comparative purposes.

Research questions four through six are associative and predictive in nature utilizing multiple independent predictor variables. As such, the multiple linear regression test statistic was employed to assess predictive robustness of the respective independent variables in each question. Predictive model fitness was assessed through the interpretation of the ANOVA table F value. An F value of $p < .05$ was considered indicative of a viable predictive model. Variable slope (t) values represented the means by which the statistical significance of independent variables will be interpreted. Values of $p < .05$ were considered statistically significant. R^2 values were utilized as the basis for effect size measurement and for comparative purposes. The formula $R^2 / 1 - R^2$ was applied to each predictor for comparative purposes to form the f^2 statistic. Effect sizes of .35 % were considered indicative of a large magnitude of predictive effect.

Research question #1

To what degree are millennials satisfied with their decision to pursue a career in law enforcement? And, does millennial degree of career satisfaction in law enforcement differ from that of their peers identified as Generation X.

The results for the first portion of the research question indicated that millennials were satisfied with their decision to pursue a career in law enforcement. The mean score (4.27) was considered statistically significant and the magnitude of effect for the first portion of the research question was very large. The results for the second portion of the research question indicated that the mean score difference between the two generational cohorts (millennial and Generation X) was not statistically significant. The magnitude of effect for the second portion of research question one was considered small.

Table 12.1 contains a comparison of study participant satisfaction with the decision to pursue a career in law enforcement by generational classification.

Research question #2

To what degree do millennials perceive that the leadership style of those in supervisory positions within the department has inspired them to remain in a career in law enforcement? And, does the millennial degree of perception that leadership style of those in supervisory positions within the department has inspired them to remain in a career in law enforcement differ from that of their peers identified as Generation X.

The results of the first portion of the research question indicated that millennials were inspired by the leadership style of their supervisor to remain in the profession. The mean score (3.81) was statistically significant and the magnitude of effect was considered large. For the second portion of the research question, the results indicated that the mean score difference between the two generational cohorts (millennials and Generation X) was statistically significant favoring millennials. The magnitude of effect for the comparison in the second portion of the research question was considered approaching medium.

Table 12.2 contains a comparison of study participant perceptions of leadership style of those in supervisory positions within the department representing inspiration to remain in a career in law enforcement by generational classification.

TABLE 12.1 Overall satisfaction comparison by generational classification

Generational cohorts	n	Mean	SD	t	g
Millennials	37	4.27	0.81	0.97	.21
Generation X	55	4.44	0.81		

TABLE 12.2 Impact of leadership style perceptions comparison by generation

Generational cohorts	n	Mean	SD	t	g
Millennials	37	3.81	0.91	2.28*	.45
Generation X	55	3.27	1.35		

*$p = .03$

Research question #3

To what degree do participants identified as millennials perceive training in handling stressful policing situations and community relations as satisfactory? And, does millennial degree of training satisfaction in handling stressful situations and community relations differ from that of their peers identified as Generation X?

The results of the first portion of the research question indicated millennials were satisfied with the training they received in handling stressful policing situations and community relations. The mean score (4.22) was statistically significant and the magnitude of effect was considered very large. For the second portion of the research question, the difference in mean scores for the two generational cohorts (millennials and Generation X) favored millennials but was not statistically significant. The magnitude of effect for the comparison in the second portion of research question three was considered small.

Table 12.3 contains a comparison of study participant perceptions of training as being satisfactory in handling stressful policing situations and community relations by generational classification.

Research question #4

Considering participant perception of sense of mission, professional respect and esteem, and role in removing criminal influences from the community, which represents the most prominent correlate and predictor of overall satisfaction with the decision to pursue a career in law enforcement for millennials?

Using the multiple linear regression statistical technique, the predictive viability of three independent variables associated with motivational factors in research question four was evaluated. The results indicated that of the three independent variables associated with motivational factors (sense of mission, professional respect and esteem, and role in removing criminal influences from the community) millennials identified sense of mission as the most prominent predictor of overall satisfaction with the decision to pursue a career in law enforcement. The magnitude of effect for sense of mission

TABLE 12.3 Comparison of perceptions of training as being satisfactory in handling stressful policing situations and community relations

Generational cohorts	n	Mean	SD	t	g
Millennials	37	4.22	0.63	0.62	.14
Generation X	55	4.11	0.90		

was considered very large. As a follow-up to the research question, the predictive model was applied to study participants identified as Generation X. The results indicated that Generation X participants identified the variable professional respect and esteem as the most prominent motivational factor predicting overall satisfaction with the decision to pursue a career in law enforcement.

Table 12.4 contains a summary of predictive finding for study participants identified as millennials in research question four.

As a follow-up to research question four, the predictive model was applied to study participants identified as Generation X.

Table 12.5 contains a summary of predictive finding for study participants identified as Generation X in research question four.

Research question #5

Considering salary, benefits, career advancement opportunities, and work schedules, which represents the most prominent correlate and predictor of overall satisfaction with the decision to pursue a career in law enforcement for millennials?

Using the multiple linear regression statistical technique, the predictive viability of four independent variables associated with hygiene factors in research question five was evaluated. The results indicated that of the four independent variables

TABLE 12.4 Predicting overall satisfaction by motivational factor for millennials

Motivational factors	β	SE	Standardized β
Intercept	1.42	0.88	
Sense of mission	0.77	0.18	.62***
Professional respect/esteem	0.16	0.09	.25
Removing criminal influence	-0.22	0.20	-.15

*p <.001

TABLE 12.5. Predicting overall satisfaction by motivational factor for Generation X

Motivational factors	β	SE	Standardized β
Intercept	2.07	0.87	
Sense of mission	0.15	0.14	.05
Professional respect/esteem	0.30	0.09	.44***
Removing criminal influence	0.26	0.16	.21

***p =.001

associated with hygiene factors (salary, benefits, career advancement, and work schedules) millennials identified career advancement and work schedules as the most prominent predictors of overall satisfaction with the decision to pursue a career in law enforcement. The magnitude of effect for both career advancement and work schedules were considered large. As a follow-up to research question five, the predictive model was applied to study participants classified as Generation X. The results indicated that Generation X participants identified the variable work schedules as the most prominent hygiene factor predicting overall satisfaction with the decision to pursue a career in law enforcement.

Table 12.6 contains a summary of predictive finding for study participants identified as millennials in research question five.

As a follow-up to research question five, the predictive model was applied to study participants classified as Generation X.

Table 12.7 contains a summary of predictive finding for study participants classified as Generation X in research question five.

Research question #6

Considering the most prominent predictors within the domains of hygiene factors and motivational factors associated with the profession of law enforcement, which represents the most prominent correlate and predictor

TABLE 12.6 Predicting overall satisfaction by hygiene factors for millennials

Hygiene factors	β	SE	Standardized β
Intercept	1.71	0.63	
Salary	-0.09	0.11	-.16
Benefits	0.15	0.13	.23
Career advancement	0.25	0.11	.38* .38*
Work schedules	0.35	0.13	

*p =.02

TABLE 12.7 Predicting overall satisfaction by hygiene factors for Generation X

Hygiene factors	β	SE	Standardized β
Intercept	2.50	0.49	
Salary	-0.11	0.11	-.16
Benefits	0.16	0.11	.24
Career advancement	0.10	0.10	.15
Work schedules	0.37	0.12	.41***

***p =.002

of overall satisfaction with the decision to pursue a career in law enforcement for millennials?

Using the multiple linear regression statistical technique, the predictive viability of one independent variable associated with hygiene factors (work schedules) and one independent variable associated with motivational factors (sense of mission) were evaluated. Each variable represented the most prominent correlate and predictor of millennials' overall satisfaction with the decision to pursue a career in law enforcement by category of factor. Millennials identified their sense of mission in serving the community as the essential reason for pursuing a career in law enforcement. Their overall satisfaction with their career in law enforcement is primarily based on their sense of mission in serving the community.

Table 12.8 contains a summary of predictive finding for study participants identified as millennials in research question six.

Discussion

The results indicated that both generational cohorts (millennials and Generation Xers) were satisfied with their decision to pursue a career in law enforcement. According to Northup (2018), job satisfaction is associated with a positive organizational culture that meets the needs of its police officers. Northup (2018) explained several ways to increase job satisfaction among police officers including "recognizing achievement, giving more responsibility to workers, providing career advancement opportunities, and offering learning opportunities" (p. 11). Retaining a balanced workforce with varying levels of experience allows for succession planning and career advancement and improves productivity and efficiency (Northup, 2018).

The results demonstrated that millennials value leadership. Millennials were inspired by the leadership style of their supervisor to remain in the profession. Law enforcement leaders must continuously adapt their leadership styles to motivate and retain changing workforce demographics. The Police Executive Research Forum (2019) found that "employees' dissatisfaction with their supervisors is one of the main catalysts of employee turnover" (p. 56). Millennials

TABLE 12.8 Predicting overall satisfaction by motivation and hygiene factors for millennials

Model	β	SE	Standardized β
Intercept	0.47	0.72	
Work schedules (Hygiene factor)	0.18	0.13	.20
Sense of mission (Motivation factor)	0.72	0.17	.59***

***$p < .001$

favor leaders who allow them to participate in decision-making, utilize their critical thinking skills, encourage personal growth, and provide immediate feedback (Jensen & Graves, 2013; Kapoor & Solomon, 2011; Naim & Lenka, 2018). According to the Task Force on 21st Century, the paramilitary rank structure utilized by many police organizations lacks inclusiveness, accordingly, adopting new leadership models, like servant leadership, provides sworn officers with the opportunity to participate in decision-making (21 CP Solutions, 2023).

Additionally, millennials value career development, expecting training and educational opportunities to continuously enhance their knowledge base and remain marketable (Naim & Lenka, 2018). According to a study by PERF (2019), 85 percent of respondents reported implementing professional development opportunities to improve retention. Young officers desire opportunities to grow and learn new skills as well as diversity of assignments.

As the results demonstrated, millennials considered the sense of mission in serving the community an essential motivational factor in pursuing a career in law enforcement. Their overall satisfaction with their career in law enforcement is primarily based on their sense of mission in serving the community. Millennials seek meaningful work and desire to help people (Morrison, 2017; PERF, 2019). Community-Oriented Policing (COP) provides officers with opportunities to serve their community beyond the crime fighter role (Pyle & Cangemi, 2019). The philosophy promotes strategies in which the police and the community develop a partnership to proactively combat quality of life issues and criminal activity (Office of Community Oriented Policing Services, 2012). COP requires a decentralized, linear structure and "greater emphasis on knowledge management, teamwork, and partnerships with the community in order for the police agency to become more proactive and adaptable in dealing with crime as well as becoming more focused on quality of life for the community" (Ford, 2007, p. 321). While most police agencies practice some form of COP, many organizations limit COP to one unit rather than allowing it to permeate the entire agency (Lawrence & McCarthy, 2013). Police executives should consider implementing the COP philosophy throughout the organization to build a culture of service which is appealing to millennials.

A key-take-away is that millennials did not identify their role in removing criminals from the community as a motivational factor in pursuing a career in law enforcement. PERF (2019) found that "fast-paced images of officers making forced entries into buildings, rappelling down walls, firing high powered weapons on the range, speeding in a power boat, or riding a horse" (p. 10) do not resonate with many of the people currently entering the workforce. The Task Force on 21st Century Policing encouraged law enforcement leaders to adopt a culture that embraces police as guardians, "working in partnership with the community to achieve safety" (21CP Solutions, 2023, p. 6).

Implications for professional policy and practice

First, law enforcement leaders should evaluate the needs of their respective department, by conducting a staffing analysis (Cain, 2019a; Orrick, 2008). It is valuable for law enforcement leaders to consider what constitutes an ideal candidate for their organization and the community and to address internal factors, external factors, and the relationships with the community before implementing any recruiting or retention initiatives. Leaders must evaluate internal factors, such as the organizational structure, morale, policies, and processes to determine whether improvements can be made in these areas. They also must evaluate if their salary schedule and other benefits, such as take-home vehicles, pension, and accrual of vacation time compare to other similarly sized agencies (Cain, 2019a; California Commission on Peace Officer Standards and Training, 2009). A survey conducted in 2022 of 1,003 state and local government employees found that respondents believed their organization could effectively improve retention by increasing salaries (74%), offering or increasing bonuses (54%), and showing more appreciation for employees (45%) (Liss-Levinson & Young, 2023).

Secondly, police executives should ensure that they are conveying the right message about police work and ensuring that potential recruits are receiving the message. Often, police recruitment literature, such as brochures, videos, and internet ads, highlight specialty units, fast-paced action, and dramatic scenes, neglecting the other, more prevalent aspects of the policing profession (PERF, 2019). As the results of this study demonstrated, millennials are interested in serving the community and potentially are more attracted to "community service and public engagement opportunities that a police career can provide" (PERF, 2019, p. 49). The results showed that they also value training and career advancement opportunities. It is valuable to ensure that these components of the profession are included in recruitment initiatives.

Millennials may be more inclined to enter police work if they had a better understanding of the policing profession and the hiring process. Effective recruitment initiatives include establishing internships programs and promoting ride-a-longs, police camps, Explorer Programs, and other activities designed to build trust and confidence in the policing profession and to expose potential recruits to the culture and expectations of policing (PERF, 2019). Younger applicants are often uninformed about disqualifying behaviors and eligibility requirements and unaware of the complexity and intrusiveness of a police background investigation (Linos & Riesch, 2020; Wood, 2017). Researchers recommended utilizing recruiters and other recruiting mediums, like social media, to clarify eligibility requirements, to explain the hiring and application process, to define disqualifying behaviors, and to reinforce the importance of making good decisions to high school and college students who are interested in a law enforcement career (Meese & Malcolm, 2018; Wood, 2017). Law enforcement executives must adopt a successful marketing strategy that includes well-produced recruitment videos and a usable and informative web page highlighting the department's achievements, technological advancements, policing philosophy, community partnerships, career opportunities, training opportunities, education incentives, salary scale, and benefit packages.

Police leaders and their recruiters must develop "outside the box" innovative approaches to recruit younger generations into policing because relying on only traditional methods such as career fairs and on-line job postings are ineffective approaches for recruiting millennials (Morrison, 2017; PERF, 2019). One innovative approach is developing a "farm system to recruit applicants, similar to efforts by colleges and universities to identify star athletes in highs schools or even middle schools" (PERF, 2019, p. 38). Law enforcement recruiters should employ their efforts in trade schools, junior colleges, and four-year colleges by developing relationships with criminal justice program directors and counselors to assist in identifying potential police candidates (Cain, 2019b). Being present on local college campuses, college events, and fundraisers provides recruiters with opportunities to meet students and foster trusting relationships (Morrison, 2017; PERF, 2019).

Conclusion

Law enforcement leaders are seeking innovative approaches to recruiting and retaining police officers for future generations. Police agencies must be committed to identifying and employing the best-qualified candidates available, not merely eliminating the least qualified. This study aimed to assist law leaders in this endeavor. The benefits of effective recruitment and selection policies are manifested in lower rates of personnel turnover, fewer disciplinary problems, higher employee morale, better community relations, and more efficient and effective service delivery to the community. Hiring and training a police officer is timely and costly, so developing an effective plan to recruit, hire, and retain the most qualified candidates is paramount to sustaining police organizations in an evolving policing climate. Turnover is costly, not just in monetary terms, but in a loss of institutional knowledge and acquired skills and abilities. To efficiently recruit future police officers and retain them, law enforcement leaders must understand the current labor force landscape.

References

21 CP Solutions. (2023). *Task force on 21st century policing: A renewed call to action*. Chicago: 21CP Solutions, LLC. https://static1.squarespace.com/static/5a

d62e3aec4eb7c4b00e03a0/t/644718fc677c5618827f6d40/1682381053513/Task_Force_Call_to_Action_Final_42523.pdf.

Arrington, G. B., & Dwyer, R. J. (2018). Can four generations create harmony within a public sector environment? *International Journal of Applied Management and Technology*, 16(1), 1–21. https://seu.idm.oclc.org/login?url=https://search-proquest-com.seu.idm.oclc.org/docview/2103082545?accountid=43912.

Benson, J., & Brown, M. (2011). Generations at work: Are there differences and do they matter? *International Journal of Human Resource Management*, 22(9), 1843–1865. https://doi-org.seu.idm.oclc.org/10.1080/09585192.2011.573966.

Cain, N. (2019a, January). A profession in crisis: Addressing recruitment and hiring practices in law enforcement. https://inpublicsafety.com/2019/01/a-profession-in-crisis-addressing-recruitment-and-hiring-practices-in-law-enforcement/.

Cain, N. (2019b, April). A profession in crisis: Proactively recruiting in schools and minoritycommunities. https://inpublicsafety.com/2019/04/a-profession-in-crisis-proactively-recruiting-in-schools-and-minority-communities/.

California Commission on Peace Officer Standards and Training. (2009). *Post recruitment strategic planning guide: Finding and keeping the right people*. http://lib.post.ca.gov/Publications/RecruitmentStrategicPlanningGuide_11-09.pdf.

Center for State and Local Government Excellence. (2018, May). *Survey findings state and local government workforce: 2018 data and 10 year trends*. https://slge.org/assets/uploads/2018/07/SLGE2018Workforce.pdf.

Chopko, B. A., Palmieri, P. A., & Adams, R. E. (2015). Critical incident history questionnaire replication: Frequency and severity of trauma exposure among officers from small and midsize police agencies. *Journal of Traumatic Stress*, 28(2), 157–161. https://doi-org.seu.idm.oclc.org/10.1002/jts.21996.

Donohue, R. (2022, December). A way forward for police recruiting. *Police Chief*. https://www.policechiefmagazine.org/way-forward-police-recruiting/.

Ford, J. (2007). Building capability throughout a change effort: Leading the transformation of apolice agency to community policing. *American Journal Community Psychology*, 39, 321–334. doi:10.1007/s10464-007-9115-2.

Fry, R. (2018). Millennials are the largest generation in the U.S. labor force. http://www.pewresearch.org/fact-tank/2018/04/11/millennials-largest-generation-us-labor-force/.

Gardner, M. & Scott, K. (2022). *Census of state and local law enforcement agencies, 2018*. United States Bureau of Justice Statistics. https://bjs.ojp.gov/sites/g/files/xyckuh236/files/media/document/csllea18st.pdf.

Goodison, S. (2022). *Local police departments, 2020*. United States Bureau of Justice Statistics.https://bjs.ojp.gov/sites/g/files/xyckuh236/files/media/document/lpdp20.pdf.

Jensen, C. J., & Graves, M. A. (2013, March). *Leading our most important resource: Policepersonnel issues in the year 2020*. https://www.nationalpublicsafetypartnership.org/Documents/Leading%20Our%20Most%20Important%20Resource%20-%20Police%20Personnel%20Issues%20in%20the%20Year%202020.pdf.

Kapoor, C., & Solomon, N. (2011). Understanding and managing generational differences in the workplace. *Worldwide Hospitality and Tourism Themes*, 3(4), 308–318. doi:http://dx.doi.org.seu.idm.oclc.org/10.1108/17554211111162435.

Lawrence, S., & McCarthy, B. (2013, November). *What works in community policing: A best practices context for measure Y efforts*. Berkley, CA: The Chief

Justice Earl Warren Institute on Law and Social Policy. https://www.law.berkeley.edu/files/What_Works_in_Community_Policing.pdf.

Linos, E., & Riesch, N. (2020). Thick red tape and the thin blue line: A field study on reducing administrative burden in police recruitment. *Public Administration Review*, 80(1), 92–103. https://doi.org/10.1111/puar.13115.

Liss-Levinson, R. & Young, G. (2023). State and local government employees: Morale, public service motivation, financial concerns, and retention. https://www.slge.org/resources/state-and-local-government-employees-morale-public-service-motivation-financial-concerns-and-retention-2.

Lyons, S., Urick, M., Kuron, L., & Schweitzer, L. (2015). Generational differences in the workplace: There is complexity beyond the stereotypes. *Industrial and Organizational Psychology*, 8(3), 346–356. doi:http://dx.doi.org.seu.idm.oclc.org/10.1017/iop.2015.48.

Maciag, M. (2018). With fewer police applicants, departments engage in bidding wars. https://www.governing.com/topics/public-justice-safety/gov-hiring-police-officers.html.

Meade, B. (2016). *Recruiting, selecting, and retaining law enforcement officers*. Police Foundation. https://www.policefoundation.org/recruiting-selecting-and-retaining-law-enforcement-officers/?gclid=EAIaIQobChMIoooushpic5QIVjIbACh0zhgW9EAAYAiAAEgJpD_BwE

Meese III, E. & Malcolm, J. (2018). Policing in America: Midsize departments as laboratories of police innovation. The Heritage Foundation. https://www.heritage.org/crime-and-justice/report/policing-america-midsize-departments-laboratories-police-innovation.

Morrison, K. (2017). *Hiring for the 21st century law enforcement officer: Challenges, opportunities, and strategies for success.* Washington, DC: Office of Community Oriented Policing Services. https://cops.usdoj.gov/ric/Publications/cops-w0831-pub.pdf.

Murray, A. (2011). Mind the gap: Technology, millennial leadership and the cross-generational workforce. *The Australian Library Journal*, 60(1), 54–65. https://doi.org/10.1080/00049670.2011.10722556.

Naim, M. F., & Lenka, U. (2018). Development and retention of Generation Y employees: A conceptual framework. *Employee Relations*, 40(2), 433–455. https://doi-org.seu.idm.oclc.org/10.1108/ER-09-2016-0172.

Northup, J. (2018). Police personnel retention challenges: Literature review and recommendations. *Police Chief*, 9, 20–27. https://www.policechiefmagazine.org/police-personnel-retention-challenges/.

Office of Community Oriented Policing Services (COPS), U.S. Department of Justice, & United States of America. (2012). *Community policing defined*. https://cops.usdoj.gov/RIC/Publications/cops-p157-pub.pdf.

Orrick, W. D. (2008). Recruitment, retention, and turnover of law enforcement personnel. https://www.nccpsafety.org/assets/files/library/Recruitment_Retention_and_Turnover_in_Law_Enforcement.pdf.

PERF (Police Executive Research Forum). (2019, September). *The workforce crisis, and what police agencies are doing about it.* https://www.policeforum.org/assets/WorkforceCrisis.pdf.

PERF (Police Executive Research Forum). (2023, April). *New PERF survey shows police agencies are losing officers faster than they can hire new ones.* https://www.policeforum.org/staffing2023.

Pyle, B. S., & Cangemi, J. (2019). Organizational change in law enforcement: Community-oriented policing as transformational leadership. *Organization Development Journal*, 37(4). https://search-ebscohost-com.seu.idm.oclc.org/login.aspx?direct=true&db=bth&AN=139880365&site=ehost-live&scope=site.

Ramchand, R., Saunders, J., Osilla, K. C., Ebener, P., Kotzias, V., Thornton, E., ... Cahill, M (2018). Suicide prevention in US Law enforcement agencies: A national survey of current practices. *Journal of Police and Criminal Psychology*, 34, 55–66. https://doi-org.seu.idm.oclc.org/10.1007/s11896-018-9269-x.

Society for Human Resource Management (SHRM). (2016). *Employee job satisfaction and engagement: Revitalizing a changing workforce.* https://www.shrm.org/hr-today/trends-and-forecasting/research-and-surveys/Documents/2016-Employee-Job-Satisfaction-and-Engagement-Report.pdf.

Wiedmer, T. (2015). Generations do differ: Best practices in leading traditionalists, boomers, and generations X, Y, and Z. *Delta Kappa Gamma Bulletin*, 82(1), 51–58. https://seu.idm.oclc.org/login?url=https://search-proquest-com.seu.idm.oclc.org/docview/1770514324?accountid=43912.

Wood, M. (2017). Making and breaking careers: Reviewing law enforcement hiring requirements and disqualifiers. *Journal of Criminal Justice Education*, 28(4), 580–597. https://doi.org/10.1080/10511253.2017.1283429.

INDEX

Note: Information in figures and tables is indicated by page numbers in *italics* and **bold**, respectively.

addiction, hypervigilance as 205–207
Akromia 108
Al Qaeda 116

body-worn cameras (BWC) 125–141, **137–140**
Brazil 125–141, **137–140**, *175*, 178–186
Brown, Michael 2, 93, 127
burnout 157–163
BWC. *see* body-worn cameras (BWC)

cameras 125–141, **137–140**
Chinese immigrants 5, 75–87
Christianity 108
Clark, Jamar 92
CLP. *see* Creative Learning Program (CLP)
community justice 5, 75–87
community policing 132–134, 225
COVID-19 pandemic 37
Creative Learning Program (CLP) 41–44
Cummings, J. P. 177

Data Envelopment Analysis (DEA) 11, 14
DEA. *see* Data Envelopment Analysis (DEA)

decentralization 133
distributive justice 182
domestic violence 7, 128, 149–153, 156–157

education. law enforcement higher 35–45, *36*
efficiency, in police structures 12–13
extremism, religious 110–113

family safety 7, 146–148
family violence 149–153, 156–157
Fernández de Kirchner, Cristina 48, 49, 70n6, 70n8
firearms, in officer suicide 148–149
Floyd, George 2, 92
force: hypervigilance and 207–208; in literature review 92–94; in street stops 91–103, **98–100**; uncontrolled use of 201–211
foreign terrorist fighters (FTFs) 117
FTFs. *see* foreign terrorist fighters (FTFs)
funeral protocol, with suicides 157–159

Garner, Eric 92
Gilmartin, Kevin 201, 202, 205, 206, 207, 209, 210, 211

Gray, Freddie 93
grip, as force 93

heutagogy 44–45
Hizb-ut Tahrir 108
Hungary 35–45, 36
hypervigilance, addictive 201–211

impact techniques 93
IMT. *see* Islamic Movement of Turkestan (IMT)
integrated public security areas (IPSAs) 10–32, **17**, **19–21**, 23, *24*, **25–27**, *28–31*, **29**
IPSAs. *see* integrated public security areas (IPSAs)
ISIS. *see* Islamic State of Iraq and Syria (ISIS)
Islam 108, 109, 110
Islamic Movement of Turkestan (IMT) 119–120
Islamic State of Iraq and Syria (ISIS) 108, 110–111, 116, 118
Israel 149

Jabhat al Nusra 116
Jaysh al-mahdi 111–112
justice: community 5, 75–87; distributive 182; procedural 129–132, 140; social 119, 121

Kyrgyzstan 107–121

Law Enforcement Mental Health and Wellness Act 164
learning, transformative 44–45
legitimacy 129–132
Local Prevention Police Units 47–69
Ludovika University of Public Service (LUPS) 40–44

McEwan, Thomas 79–80
media: suicide death and 159–161
mental illness 180–184. *see also* post-traumatic stress disorder (PTSD)
migration: community justice and 75–87; illegal 36–37
murder/suicide 156–157

National University of Lanús 47–69
neighbourhood proximity 57–58
Netherlands 196

New South Wales (NSW) 13
non-traffic situation, officer behavior in 91–103, **98–100**
NSW. *see* New South Wales (NSW)

Obama, Barack 2, 125
Ontario, Canada 13
Operational Research (OR) 14
OR. *see* Operational Research (OR)

pain compliance 93
peer support group 165–166
pension eligibility 190–191
performance evaluation, of integrated public security areas 10–32, **17**, **19–21**, 23, *24*, **25–27**, *28–31*, **29**
police perceptions, of community justice 79–82
Portugal 14
post-traumatic stress disorder (PTSD) 154, 163, 189–198, **193**, 193–194, **195**, 196–197, 198, 216
presence, as force 93
procedural justice 129–132, 140
PROMETHEE II 10–32, **17**, **19–21**, 23, *24*, **25–27**, *28–31*, **29**
psychological examination, pre-employment 161–162
PTSD. *see* post-traumatic stress disorder (PTSD)
Pulse night club shooting 191–192

radicalization 107–121
recruitment 38–46, 86–87, 111–121, 214–227, **220**, **222**, **223**
religious extremism 110–113
religious radicalization 107–121
retention 214–227, **220**, **222**, **223**
Rice, Tamir 93
Rio de Janeiro 3, 4, 11, 12, 15, 16–32
rotations, compulsive 57–58
Russia 37–38

Salcedo, Daniel 49, 70n10
Sandy Hook Elementary School shooting 196
Scioli, Daniel 47, 49, 65, 70n8, 70n18
screening, suicide and 161–164
shootings, mass 191–192
social justice 119, 121
social media 159–161
Solá, Felipe 48

Soviet Union 108, 109
Stornelli, Carlos 48
substance use and abuse 154–156
suicide, officer 146–166, 173–186, **175**
Syria 111–116

Taylor, Breonna 92
technology 2–3
terrorism 110–117
threat misperception 204–205
trauma, hypervigilance and 211n5
Turkestan 119–120
Turkey 13–14
Tyler, Tom 131–132

Ukraine-Russian war 37–38

United States 75–87, 91–103, **98–100**, 125–126, 191–192, 193–194

Varela, Cristian 58
verbal attacks, in street stops 91–103, **98–100**
verbalization, as force 93

Wahhabization 112
wellness culture 164–165
Wilson, Darren 2, 125
workers' compensation 190–191, 192, 193, 194, 195, **195**, 198
workforce crisis 38–39, 214–227, **220, 222, 223**